Education, Curriculum and Educology

by

James E. Christensen

First published as a Smashwords™ e-book in 2014.

Education, Curriculum and Educology

Copyright © 2014 James E. Christensen

Printed by Kindle Direct Publishing

Available from Amazon.com and other retail outlets

Preface

My intention in writing this book has been to achieve some much needed clarity in spoken and written discourse about education and curriculum. The language used in discourse about education and curriculum is cluttered with metaphorical, ambiguous and puzzling expressions. Teachers are advised to help their students to achieve "deep understanding." They are told that they should engage in "explicit teaching." They are counseled to practice "intentional instruction." They are instructed to use "productive pedagogies." They are urged to use "student centered" teaching strategies. They are told to use "direct instruction."

There is a great need to clarify what these terms and statements mean, if they mean anything at all. Without clarity and unambiguous meaning in discourse about education, there is little hope for establishing knowledge about education. Without knowledge about education, there is little basis for making rational judgments about education. Effective rational action in relation to education, without knowledge about education, is impossible. We can't be of much help if we don't know what to do to help.

From my studies, research and experience, I have found sufficient and necessary evidence to warrant the assertion that knowledge about education is possible. I have also found that the first step towards developing knowledge about education is establishing clarity and disambiguation in discourse about education. Once we are clear in what we are talking and writing about, then the conceptual foundation is laid for finding the appropriate evidence to determine whether what we are saying and writing is true. Achieving clarity in meaning of a statement logically precedes judging the truth value of a statement. A statement must make sense before it can be true.

Introduction

This book is written from an educological perspective. The educological perspective looks at education as the dependent variable, and it inquires about how all other factors, phenomena and states of affairs affect the educational process. The educological perspective leads one to think about education,

(1) not in terms of the sociology of education, but in terms of the educology of society;

(2) not in terms of the psychology of education, but in terms of the educology of mind, mental processes, motivation, human development and conduct;

(3) not in terms of the economics of education, but in terms of the educology of economic arrangements;

(4) not in terms of the politics of education, but in terms of the educology of political states of affairs;

(5) not in terms of the anthropology of education, but in terms of the educology of cultural processes;

(6) not in terms of comparative education, but in terms of comparative educology, or more appropriately, the educology of societies and cultures.

The term *educology* means the fund of knowledge about the educational process. The fund includes all warranted assertions, valid explanatory theories and sound justificatory arguments about the educational process. *Educology* is a combinative term that derives from the terms *education* and *–logy*. The term has been in use since the seminal work in educology by Professor Lowry W. Harding at Ohio State University in the 1950s and by Professor Elizabeth Steiner [Maccia] and George Maccia at Indiana University in the 1960s. The discipline requisite for producing educology includes that which is necessary for conducting analytic, normative and empirical inquiry or research. The educological perspective is inclusive of the historical, analytical philosophical, normative philosophical, scientific and praxiological perspectives in discourse about the educational process. Rational, constructive action within the educational process derives from sound educological understanding. Through studying educology, one can develop educological understanding towards several ends, e.g. towards

(1) heightened sensitivity for educational situations,
(2) effective participation within educational situations,
(3) articulation of sound explanatory and justificatory theories about educational situations and
(4) rational and intelligent resolution of problems connected with educational situations.

Table of Contents

Chapter 2: Uses for the Critical Categories   45

Chapter 4: Issues Arising from Discourse about Curriculum 173

Chapter 1: Fourteen Critical Categories

An important educological issue is the clarity of discourse about education and curriculum. Discourse about education and curriculum has historically been especially prone to generating confusion. This is because the terms *education* and *curriculum* have often been used in ways to make them malfunction. They have been made to do multiple duties, in that they have been made to carry multiple meanings simultaneously. Their equivocation and ambiguity in discourse about educational phenomena has resulted in category mistakes, conflation of meanings and misconceptions. The consequences of category mistakes and conflation have included

    (1) confused thinking about education and curriculum,
    (2) obstructions to progress in developing new knowledge about education and curriculum and
    (3) wasted resources and effort in the educational process.

What is needed is a system of conception which unambiguously relates, yet distinguishes, education, curriculum, knowledge, knowing and understanding. The set of concepts critical for this system of conception includes the following:

    (1) field of phenomena
    (2) aspect of a field of phenomena
    (3) knowledge about a field of phenomena
    (4) fund of knowledge about a field of phenomena
    (5) inquiry about a field of phenomena
    (6) discipline of inquiry about a field of phenomena
    (7) kinds of knowledge about a field of phenomena
    (8) publicly verifiable vs. privately verifiable knowledge
    (9) purposes of knowledge
  (10) knowing about a field of phenomena
  (11) forms of knowing
  (12) levels of knowing
  (13) kinds of knowing
  (14) understanding and knowing

These concepts are critical categories because they have the power to produce discourse about education and curriculum that has clarity, that averts category mistakes and that forestalls conflation of meanings.

Critical Category 1: Field of Phenomena

The first critical category to be distinguished is a field of phenomena. A field is a realm, a domain, an area, a portion or a division. A field of phenomena is a set of occurrences, happenings,

Figure 1.1: Field of Phenomena

Phenomena in the field of education	
Field of education	**Field of educational phenomena**
	Field of phenomena in education
	People, entities, practices, activities, events, relationships, policies, rules, regulations in the process of teaching, studying and intentionally learning under guidance something in some setting, including physical, geographic, social, cultural (including political, religious, economic) settings

behaviors, practices, events, policies, relations. When the term *education* is being used to name the educational process, then the term *education* is being used to name a field of phenomena. The educational process is a field of phenomena in which someone intentionally teaches and someone intentionally studies under guidance with the intention to learn some content within the context of some physical, geographical, social and cultural setting. The field of phenomena named by the term *education* includes events such as someone assuming the role of teacher, someone taking on the role of pupil or student, some content being selected and organized for teaching and studying and some configuration of settings (physical, geographical, social, cultural) that influences the processes of teaching and studying.

Critical Category 2: Aspect of a Field

A field of phenomena has aspects. An aspect is a feature, a part, an element or a component. An aspect of a field of phenomena is an element of the total set of phenomena included in the field. For example, the term *curriculum* names an aspect of the total field of phenomena that is education.

Figure 1.2: Aspects of the Field of Education

Aspects of the field of education	
Meaning of the term *aspects of the field of education*	**Examples of aspects of the field of education**
An element or component of the domain of educational phenomena	**Teachers, students, content, settings, teaching, studying, intentionally learning under guidance, syllabus and syllabi, curriculum and curricula, unit plans, lesson plans, assessment tasks, intended learning outcomes, goals, goal structures, group organization, teaching methods, studying methods, teaching styles, studying styles, functions of language used in teaching and studying, resources used in teaching and studying, official education, unofficial education**

Examples of aspects of the field of educational phenomena include teachers, students, content, settings for teaching and studying, teaching, studying, intentionally learning under guidance, curriculum and curricula, syllabus and syllabi, unit plans, lesson plans, assessment tasks, intended learning outcomes, goals, goal structures, organization of students into groups, teaching methods, teaching styles, studying methods, studying styles, functions of language used in teaching and studying, resources used in teaching and studying, official education, unofficial education, teaching and studying mathematics, teaching and studying dressage, teaching and studying welding, teaching of and studying by children with special needs, and the list goes on and on.

Critical Category 3: Knowledge about a Field of Phenomena

The term *knowledge* has several common usage meanings. In one common usage, the term *knowledge* names true statements about something. That common usage sense is intended in this explication. Knowledge about a field of phenomena is true statements about the field. Knowledge about education is true statements about the field of educational phenomena. The statements,

(S-1) "Many students feel pleasure, self satisfaction and happiness as they come to master new understandings and skills,"
(S-2) "Most teachers use asking questions as one of their teaching methods,"
(S-3) "Students who study reading in classes smaller than 20 perform oral reading more fluently than students in classes larger than 20,"

if true, are examples of knowledge about education. Knowledge about education is located in books, articles and any other medium where warranted assertions may be recorded.

Critical Category 4: Fund of Knowledge

Knowledge (true statements) can be assembled into funds of knowledge. A fund is a collection, an accumulation, a stock, a sum or a set. As more and more knowledge claims about education are in some way shown to be true, a collection of true statements is gradually built up into a fund of knowledge about educational phenomena. This fund may function as descriptions, character-izations, explanations, predictions, justifications and prescriptions of that which occurs in the field of educational phenomena.

Figure 1.3: Fund of Knowledge about Education

Fund of knowledge about education	
Fund of knowledge about education	**Collection of true statements about the field of educational phenomena**

Possible names for the fund of knowledge about educational phenomena include the terms *pedagogy*, *ethology*, *andragogy* and *educology*. The term *pedagogy* has been in use since the eighteenth century (Wolfgang Brezinka, 1992), and it derives from the Greek term *paidos*, meaning children. The concept of the term *pedagogy* relates closely to the idea of knowledge about the education of children. Hence it is too narrow in its conception to include knowledge about all levels, forms and functions of education. What's more, in current times, the term *pedagogy* has been made to malfunction, in that it is commonly used to name teaching strategies as well as knowledge about teaching strategies.

A second candidate, *ethology*, was proposed by J.S. Mill in the nineteenth century (*System of Logic*, 1846, Book VI, Chapter V, Paragraph 4). Mill was concerned about the problem of explaining how different nations developed distinct national characters and how the process of mass character formation functioned. The term *ethology* derives from the Greek term *ethos*, meaning character of a group. The concept of the term *ethology* relates to knowledge about the character development of societies and nations. It implies knowledge about all learning, whether guided or unguided, deliberate or unintentional. Thus, the concept of *ethology* is too broad for the term to be used to mean, and only mean, knowledge about education.

The term *andragogy* has been proposed as a name for knowledge about adult education (M.S. Knowles, 1970; K.P. Cross, 1992). The term is derivative of the Greek combinative term *andr-*, meaning man or male, and *-logy*, meaning knowledge. Etymologically the concept of the term *andragogy* relates more closely to knowledge about the education of men or males than to knowledge about the education of adults. But in either case, its implication is too narrow to mean knowledge about the education of anyone and everyone, including children, adolescents, young adults, mature adults, senescent adults, males and females.

Another term which has been proposed to name the fund of knowledge about education is *psychopedagogy* (E. Stones, 1979). Psychopedagogy, Stones has argued, is a combination of psychological knowledge and knowledge about the practice of teaching. The implications of psychopedagogy are both too inclusive and too exclusive. The concept of psychopedagogy is too exclusive to include all knowledge about the educational process, and it is too inclusive in that it includes knowledge about mind, mental processes, motivations, human development and conduct.

A fifth candidate yet remains. The term *educology* is a combinative term which derives from *education*, meaning the process of someone undertaking to learn something under guidance in some setting, and *-logy*, meaning knowledge. The concept of the term *educology* means, and only means, knowledge about education (Elizabeth Steiner [Maccia], 1964, 1977, 1981). Steiner initially used the term *educatology* but later revised it to *educology*. The origins of the term *educology*, coined in 1951 by Prof. Lowry M. Harding (1951, 1956, 1964, 1965), are traced in the Preface of *Perspectives on Education as Educology* (J.E. Christensen, Ed., 1981).

The term *educology* functions much like the terms *anthropology*, *sociology* and *psychology*. Each names a fund of knowledge about some set of phenomena. The term *anthropology* names the fund of knowledge about the customs, norms and ways of life of humankind. The term *sociology* names the fund of knowledge about society. The term *psychology* names the fund of knowledge about mind, emotions, motivations, human development and conduct.

Figure 1.4: Educology as Knowledge about Education

Fund of knowledge about education	
Fund of knowledge about education	**Collection of true statements about the field of educational phenomena**
	Educology

Educology is related to education and curriculum in the same way that zoology is related to animals and vertebrates or sociology is related to society and social class. Educology, zoology and sociology are funds of knowledge. Education, animals and society are fields of phenomena. Curriculum, vertebrates and social class are aspects of fields of phenomena.

Figure 1.5: Fund, Field and Aspect

Funds of knowledge	Fields of phenomena	Aspects of fields of phenomena
Educology	Education	Curriculum
Zoology	Animals	Invertebrates
Sociology	Society	Social class

Critical Category 5: Inquiry about a Field of Phenomena

Inquiry, in general, is a set of activities of asking questions, answering questions and searching for evidence to support the truth value of answers to questions. The outcome of successful inquiry is true statements (or knowledge) about something. The knowledge can be, for example, about the logical relationships of the meaning of terms (as in the fund of knowledge that is mathematics). It can be about some field of phenomena (as in the fund of knowledge that is zoology). It can be about things that are worthwhile or valuable (as in the fund of knowledge that is normative philosophy).

Inquiry about education, in particular, is the activity of asking, answering and verifying (finding sufficient and necessary evidence in support of) answers to questions about the field of educational phenomena. The product of successful inquiry about education is educology (knowledge about education). Common usage names for inquiry about education include *educational inquiry*, *educational studies* and *educational research*. In the interest of clarity, more appropriate names for inquiry about the educational process are *educological inquiry*, *educological research* and *educological studies*, just as the name *sociological research* is more appropriate than *societal research* or *social research* (J.E. Fisher, 1981).

Figure 1.6: Educological Inquiry or Educological Research

Educological inquiry or research	
Educological inquiry or research	**The activity of asking, answering and verifying (finding sufficient and necessary evidence in support of) answers to questions about the field of educational phenomena (or some aspect of the field) for the purpose of producing educology (knowledge about education)**

Critical Category 6: Discipline of Inquiry about a Field of Phenomena

It is the business of educological researchers and inquirers to construct discourse, in the sense of sets of statements, that adequately characterizes educational phenomena. In their work, educological researchers must take care in the gathering of evidence so that the statements which they claim to be true can be demonstrated in some way to be true (or at least are not yet demonstrated to be false). They must follow appropriate rules, logical operations and procedures so that the characterizations of phenomena which they construct in language are justified. The set of rules that they follow in substantiating knowledge claims (statements asserted to be true) about the field of educational phenomena is their discipline. There are at least six sets of rules (and therefore six disciplines) for conducting educological research or inquiry (J.E. Christensen, 2013).

Figure 1.7: The Discipline of Educological Inquiry

Discipline for conducting educological inquiry or research	
Discipline of inquiry about educational phenomena	Sets of rules, logical operations and procedures which are followed to verify knowledge claims about the field of educational phenomena

Critical Category 7: Kinds of Knowledge about a Field of Phenomena

Knowledge, in the sense of true statements, can be distinguished with respect to the kind of evidence that counts in the verification of the statements. For example, empirical statements require the evidence of observable phenomena. Analytic statements require the evidence of the necessary implications of concepts and propositions. Normative statements require the evidence of necessary implications of concepts and propositions and acts as objects.

With regard to educology, at least six kinds of knowledge about education are possible: empirical$_1$, empirical$_2$, empirical$_3$, analytic, normative and ontological. The six kinds are distinguished with respect to the standard of verification that each requires. A standard of verification is a principle of verification that is used to judge whether a statement is true or false (J. Christensen and J. Fisher, 1979).

At least six different principles of verification can be distinguished. Therefore, at least six kinds of knowledge (i.e. true statements) about education can be established.

The six principles of verification that determine the six kinds of knowledge are:

(1) the principle of introspection$_1$;
(2) the principle of introspection$_2$;
(3) the principle of extrospection;
(4) the principle of deduction (necessity reasoning);
(5) the principle of evaluation (normative reasoning);
(6) the principle of revelation.

The six principles of verification and the six possible kinds of knowledge about education can be related in the following way.

Empirical$_1$ knowledge about education is any set of true empirical$_1$ declarative sentences about education. They are verifiable by the principle of introspection$_1$. This is the principle of verification that is used to establish the correspondency relationship between empirical$_1$ statements about education and the perceivable evidence of mental objects in education (J. Christensen, 2013).

Empirical$_2$ knowledge about education is any set of true empirical$_2$ declarative sentences about education. They are verifiable by the principle of introspection$_2$. This is the principle of verification that is used to establish the correspondency relationship between empirical$_2$ statements about education and the kinceivable evidence of physiological objects in education (J. Christensen, 2013).

Empirical$_3$ knowledge about education is any set of true empirical$_3$ declarative sentences about education. They are verifiable by the principle of extrospection. This is the principle of verification that is used to establish the correspondency relationship between empirical₃ statements about education and the senceivable evidence of physical objects in education (J. Christensen, 2013).

Analytic knowledge about education is any set of true analytic declarative sentences about education. They are verifiable by the principle of deduction (necessity reasoning). This is the principle of verification that is used to establish the coherency relationship between analytic statements about education and the conceivable evidence of logical objects in education (J. Christensen, 2013).

Normative knowledge about education is any set of true normative declarative sentences about education. They are verifiable by the principle of evaluation (evaluative reasoning). This is the principle of verification that is used to establish the coherency relationship and the adherency relationship between normative statements about education and the conceivable evidence of logical objects and acts as objects in education (See Paul W. Taylor, 1961).

Ontological knowledge about education is any set of true ontological declarative sentences about education. They are verifiable by the principle of revelation. This is the principle of verification that is used to establish the adherency relationship between ontological statements about education and the divinational evidence of objects other than logical objects, physical objects, mental objects, physiological objects and acts as objects in education. Another name for ontological statements is metaphysical statements (J. Christensen, 2013). (See Figure 1.8.)

In Figure 1.8,

(1) The expression *kinds of knowledge about education* means the same as the set of words *categories of verified declarative sentences about education.*

(2) The term *principles of verification* means the same as the set of words *standards for judging whether statements are true.*

(3) The expression *ways of collecting evidence about education* means the same as the set of words *processes of sensation and intellection of objects that count in verification of statements about education.*

Figure 1.8: Kinds of Knowledge about Education

Kinds of knowledge about education	Principles of verification for knowledge about education	Ways of collecting evidence for verification of knowledge about education	Kinds of evidence for verification of knowledge about education	Relationships between knowledge and education
Empirical$_1$ knowledge	Principle of introspection$_1$	Perception	Mental objects	Correspondency relationship
Empirical$_2$ knowledge	Principle of introspection$_2$	Kinception	Physiological objects	Correspondency relationship
Empirical$_3$ knowledge	Principle of extrospection	Senception	Physical objects	Correspondency relationship
Analytic knowledge	Principle of deduction (necessity reasoning)	Conception	Logical objects	Coherency relationship
Normative knowledge	Principle of evaluation (evaluative reasoning)	Conception	Logical objects and acts as objects	Coherency relationship and adherency relationship
Ontological knowledge	Principle of revelation	Divination	Other than mental objects, physiological objects, physical objects, logical objects and acts as objects	Adherency relationship

Figure 1.9: Conditions for Verification of Knowledge about Education

Kinds of knowledge (true statements) about education	Conditions for verification of kinds of knowledge (true statements) about education
Empirical$_1$ knowledge (true statements)	Empirical$_1$ meaning Principle of introspection$_1$ Perception way of collecting evidence Mental object evidence Correspondency relationship
Empirical$_2$ knowledge (true statements)	Empirical$_2$ meaning Principle of introspection$_2$ Perception way of collecting evidence Physiological object evidence Correspondency relationship
Empirical$_3$ knowledge (true statements)	Empirical$_3$ meaning Principle of extrospection Senception way of collecting evidence Physical object evidence Correspondency relationship
Analytic knowledge (true statements)	Analytic meaning Principle of deduction (necessity reasoning) Conception way of forming evidence Logical object evidence Coherency relationship
Normative knowledge (true statements)	Normative meaning Principle of evaluation (evaluative reasoning) Conception way of forming evidence Logical object evidence and act as object evidence Coherency and adherency relationships
Ontological (metaphysical) knowledge (true statements)	Ontological (metaphysical) meaning Principle of revelation Divination way of collecting evidence Other than mental, physiological, physical, logical object and other than act as object Adherency relationship

(4) The expression *kinds of evidence about education* means the same as the set of words *categories of objects which are presented in the verification of statements about education*.

(5) The expression *relationships between knowledge and education* means the same as the set of words *logical connections between verified declarative sentences about education and objects that occur in education*.

The conditions for verification of knowledge about education are summarized in Figure 1.9.

So, educology is the product of systematically asking questions about education, answering those questions and successfully verifying those answers. The rules followed in the verification of statements are the discipline of the inquiry. The product of successful inquiry about education is verified answers. Verified answers are verified statements. Verified statements are statements that are true, and true statements are knowledge. Knowledge about education is educology. Educology, therefore, is the outcome of forming verified statements about education by asking questions and making statements about education and adducing necessary and sufficient evidence from education.

Educological inquiry is the asking and stating empirically$_1$, empirically$_2$, empirically$_3$, analytically, normatively and ontologically about education. Successful educological inquiry can produce at least six different kinds of true statements about education, therefore educological inquiry implies the use of six disciplines to form at least six kinds of knowledge about education, or six kinds of educological knowledge, or six kinds of educology.

Critical Category 8: Publicly Verifiable vs. Privately Verifiable Knowledge

There is a serious objection which can be raised to counter the claim that educology includes ontological (metaphysical) knowledge. Suppose that the concept of educological inquiry is taken to imply inquiry that, if successful, produces publicly verifiable knowledge, and the concept excludes inquiry that, if successful, produces privately verifiable knowledge. If this distinction is made, then educological inquiry implies analytic, normative, empirical$_1$, empirical$_2$ and empirical$_3$ inquiry about education. But it does not imply ontological inquiry.

Why is it that ontological inquiry can not produce publicly verifiable knowledge? Consider this example. The statement, *It is God's will that I teach*, is ontological. It has an ontological or metaphysical meaning. It requires the use of the principle of revelation to verify it. A person must engage in the process of divination to collect the evidence, and the evidence is other than mental, physiological, physical and logical objects and acts as objects. That is, the evidence is outside of public human experience. It is not in the natural world, and it is therefore not open to scrutiny by the public. In this context, public scrutiny means accessible by senception, perception, kinception and/or conception (J. Christensen and J. Fisher, 1979; J. Christensen, 2013), i.e., the ways of collecting the evidence which exist in the natural world. The evidence for ontological (metaphysical) statements lies in the supernatural (other than natural) world, which is hidden from public scrutiny and available only through private divination. If educology is taken to imply only publicly verifiable knowledge about education, ontological statements are necessarily excluded from educology. Educology, then, would be the product of asking and stating empirically$_1$, empirically$_2$, empirically$_3$, analytically and normatively, but not ontologically, about education.

Some use the term *publicly verifiable knowledge* to mean, and only mean, statements that are verifiable by senception and conception. The concept of *publicly verifiable knowledge* has been extended in this text to include statements which are verifiable by perception and kinception. The reason for this extension of meaning is that perception and kinception are common human experiences. Furthermore, statements which are verifiable by perception and kinception can be corroborated by following the rules of probability reasoning, thereby bringing the statements into the public domain. Probability reasoning is not applicable to the verification of ontological statements, thus such statements remain in the private domain.

Probability reasoning, or induction, is drawing an inference from a set of facts (i.e. true statements) so as to form a conclusion which is probably true, not necessarily true. Necessity reasoning, or deduction, is drawing an inference from a set of facts so as to form a conclusion which is necessarily true, not probably true.

It is a popular misconception that deduction is reasoning from generalizations to specifics, and that induction is reasoning from specifics to generalizations. These are not adequate characterizations of deduction and induction because they do not correctly identify the distinguishing characteristics of deduction and induction. Deduction is necessity reasoning. Induction is probability reasoning.

Critical Category 9: Purposes of Knowledge

The concept of purpose belongs to the same family of concepts as reason, cause, intent, aim and goal. A purpose is an intention to achieve a set of deliberately chosen outcomes or states of affairs. At least six purposes of knowledge about education can be distinguished:
  (1) description,
  (2) characterization,
  (3) explanation,
  (4) prediction,
  (5) prescription and
  (6) justification.

Description. The concept of a description belongs to the same family of concepts as an account, a representation, a record and a depiction. A description is a set of statements which represents objects, entities and states of affairs. Knowledge about education which is produced for the purpose of description is knowledge that is intended to state accurately about educational phenomena as they exist, occur and function, or as they have existed, occurred or functioned. An educological description answers the question,
  "What is happening (or has happened) within the field of phenomena that constitutes education?"

Characterization. The concept of characterization implies the process of characterizing, and the concept of characterize belongs to the same family of concepts as typify, embody and exemplify. A characterization is a set of statements which identifies the distinguishing features of something or some state of affairs. Distinguishing features are those aspects of something which make that something different from other things. Knowledge about education which is produced for the purpose of characterization is knowledge that is intended to state accurately about the distinguishing features or aspects of some set of educational phenomena or some state affairs within the educational process. It is knowledge that clearly distinguishes one entity or state of affairs from another. An educological characterization answers the question,

"What makes one aspect of education distinctive from other aspects within the field of phenomena that constitutes education?"

Explanation. The concept of explanation belongs to the same family of concepts as accounting for, giving reasons for and identifying causes of something. An explanation is a set of statements that provides reasons for why something or some state of affairs exists, occurs or happens, or has existed or happened. An educological explanation answers the question,

"Why does something happen (or has happened) in the field of phenomena that constitutes education?"

A set of explanatory reasons is a set of statements which acts as premises in a deductive argument. But instead of starting with a set of premises, then reasoning to a necessarily true conclusion, explanation starts with a true statement, then reasons backwards (or retroductively) to identify the premises which lead to the conclusion that the original true statement is necessarily true. Explanation is not formed by deduction, but rather, it is formed by retroduction. In deduction, the premises lead to a necessarily true conclusion. In retroduction, the conclusion leads to necessarily true premises.

Another way to think of an explanation is to conceive of it as a theory (an explanatory theory), which accounts for why some statement is true, as opposed to a justificatory theory, which provides an argument for why something is good or ought to be done. An explanation is neither true nor false. Rather, it is valid or invalid, based on whether the retroductive argument is coherent or incoherent. See Figure 1.10.

Knowledge about education that is produced for the purpose of explanation is knowledge that is intended to account for why a set

Figure 1.10: Kinds of Reasoning

Kinds of reasoning		
Deduction: *Necessity reasoning*	**Retroduction:** *Explanatory reasoning*	**Induction:** *Probability reasoning*
Reasoning from a set of premises to a necessarily true conclusion	Reasoning from a conclusion to a set of necessarily true premises	Reasoning from a set of premises to a probably true conclusion
Deductive form of argument: If statements A, B, C ... N are true, then statement Z is necessarily true.	*Retroductive form of argument:* If statement Z is true, then statements A, B, C ... N are necessarily true. *Explanatory theory*: In the retroductive argument, statements A, B, C ... N form an explanatory theory for statement Z. They account for why statement Z is true.	*Inductive form of argument*: If statements A, B, C ... N are true, then statement Z is probably true.

of true statements about educational phenomena, or state of affairs in the educational process, are true.

Prediction. The concept of prediction belongs to the same family of concepts as prognostication, forecasting, forewarning, and foretelling. A prediction is a set of statements that declares what is going to happen in the future. Predictive knowledge is expressed as statements in the form,

"If conditions A exist, then conditions B will be the result."

Knowledge about education that is produced for the purpose of prediction is knowledge which is intended to state that, given a specified set of conditions within the educational process, a set of specified consequences will, to some degree of probability, result in the educational process. An educological prediction answers the question,

"Given a specified set of circumstances, what will happen in the field of phenomena that constitutes education?"

Prescription. The concept of prescription belongs to the same family of concepts as advice, suggestion, recommendation and imperative. A prescription is a set of statements that directs a course of action to take in order to achieve a desired result. Prescriptive knowledge is expressed as statements in the form,

"If conditions Z are desired, then actions $A, B, C, ... N$ must be taken."

Knowledge about education that is produced for the purpose of prescription is knowledge which is intended to state that, if one desires a set of circumstances or state of affairs in education, then a set of specified actions must be performed to achieve the desired conditions. An educological prescription answers the question,

"What needs to be done to achieve a desired state of affairs in the field of phenomena that constitutes education?"

Justification. The concept of justification belongs to the same family of concepts as vindication, warrants and defense. A justification is a set of statements which forms an argument that there are good reasons for accepting a value judgment (Paul W. Taylor, 1961, p. 70). Knowledge about education that is produced for the purpose of justification is a set of statements which forms a justificatory argument to support value judgments about decisions, acts, dispositions and attitudes within, and for, the educational process. An educological justification answers the question,

"Why is some state of affairs good or bad (or relatively better or worse) in the field of phenomena that constitutes education?"

Critical Category 10: Knowing about a Field of Phenomena

The term *knowledge* has a least two common usage meanings. It is used to name true statements, and it is used to name cognitive function. Knowledge as true statements, or propositional knowledge, is located in books and other ways of making records of warranted propositions. Knowledge as cognitive function, or knowing, is located in people, or more accurately, in the functioning of people.

An example will help to clarify the distinction between knowledge and knowing. Look at your hand. Your hand exists in time and space. It is part of physical reality. It is one of many phenomena in physical reality. Now look at your hand and snap your fingers. Finger snapping is one of the many functions of the hand. Do you know how to snap your fingers? Yes, you do know how, and you can verify that you know by people observing (or senceiving) the physical evidence (the motion and the sound) of your fingers snapping. Where is your knowing located? It is located in your repertoire of functions. Your knowing is located in your set of cognitive functions. Now look at the sentence,

"Finger snapping is one of the many functions of the hand."

Is the statement true? Yes, it is true, and we can verify that it is true by using the principle of observation (extrospection) to use the process of observing (or senceiving) the physical evidence (the motion and sound) of the hand snapping its fingers. The sentence,

"Finger snapping is one of the many functions of the hand,"
is a warranted assertion. Warranted assertions are knowledge. Where is this knowledge located? Right here, on this page. You can see the true statement,

"Finger snapping is one of the many functions of the hand."

Knowledge is located in the medium in which the knowledge is recorded. Knowing is located in the function of people, and more specifically in their cognitive function. When people die, their knowing dies with them. But knowledge does not die. Knowledge lasts as long as the medium lasts in which the knowledge is recorded.

A useful way to regard knowing is to conceive of it as the realized ability to perform adequately in relation to a field of phenomena. It is necessary to say "realized ability" in order to distinguish it from potential ability. A realized ability is a competence which has been developed into an actuality. For example, all of us have the ability to speak Turkish, in the sense that we have the potential to develop that competence. But at the moment, we may not speak it. That is, not all of us have realized the ability. Not all of us know. Potentialities relate to abilities not yet developed. Knowing is ability which has been developed, made an actuality or realized.

While knowing and adequate performance are closely related, they are not identical. Knowing is the realized ability to perform adequately in relation to some field of phenomena or state of affairs. Adequate performances are indications of knowing, but there can be instances of inadequate performance, even though the person knows. This may be the result of mistake, fatigue, injury or even intention. A person can know something and deliberately not show it.

A special case of this is the basis for Dalton Trumbo's novel, *Johnny Got His Gun* (1939). The protagonist, Joe Bonham, a young Canadian soldier in the First World War, suffers such horrific wounds that he finds himself in hospital without legs, arms, eyes, nose, voice or hearing. Still, his mind is intact. He knows how to talk, swim, ride horses, pick apples. However his adequate performances in relation to his environment are limited to emotional, imaginal, physiological, conative and linguistic (and only silent, inward linguistic) performances. He does know Morse code, and he taps out messages with the movement of his head against his bed frame. The tapping is both a physical and linguistic performance. Any other physical performances are very limited because of his injuries and amputations.

We can know about many things. And one of the many things which we can know about is the field of education. Knowing about the field of phenomena that is education is having a set of realized abilities to perform adequately in relation to education. These abilities include linguistic performances such as talking and writing adequately about education. Undertaking discourse about education is an act of conceiving educologically. Such linguistic performances also include talking adequately while engaged in the process of education in the role, for example, of teacher, pupil, counselor, tutor or coach. Other kinds of knowing about education include adequate physical performances such as gestures and movements performed while engaged in the educational process. They include adequate emotional performances such as feelings of involvement and emotions of caring while engaged in the process of education. They include adequate imaginal performances such as empathizing and anticipating while engaged in the educational process. And they include adequate conative performances, as in choosing a particular curriculum from a range of alternative curricula for a particular group of pupils.

Critical Category 11: Forms of Knowing about a Field of Phenomena

The forms of people's knowing (i.e. the forms of people's cognitive function) are the ways in which they can manifest their cognitive function. Forms of knowing are different ways in which cognitive performances can be realized and demonstrated. At least six forms are distinguishable: linguistic, emotional, imaginal, physical, physiological and conative.

Linguistic Knowing. Linguistic cognitive performances are those by which people signify meaning with symbols. They include speaking, reading, writing, reasoning in sentences and reasoning with mathematical symbols, and they include performing logical operations such as deduction, reduction, induction, retroduction, evaluation and justification. They may be silent, told inwardly, or they may be spoken aloud, or written, or they may be signed with gestures, as in American Sign Language. An example of linguistic educological knowing is a supervising secondary school science teacher describing to a student teacher how to give guidance to a set of secondary school students about how to conduct an experiment to determine whether carbon dioxide supports combustion.

Emotional Knowing. Emotional cognitive performances are feelings of emotion in relation to some state of affairs. Examples of emotional knowing include a learned emotional response to a rendition of Vivaldi's musical piece, *Four Seasons*. A second example is remaining calm and suppressing panic as one participates in the evacuation of a burning building. An example of emotional educological knowing is a teacher maintaining confidence, serenity and equanimity among a group of hostile, unruly and rebellious pupils.

Imaginal Knowing. Imaginal performances are the acts of forming (or perceiving) images, shapes, imagined sounds and imagined relationships in one's awareness or consciousness. Someone who forms a picture of a cow in the consciousness (but is not viewing, or seeing a cow with the eye) is performing imaginally. Likewise, imagining a tune or musical piece by recalling it or creating it (but not audibly singing it or hearing it with the ear) is an imaginal performance. Imagining where your opponent in a tennis game is going to drive the next shot is an imaginal performance. An example of imaginal educological knowing is imagining accurately, as a teacher of English literature, how your Year 10 high school students might feel as they read *A Tale of Two Cities* by Charles Dickens.

Physiological Knowing. Physiological performances are, for example, through choice, deliberately slowing one's heart rate, diminishing one's blood pressure, suppressing one's tears, blocking out pain, controlling urination & bowel movements or achieving sexual orgasm. A clear case of physiological educological knowing is exemplified by Deborah Sundahl, Carol Queen and Shannon Bell in their video in which, for educational purposes, they demonstrate effective techniques for achieving female sexual orgasm and ejaculation (D. Sundahl, 2004).

Physical Knowing. Physical performances are organized and coordinated movements and gestures, such as swimming, driving a car, bouncing a basketball, operating a crane, piloting a boat, flying an aircraft, diving from a high tower into a pool. An example of physical educological knowing is demonstrating to a set of pupils how to move their feet and arms and how to hold their bodies while dancing the cha-cha.

Conative Knowing. Conative performances are acts of volition or will. Conation is the state of mind of having purpose, and conative knowing is choosing or willing. Conative knowing is an adequate performance of will in relation to some set of circumstances or state of affairs. Conative knowing is a state of <u>knowing-to</u>, as distinct from <u>knowing-that</u> or <u>knowing-how</u>. Individuals have achieved a state of <u>knowing-to</u> when they can say (and mean it), "I am willing to do that." That state of willingness, or <u>knowing-to</u>, is the same as conative knowing (G. Maccia, 1973c).

Critical Category 12: Levels of Knowing

There are degrees of extent to which one knows. Levels of knowing are degrees of extent to which one has realized the ability to perform in a well informed, purposeful and adequate manner in relation to some state of affairs. Degrees of extent of knowing are levels of knowing. At least three levels of knowing can be distinguished:
    (1) Level 1 or preconventional knowing,
    (2) Level 2 or conventional knowing,
    (3) Level 3 or postconventional knowing.
The three levels of knowing relate to the distinctions of
    (1) beginner or novice (Level 1),
    (2) intermediate and expert (Level 2) and
    (3) expert innovator (Level 3).
One who has preconventional knowing about education is just at the beginning of learning some kind and form of knowing about education. The person has not yet achieved the conventions. At the conventional level, the person has learned the conventions, and the level includes both intermediate and expert performances. The postconventional level is being manifested when the knower is creating innovations which have not yet become accepted conventions. Innovative expert performers within the educational process and educological researchers who are engaged in neo-search about the educational process, if successful are performing at the postconventional level of knowing. They are setting new standards or new conventions of knowing about education.

Level 1 Knowing. At Level 1 knowing, that of preconventional knowing, individuals experience high degrees of disorganization, make many mistakes and have a low degree of control. It is a level in which there are many trials and errors, and much exertion of self-conscious effort. In coming to know how to ride a bicycle, for example, Level 1 knowing is the stage of wobbling around and falling over frequently. In coming to know how to add, Level 1 knowing is the stage of setting out four beans and five beans and counting all of the beans individually in the two groups in order to determine that four plus five makes the sum of nine. In the task of writing instructional unit plans and lesson plans for a Year 4 primary school class, Level 1 knowing is the stage at which the novice teacher has no idea where to begin, or what the differences among a curriculum, a syllabus, a unit plan and a lesson plan might be, or what sequence of guided study tasks may be appropriate for a Year 4 primary school class. Level 1 knowing is the level of knowing at which the novice or beginner performs.

In the transition between Level 1 and Level 2 knowing, the degree of control becomes extended and refined. Fewer mistakes are made, and conventions in performance are well on their way to becoming habituated, but there are still self-conscious uses of the conventions. Control is being achieved, but only with considerable concentration. With respect to bicycle riding, for example, the transition from Level 1 to Level 2 knowing is characterized by steady riding and little wobbling, but control is not yet automatic. The rider puts in a great deal of concentration in order to coordinate the movement of foot, leg, arm and trunk in order to assure balance. In the case of someone learning to add, the transition from Level 1 to Level 2 knowing is characterized, for example, by the ability to add two and three digit numbers fairly efficiently, but not able to go beyond three digits. In the case of the novice teacher in transition from Level 1 to Level 2 knowing, the novice can write a rudimentary unit plan and write a basic lesson plan that is logically linked to the unit plan.

Level 2 Knowing. Once the transition is made, and knowing at Level 2, or conventional knowing, is achieved, one's performance becomes habituated and automatic. The conventions of any particular knowing have become mastered. Control within the limits of established conventions is achieved to a high degree, and there is little or no self-conscious effort exerted in the control. Adequate performance of conventions has become routine. In the example of riding a bicycle, the rider maintains balance, speed and control without having to concentrate. It has become automatic to coordinate all of the necessary body movements for cycling. With regard to the case of addition, Level 2 knowing is characterized by being able to make the correct shape and orientation of numerals, state and use face and place value of numerals, place decimal points correctly and use the basic addition facts efficiently so that one can add any number to any number. The conventions of addition are used quickly, efficiently and accurately. With respect to curricula, syllabi, unit planning and lesson planning, at Level 2 conventional knowing, the teacher can routinely and quickly use curriculum and syllabus documents to write an instructional unit plan appropriate for a Year 4 primary school class and design a set of lesson plans which link consistently, sequentially and appropriately to the unit plan.

Level 3 Knowing. Knowing at Level 3 is cognitive function which has extended beyond established conventions. Achievement of Level 3 knowing, or postconventional knowing, requires inquiry, innovation and creativity so that one breaks new ground and forms new standards of performance which extend beyond the conventions of Level 2 knowing. In bicycle riding, it might be, for example, the development of a set of new techniques and expertise in cycling (e.g. lifting up the back wheel and doing a triple pirouette on the front wheel). In mathematics, it might be the development of a new algorithm for doing a mathematical operation. In unit planning and lesson planning, the teacher may be developing an innovative systematic approach to curriculum planning, unit planning and lesson planning which links to a model of teaching or a system of instruction which the teacher has investigated experimentally, empirically verified as being effective and documented in a research report. The new standards of performance which might be established at Level 3 knowing could even contravene or reject the accepted conventions of Level 2 knowing.

Figure 1.11: Three Levels of Knowing and Six Forms of Knowing

Three levels & six forms of knowing						
Levels of knowing	**Forms of knowing**					
	(1)	(2)	(3)	(4)	(5)	(6)
	Linguistic knowing	Emotional knowing	Imaginal knowing	Physiological knowing	Physical knowing	Conative knowing
(A) Level 3: Post-conventional	A-1	A-2	A-3	A-4	A-5	A-6
(B) Level 2: Conventional	B-1	B-2	B-3	B-4	B-5	B-6
(C) Level 1: Pre-conventional	C-1	C-2	C-3	C-4	C-5	C-6

Figure 1.11 illustrates the possible combinations of levels of knowing and forms of knowing. For example, *A-2* in Figure 1.11 signifies Level 3 postconventional knowing in an emotional form. *B-6* signifies Level 2 conventional knowing in a conative form. *C-1* signifies Level 1 preconventional knowing in a linguistic form.

Critical Category 13: Kinds of Knowing

In addition to levels of knowing and forms of knowing, there are kinds of knowing. Kinds of knowing are distinguishable with respect to the state of affairs in relation to which the knowing is performed. At least three kinds can be distinguished: qualitative, quantitative and procedural knowing. Qualitative knowing is the realized ability to perform adequately in relation to unique states of affairs. Quantitative knowing is the realized ability to perform adequately in relation to states of affairs as categories. Procedural knowing is the realized ability to perform adequately in relation to a set of sequenced activities intended to achieve desired goals or outcomes.

Qualitative Knowing. Qualitative knowing about education is the learned ability to perform in a well informed, purposeful and adequate way in relation to unique states of affairs within education. Qualitative knowing is a state of knowing-that-one, as distinct from knowing-that (G. Maccia, 1973c). It is, in Maccia's terms, a "basic knowing" (G. Maccia, 1973c), which is relevant to unique entities and states of affairs. Individuals have achieved a state of knowing-that-one when they can say (and mean it), "I know that one" (G. Maccia, 1973c). For example, Mr. Kennedy, a middle school teacher, recognizes, is well acquainted with and appreciates Michael's moods, motivations, aspirations and capabilities, not as an adolescent or a middle class child or a student in his eighth year of school, but as Michael, in all of his uniqueness. This is an example of Mr. Kennedy's qualitative educological knowing. He might be able to manifest this qualitative knowing of Michael in talking with Michael (linguistic knowing), in anticipating Michael's conduct (imaginal knowing), in making gestures to Michael (physical knowing), in having a certain set of purposes in mind for Michael (conative knowing). Qualitative knowing of education gives the knower (e.g. parent, uncle, school teacher, student, counselor, coach, trainer, administrator, curriculum developer, educological researcher) sensitivity for the educational process and for individuals, entities and features within the process so that unique, significant and important aspects of the process can be discerned and appreciated by the knower.

At least three subcategories of qualitative knowing can be distinguished, viz. recognitive, acquaintive and appreciative (G. Maccia, 1973a,b,c, 1977). Individuals have achieved qualitative recognitive knowing when they can recognize a state of affairs and discern it from that which is not that state of affairs, and vice versa, viz. discern that which is not that state of affairs from that which is. Individuals have achieved qualitative acquaintive knowing when they, at first hand, experience a state of affairs and become familiar with the essential and unique qualities of that given state of affairs (i.e. entities, activities, relations). The ability to identify the unique qualities of a known state of affairs by denotative use of language (J. Christensen, 2013) characterizes qualitative acquaintive knowing. Individuals have achieved qualitative appreciative knowing of a state of affairs when they are acquainted with the something, can select elements that are appropriate to the something and can select relations which are appropriate to the something. It is a "discerning judgment ... that appraises the adequacy of part-whole entities and connections" (G. Maccia, 1973c, p. 3).

In summary, qualitative knowing can be manifested in all three levels and in all six forms of knowing, and it is qualitative educological knowing which gives individuals their sensitivity to discerning states of affairs in the educational process.

Quantitative Knowing. Quantitative knowing about education is the ability to perform in a well informed, purposeful and adequate way in relation to states of affairs within education as members of categories. In contrast to qualitative knowing, which is a state of knowing-that-one, quantitative knowing is a state of knowing-that (G. Maccia, 1973c). People have achieved a state of knowing-that when they say (and mean it), "I now know that is so." The teacher, Mr. Kennedy, can, for example, classify Michael's conduct as typical of thirteen year olds. He can categorize Michael's capabilities as characteristic of middle level achievers and relate his aspirations and motivations to what one might expect of male, middle class adolescents. He may manifest this quantitative knowing in

(1) writing a report (linguistic knowing),
(2) having a feeling of familiarity about Michael's conduct as typical of boys of his age, social class and cultural heritage (an emotional knowing),
(3) imagining how Michael will resemble his mates in a year's time (imaginal knowing),
(4) making gestures towards boys of Michael's kind (physical knowing) and
(5) forming purposes for instruction appropriate to Michael as a member of the category of male adolescents (conative knowing).

Quantitative knowing gives the knower adequacy and power with respect to theory (i.e. quantitative knowing gives theoretical adequacy). The knower with quantitative knowing about education can describe, characterize and explain (i.e. theorize) about the educational process in terms of categories and classifications of features or aspects of the educational process. Knowers can do this with appropriate evidence and sound inferences, if they have quantitative knowing.

At least three subcategories of quantitative knowing can be distinguished, viz. instantive, theoretical and criterial knowing (G. Maccia, 1973c). Knowing-that is "non-basic knowing" (following K. Lehrer and T. Paxon, 1968). Whereas a "basic knowing" is relevant to the unique, a "non-basic knowing" is relevant to the general, i.e. to a category. Knowing-that-one is "true belief that is completely justified and which justification does not depend upon any other statement or belief," but knowing-that is "true belief that is completely justified and that justification is not defeated by any other justifying statement or belief" (G. Maccia, 1973c, pp. 2, 4). Individuals have quantitative instantive knowing when they are able to make an assertion that is warranted by referencing the assertion with adequate authority. Individuals can be said to have quantitative theoretical knowing when they are able to make an assertion and warrant the assertion by appropriate evidence or evidential argument. And individuals have quantitative criterial knowing when they can make an assertion and warrant the assertion by justificatory argument.

Procedural Knowing. Procedural knowing is the ability to use a set of performances to achieve a desired result. Procedural knowing is knowing-how-to-do-that and also knowing-what-to-do as opposed to knowing-that-one and knowing-that (G. Maccia, 1973c). Individuals have achieved a state of knowing-how when they can say (and mean it), "I can now do that." Knowing-how can be manifested in all forms of knowing, viz. linguistic, emotional, imaginal, physical, physiological and conative knowing. For example, the performances implied by the statement, "I can do that," include the ability to solve quadratic equations, speak Russian and write essays on existentialism. A case of procedural educological knowing is the example of Mrs. Gum. Mrs. Gum, a primary school teacher, for example, starts class by having the children assemble in a line outside the classroom, enter the classroom single file and take their seats as assigned seats. She has found that this set of procedures achieves an orderly entry into the room and focuses the attention of the pupils upon what is to happen next in the lesson. In this example, Mrs. Gum is manifesting procedural educological knowing. When she is giving directions, the procedural knowing is being manifested as linguistic procedural knowing. It can also be manifested in gestures (physical knowing), in feelings (emotional knowing), in anticipation (imaginal knowing) and in purposes (conative knowing). Procedural knowing is the basis for effective action within the educational process.

At least four subcategories of procedural knowing can be distinguished. First, there is protocolic procedural knowing. This knowing is an ability to execute some performance smoothly, appropriately and repeatedly. It is a state of knowing-how-to-do-that. It is a single-pathed performance characterized by goal attainment through invariant sequences of activity (inclusive of the six forms of knowing). The other three subcategories (adaptive, innovative and creative procedural knowing) are subsets of knowing-what-to-do. A state of knowing-what-to-do is the realized ability to specify the manner by which some performance is to be altered in realizing a goal, and it is manifested by mapping sequences for executing alternative novel performances. Individuals have adaptive procedural knowing (G. Maccia, 1973c, calls this "conventional procedural knowing") when they have the ability to execute a multi-pathed performance smoothly and to attain a goal through adaptive sequences of movement. Individuals have innovative knowing when they have the ability to transfer elements of one performance to another and to attain goals by improving or inventing different ways of performance. Creative knowing is manifested as the ability to transform elements of performance into unique forms and to unite disparate ways of realizing goals. Adaptive, innovative and creative procedural knowing are operating at the postconventional level of knowing.

Adaptive, innovative and creative knowing can not be taught, only achieved. But what can be taught, studied and learned under guidance is the means by which to recognize adaptive, innovative and creative knowing (an important knowing for a teacher or an evaluator). And, of course, once adaptive, innovative and creative knowing have been achieved by someone, others can follow along, because the new knowing becomes conventional knowing. Those who follow can learn the conventional knowing which has been formed through adaptation, innovation and creation by the originator of the knowing. Conventional knowing can always be taught, studied and learned.

Of the three kinds of knowing, qualitative knowing (knowing-that-one) includes
- recognitive,
- acquaintive and
- appreciative knowing.

Quantitative knowing (knowing-that) includes
- instantive,
- theoretical and
- criterial knowing.

Procedural knowing (knowing-how-to-do) includes
- knowing-how-to-do-that and
- knowing-what-to-do.

Knowing-how-to-do-that includes only
- protocolic knowing.

Knowing-what-to-do includes
- adaptive,

- innovative and
- creative knowing.

The relationships of qualitative, quantitative and procedural knowing are summarized in Figure 1.12.

Figure 1.12: Three Kinds of Knowing

Kinds of Knowing			
Qualitative	**Quantitative**	**Procedural**	
Knowing-that-one	**Knowing-that**	**Knowing-how-to-do**	
		Knowing-how-to-do-that	**Knowing-what-to-do**
Recognitive Acquaintive Appreciative	Instantive Theoretical Criterial	Protocolic	Adaptive Innovative Creative

In relation to the forms and levels of knowing, qualitative knowing (knowing-that-one, including recognitive, acquaintive, appreciative) can be manifested in all six forms of knowing and all three levels. Recognitive and acquaintive knowing function at the level of apprehension (denotative use of language). Appreciative knowing operates at the level of comprehension (denotative and connotative use of language). Quantitative knowing (knowing-that) is a complex system of all forms of knowing in which linguistic knowing operates as a guide for the other forms of knowing. Quantitative knowing can function at the apprehension and comprehension levels. Protocolic procedural knowing (knowing-how-to-do-that) can be any of the six forms of knowing, and it operates at the preconventional and conventional levels of knowing. Knowing-what-to-do, including adaptive, innovative and creative knowing, can be any of the six forms, and it operates at the level of postconventional knowing.

Summary. In summary, knowing is cognitive function. Cognitive function is learned, not instinctual. It is the learned ability to perform in a well informed, intelligent, purposeful and adequate way in relation to some state of affairs. There are at least six forms of knowing. The six forms of knowing are distinguishable with respect to the manner in which the knowing is manifested. There are at least three levels of knowing. The three levels of knowing are distinguishable with respect to the degree of expertise with which the knowing is performed. There are at least three kinds of knowing. The three kinds are distinguishable with respect to the state of affairs in relation to which the knowing is performed.

The combination of forms, levels and kinds of knowing constitutes the range of knowing. A range of knowing may vary from restricted to extended. It is possible for a person to develop linguistic knowing without physical knowing, or procedural linguistic knowing without procedural physical knowing. For example, there have been historical examples of swimming coaches who could not swim themselves, but who were very competent in coaching competitive swimmers. There have been teachers who have taught young people how to play netball, but they never played the game themselves.

The range of people's knowing determines their understanding. That is to say, when we say that someone has a good understanding of something, we mean that the person has an extensive range of knowing about that something. See Figures 1.13a,b,c.

In Figure 1.13c, preconventional linguistic quantitative knowing at Level 1 (*C-1-b*), for example, is very restricted. In Figure 1.13b, at Level 2 (*B-1-b*), it is well developed and in accordance with conventions. In Figure 1.13a, at Level 3 (*A-1-b*), it is creative and innovative. So it is with each of the other levels and forms. The first level is the preconventional. The second is the conventional. And the third is the postconventional. These combi-

Figure 1.13a: Range of Knowing as Combinations of Levels, Kinds and Forms of Knowing (Level 3 Knowing)

Range of Knowing (Combinations of Levels, Forms and Kinds of Knowing – Level 3 Knowing)				
Levels of Knowing	**Forms of Knowing**	**Kinds of Knowing**		
		(a) *Qualitative*	**(b)** *Quantitative*	**(c)** *Procedural*
(A) *Third Level: Post-conventional Knowing*	**(1)** *Linguistic*	A-1-a	A-1-b	A-1-c
	(2) *Emotional*	A-2-a	A-2-b	A-2-c
	(3) *Imaginal*	A-3-a	A-3-b	A-3-c
	(4) *Physio-logical*	A-4-a	A-4-b	A-4-c
	(5) *Physical*	A-5-a	A-5-b	A-5-c
	(6) *Conative*	A-6-a	A-6-b	A-6-c

Figure 1.13b: Range of Knowing as Combinations of Levels, Kinds and Forms of Knowing (Level 2 Knowing)

<table>
<tr><th colspan="5">Range of Knowing
(Combinations of Levels, Forms
and Kinds of Knowing – Level 2 Knowing)</th></tr>
<tr><td rowspan="2"></td><td rowspan="2"></td><td colspan="3">Kinds of Knowing</td></tr>
<tr><td>(a)
Qualitative</td><td>(b)
Quantitative</td><td>(c)
Procedural</td></tr>
<tr><td>Levels of Knowing</td><td>Forms of Knowing</td><td></td><td></td><td></td></tr>
<tr><td rowspan="6">(B)
Second Level: Conventional Knowing</td><td>(1)
Linguistic</td><td>B-1-a</td><td>B-1-b</td><td>B-1-c</td></tr>
<tr><td>(2)
Emotional</td><td>B-2-a</td><td>B-2-b</td><td>B-2-c</td></tr>
<tr><td>(3)
Imaginal</td><td>B-3-a</td><td>B-3-b</td><td>B-3-c</td></tr>
<tr><td>(4)
Physio-logical</td><td>B-4-a</td><td>B-4-b</td><td>B-4-c</td></tr>
<tr><td>(5)
Physical</td><td>B-5-a</td><td>B-5-b</td><td>B-5-c</td></tr>
<tr><td>(6)
Conative</td><td>B-6-a</td><td>B-6-b</td><td>B-6-c</td></tr>
</table>

Figure 1.13c: Range of Knowing as Combinations of Levels, Kinds and Forms of Knowing (Level 1 Knowing)

Range of Knowing (Combinations of Levels, Forms and Kinds of Knowing – Level 1 Knowing)				
		Kinds of Knowing		
Levels of Knowing	Forms of Knowing	(a) *Qualitative*	(b) *Quantitative*	(c) *Procedural*
(C) *First Level: Preconventional Knowing*	(1) *Linguistic*	C-1-a	C-1-b	C-1-c
	(2) *Emotional*	C-2-a	C-2-b	C-2-c
	(3) *Imaginal*	C-3-a	C-3-b	C-3-c
	(4) *Physio-logical*	C-4-a	C-4-b	C-4-c
	(5) *Physical*	C-5-a	C-5-b	C-5-c
	(6) *Conative*	C-6-a	C-6-b	C-6-c

nations of levels, forms and kinds constitute the range of knowing of any individual. Individuals have upper and outer limits to the levels, forms and kinds of knowing which they have achieved at any given point in life. These upper and outer limits are the extent of any individual's range of knowing. In relation to basketball, for example, there are some people who can tell you all about the various teams, but they do not play the sport themselves. Their linguistic quantitative knowing of basketball is well developed, but not their physical procedural knowing. There are others who play the sport well. They have extensive command of defensive and offensive tactics and strategies. They anticipate well the moves of their fellow team members and the moves of their opponents. They also have a strong attachment and commitment to the game. Such people have well developed physical, physiological, imaginal, emotional and conative knowing of basketball. Their range of knowing is extensive.

With regard to knowing about education (or educological knowing), to claim that people know extensively about education implies that their range of adequate performances in relation to the educational process are extensive. They can talk and write about it adequately. They can engage in the process adequately. They are expert conceivers and observers of the process, and they are expert participants and practitioners in the process. They have realized a very wide range of adequate linguistic, imaginal, emotional, physical, conative and even physiological performances in relation to the field of phenomena that is education. They consistently perform at the conventional and postconventional levels of knowing. They are educological experts. They understand education very well.

Critical Category 14: Understanding and Knowing

Understanding is, of course, closely related to knowing, and especially to linguistic knowing. Understanding is some range of knowing, i.e. some combination of levels, kinds and forms of knowing. Understanding arises from realizing the ability to signify meaning to one's self with symbols (i.e. to in-tell). It is through symbolizing (conceiving) that one can make sense out of states of affairs and thus come to understand one's environment and one's self in relation to that environment. The development of understanding requires experience (in the sense of transactions with one's environment) and an ability to conceive about that experience, either out-loud (talking with meaning out-loud or signing with gestures as with American Sign Language), in-loud (speaking with meaning silently to one's self), or writing, or all three.

At least three levels of understanding can be distinguished. They are the levels of
- prehension,
- apprehension and
- comprehension.

In the development of understanding, enunciation precedes adjudication. That is to say, the act of conceiving or saying with meaning (either out-loud or in-loud) about a matter takes place before one is able to engage in the act of exercising competent and adequate judgment about a matter or some state of affairs. Furthermore, the act of saying with little or even no meaning precedes the act of saying with meaning, in the normal course of developing understanding. Saying with meaning is conceiving. Saying without meaning is uttering sounds, or making senseless noise (i.e. senseless, at least, to the individual who is producing the utterance). The three levels of understanding (prehension, apprehension, comprehension) relate to the acts of uttering and conceiving, and they also relate to the acts of enunciating and adjudicating. Prehension is operating with language at the level of uttering without conceiving much meaning. Apprehension is conceiving symbols with meaning, but the meaning is restricted largely to denotative meaning. Comprehension is conceiving with both denotative and connotative meaning. It is the most expanded level of understanding. See Figure 1.14.

At the level of prehension (Level 0), an individual, for example, might be able to say (or write) the statement,

Education is a process in which someone teaches and someone studies something in some setting,

but the individual does so without conceiving the meaning of the statement. Prehension is the act of uttering. For the individual who produces the utterance, there is little sense in it, as yet. The level of prehension is the lowest level of understanding. It is the beginning, or dawning, of understanding, and it is a necessary prerequisite level which an individual normally must develop prior to any higher levels of understanding.

At the next level, the level of apprehension (Level 1 under-standing), an individual is operating with language at the level of saying or talking (out-loud or in-loud) or writing with meaning. However, even though apprehension is conceiving (using symbols with meaning), the meaning is restricted largely to denotative meaning. Individuals can connect their language with specific objects and particular actions, but not extend the meaning beyond the level of denotations. Denotative meaning is the relationship between an object and a word. A tree is a denotation of the word *tree*. To denote with the word *tree* is to say the word *tree* and mean the object, tree.

Figure 1.14: Levels of Understanding as Prehension, Apprehension and Comprehension

Levels of Understanding		
Level 2	Comprehension	Level of using language to conceive denotative and connotative meaning
Level 1	Apprehension	Level of using language to conceive denotative meaning
Level 0	Prehension	Level of uttering language without conceiving meaning

One can point to (or denote) objects with words, and one way in which we commonly define meanings is to point to the things or categories of things which words name. This is the act of defining a word's meaning denotatively. So, denoting is pointing to objects with words.

Denotations are objects referred to by words. And denotative meaning is the relationship between an object and a word in which the meaning of the word is the object to which the word refers. It is possible (and fairly common) for an individual to know how to use a word correctly, but not know how to define the meaning of the word with another set of words. And it is possible to know how to use a sentence correctly, but not know how to explicate the meaning of the sentence. In such cases, individuals are using language (or systems of symbols) denotatively. They can point to objects and states of affairs with words. They can name, identify, describe and to some extent explain actions, the workings of objects and states of affairs. They can even predict, manipulate and control states of affairs. But their language is functioning within the restricted use of denotative meaning.

Individuals who are operating at the level of apprehension can, for example, say or write the statement,

Education is a process in which someone teaches and someone studies something in some setting,

and conceive the meaning of the statement to the extent of being able to point to actual instances of teachers, students, content and settings. The ability to point to objects, actions and states of affairs with words characterizes understanding at the level of apprehension.

At the third level of understanding (Level 3 understanding), that of comprehension, individuals are operating with language at the level of saying or talking (out-loud or in-loud) or writing with denotative and connotative meaning. Individuals operating at the level of comprehension can do more than point to specific objects, actions and relations. They can extend beyond the level of denotations to that of connotations. Connotative meaning is the relationship between a word (or a set of words) and another word (or set of words). The set of words,

a woody perennial plant having a single usually elongated stem generally with few or no branches on its lower part

is a connotation of the word *tree*. To connote with the word *tree* is to say the word *tree* and mean the set of words *a woody perennial plant having a single usually elongated stem generally with few or no branches on its lower part.*

One can point to, or connote, other words with words, and a second way of defining (besides pointing to objects) is to point to other words which can be used in place of a word (or a term). This is the act of defining the meaning of a word connotatively. So, connoting is pointing to words with words. Connotation is a set of words which can be used in place of a word. And connotative meaning is a relationship between a set of words and another word in which the meaning of the word is the set of words which can be used in its place.

At the level of comprehension, individuals are able to say, for example, the statement,

Education is a process in which someone teaches and someone studies something in some setting,

and to conceive the meaning of the statement both denotatively and connotatively. The individuals are able to point to actual instances of teaching and not teaching, or studying and not studying, or content and not content, or educational settings and not educational settings. To do these things is to conceive denotatively. They are also able to say with other words what the statement,

Education is a process in which someone teaches and someone studies something in some setting,

means and implies. They can, for example, say or write,

A teacher is anyone who acts deliberately in a way to help someone learn something. For example, a father who shows his son how to slide a worm onto a fishing hook so that it stays, then gives practice and supervision until his son can expertly slide a worm onto a hook, is engaging in teaching. He is using the teaching methods of describing, demonstrating, explaining, assigning guided practice, supervising and evaluating. The son is engaging in education as a pupil. He is using the study methods of observing, listening and practicing under guidance. The content is the fund of knowledge about how to put bait on a hook. The outcome of the educational transaction is that the boy knows something he didn't know before. He extends his range of knowing. He develops his physical procedural knowing at the conventional level in relation to putting a worm on a fishing hook. The social setting is the family. The physical setting is a boat on a river. The cultural setting is that of recreational fishing in contemporary Australian society.

To be able to say or write the above paragraph (and mean it) is to conceive about education connotatively. The people who can say or write that paragraph, mean it, make judgments based on the meaning of the statements and elaborate upon it without help or prompting, are manifesting extensive linguistic quantitative educological knowing at the conventional level. They are conceiving denotatively and connotatively about education. They have a linguistic comprehension of education, or a linguistic educological comprehension. Comprehension includes both denotative and connotative conception.

There is uttering, and there is conceiving. Uttering is making the sound of a word without understanding or knowing its meaning. Conceiving is using a word with meaning and understanding.

The three levels of understanding relate to the activities of uttering and conceiving in this way. The first level of understanding (prehension) is the same as uttering, and the second and third levels (apprehension and comprehension) are both different kinds of conception. Apprehension is conceiving denotatively. Comprehension is conceiving denotatively and connotatively.

The levels of understanding relate to the acts of enunciation and adjudication. Enunciation is saying or making a pronounce-ment about something, and enunciation is part of all three levels of understanding. Adjudication, or making judgments about some-thing, is made possible by the three levels of understanding. At the level of prehension, well informed judgments are not possible, but prehension is a necessary foundation for the development of adjudication. As understanding develops through to the two higher levels (apprehension and comprehension), the capacity to make well informed judgments about something (e.g. objects, relations, states of affairs, procedures) also develops.

Levels of understanding are related to levels of knowing, forms of knowing and kinds of knowing in this way. Understanding enables an individual to describe, characterize, explain, predict, prescribe and justify states of affairs. It also enables an individual to influence and control (to some extent) states of affairs through anticipation, prescription and intervention. The realized abilities to describe, characterize, explain, predict, justify and prescribe are all linguistic abilities. That is, they are instances of linguistic knowing. The realized ability to intervene may be of any form, e.g. linguistic, physical, physiological, emotional, imaginal, conative. Understanding, then, is linguistic knowing at the two upper levels of conventional and postconventional knowing, in all kinds of knowing, plus any or all of the other possible forms of knowing. Understanding is a range of knowing in which linguistic knowing guides the other forms and kinds of knowing that are functioning within one's range of knowing. This range of knowing, which is understanding, is located within the functioning of individuals. Human development, taken as the extension of cognitive function, is the process in which this range of knowing, which is understanding, develops from (1) a restricted and relatively uncomplicated, undifferentiated function into (2) an extensive, highly complicated and extremely differentiated function.

An extensive understanding consists of an extensive combination of forms, kinds and the two upper levels of knowing. A restricted understanding consists of a restricted combination of forms, kinds and levels of knowing. In short, what is understanding? It is a range of knowing.

Chapter 2: Uses for the Critical Categories

The fourteen critical categories can be used in inquiry, analysis and discourse about curriculum and education in a variety of ways. For example, they can be used to select an appropriate name to denote knowledge about education and knowledge about curriculum. They can be used to clarify the relationship between curriculum and the educational process. They can be used to clarify what it is we denote with the terms *education* and *curriculum*. They can be used to identify and characterize the basic components of education, the basic functions of education and the derivative features of education. They can be used to identify and characterize different sets of teaching and studying strategies in education. And they can be used to identify and characterize the basic components of a sound curriculum.

A Name for Knowledge about Curriculum

The fourteen critical categories can be used in inquiry about curriculum in a variety of ways. One use is to clarify existing discourse about curriculum. An important step in the clarification process is to address the question,

"What is an appropriate name for knowledge about curriculum?"

Candidates which exist in common usage at the moment are the terms

- *curriculum*,
- *curriculum inquiry*,
- *curriculum theory* and
- *curriculum studies*.

In relation to this question, consider for a moment why zoology is not named *animals*. To do so would be to conflate a field of phenomena (animals) with a fund of knowledge about that field (zoology). Now consider why zoology is not named *vertebrates*. This would be the conflation of an aspect or feature of a field with the fund of knowledge about the field.

Such conflations do not exist in zoology because they are obvious category mistakes. The language of zoology is developed well enough to distinguish clearly among fund of knowledge, field of phenomena and aspects of a field of phenomena. But in relation to curriculum, such conflations do exist. The language that is used in discourse about curriculum and education is not developed well enough to make clear distinctions and to avoid conflations of distinct categories. Some critical distinctions need to be made to clarify discourse about curriculum.

For example, the fund of knowledge about curriculum is named by the term *curriculum*. This is the same as naming zoology with the term *vertebrates*. It conflates an aspect (curriculum) of a field of phenomena (education) with the fund of knowledge about the field (educology). This is why the term *curriculum* is an inappropriate name for the fund of knowledge about curriculum.

None of the other terms in common usage is appropriate either. In the case of *curriculum inquiry*, the term *inquiry* names an activity, viz. that of conducting research. An activity is not a fund, and the problem is to find an appropriate name for the fund of knowledge about curriculum. With the term *curriculum studies*, the term *studies* functions ambiguously. It simultaneously names the activity of conducting research and the activity of undertaking to learn something under the guidance of someone. Neither activity is a fund.

The term *curriculum theory* comes closest to the mark because the term *theory* names a fund of a certain category of statements. The term *theory* denotes both explanatory theory and justificatory theory. An explanatory theory is a retroductive argument that offers a set of premises to account for a known fact. A justificatory theory is a normative argument that offers a set of reasons for the conclusion that some state of affairs is good or bad, or relatively good or bad. But there is more to knowledge about curriculum than explanations of known facts and justifications for states of affairs. A fund of knowledge includes accurate descriptions (facts), adequate characterizations (identification of distinguishing features), adequate explanations (explanatory theories), adequate predictions, adequate prescriptions and adequate justifications (justificatory arguments). Thus the category of statements denoted by the term *curriculum theory* is too exclusive; it excludes a considerable part of the fund of knowledge about curriculum.

The problem is resolved by naming

(1) the field of phenomena with the term *education*,
(2) the aspect of the field with the term *curriculum* and
(3) the fund of knowledge about the aspect with the term *educology*.

This is achieved with the term *educology of curriculum*. This name necessarily implies the fund of knowledge about the relationship of curriculum to education.

Curriculum as an Aspect of Education

Another important step in the process of clarifying discourse about curriculum is to address the question of

"How does education as a field of phenomena relate to curriculum as an aspect of that field?"

This question requires clarification of the meanings of the terms *education* and *curriculum*, and it requires characterization of relationships between the two.

Clarification of the Concept of Education

Among the challenges in developing a satisfactory solution to this question is the ambiguity and malfunction of the term *education*. The term *education* is commonly used to name at least five different things. For example, it is commonplace for a teacher to say,

(S-1) "My profession is education."

In sentence S-1, the term substitution of *teaching* for *education* can be made without changing the meaning:

Term substitution in S-1: "My profession is [*teaching*]."

The fact that there is no change in meaning indicates that in the context of this sentence, the terms *teaching* and *education* are naming the same process. One common usage of the term *education*, then, is in the sense of teaching.

Now consider Thomas Hughes' comment on the education of an Englishman:

(S-2) "Life isn't all beer and skittles; but beer and skittles, or something better of the same sort, must form a good part of every Englishman's education" (from *Tom Brown's School Days*, 1857, Pt. I, Ch. 2).

If the term *education* is substituted by the term *teaching* in this statement, it still makes sense, but a more suitable substitution recommends itself. Put *learning* in the place of *education*, and the meaning of the statement remains closer to the original:

Term substitution in S-2: "Life isn't all beer and skittles; but beer and skittles, or something better of the same sort, must form a good part of every Englishman's [*learning*]."

From this substitution, a second common usage meaning of the term *education* becomes apparent, viz. *learning*.

But in what sense of learning? The term *learning* suffers the process-product confusion, i.e. the term *learning* has at least two senses:

(1) the process of learning and

(2) the product of learning.

One conception of learning, the process of learning, relates to the steps that people go through, their trials and errors, mistakes and successes, in coming to know something, to do something well or to understand something. A second conception of learning, the product of learning, relates to the outcome of having gone through the steps. It is the realized ability to do something well, the knowing (i.e. the knowing-that-one, the knowing-how-to, the knowing-what-to-do, the knowing-to-do), or the understanding. Learning in the first sense implies the process of coming to know. Learning in the second sense implies the product of the process, i.e. the knowing, the understanding, the realized ability to perform adequately in relation to some state of affairs.

So, to say that a common usage meaning of the term *education* is learning requires us to consider which sense of learning. The technique of term substitution shows that it is both senses of learning that are implied, depending on the context. This is illustrated, for example, in the sentences,

(S-3) "Nothing in education is so astonishing as the amount of ignorance it accumulates in the form of inert facts" (Henry Brooks Adams, *The Education of Henry Adams*, 1907, Ch. 25).

(S-4) "It is only the ignorant who despise education" (Publilius Syrus [Translated by Darious Lyman], ca. 50 B.C., *Maxim 571*).

The sense of learning implied by the term *education* in the first sentence (S-3) is the process of coming to know. This can be demonstrated by term substitution.

Term substitution in S-3: "Nothing in [*the process of coming to know*] is so astonishing as the amount of ignorance it accumulates in the form of inert facts."

The sense of learning implied by the term *education* in the second sentence (S-4) is the product of having come to know, viz. knowing, knowledgeability, competence, understanding.

Term substitution in S-4: "It is only the ignorant who despise [*knowing, knowledgeability, competence, understanding*]."

At least two other common usages of the term *education* are distinguishable. Sometimes the term *education* is used to mean the combination of guiding someone in the process of her or his learning and that someone deliberately undertaking to be guided in her or his learning. In this usage, the term *education* is made to mean the combination of teaching by one person and trying to learn (studying under guidance) by a second person. This fourth sense is implied, for example, in the sentence

(S-5) "... one of the central functions ... of education is the introduction of pupils to forms of thought and knowledge which we think peculiarly valuable" (P.H. Hirst, 1974, p. 69).

This fourth meaning of *education* is made apparent by the following term substitution.

Term substitution S-5: "... one of the central functions ... of [*teaching and studying under guidance*] is the introduction of pupils to forms of thought and knowledge which we think peculiarly valuable."

The fifth sense of the term *education* that is established in common usage is that of knowledge about the process of teaching and studying under guidance. For example, in universities we find units named

- *College of Education,*
- *School of Education,*
- *Graduate School of Education,*
- *Faculty of Education,*
- *Division of Education* and
- *Department of Education.*

And people are awarded degrees and diplomas in *Education*. In the sentence,

(S-6) "Mr. Gamma holds a Ph.D. in Education,"

the following term substitution can be made without changing the meaning.

Term substitution in S-6: "Mr. Gamma holds a Ph.D. in
[*knowledge about teaching and studying under guidance*]."

A second substitution is also possible, and it, too, does not change the meaning:

Term substitution in S-6: "Mr. Gamma holds a Ph.D. in
[*educology*]."

From common usage, therefore, there are four possibilities from which a choice could be made to identify a field of phenomena for study or inquiry. The candidates are

(1) education as the process of coming to know,
(2) education as the product of coming to know,
(3) education as teaching and
(4) education as teaching and studying under guidance (with the intention to learn).

The fifth sense of the term *education* (i.e. educology) is not a candidate because it does not name a field of phenomena. Rather, it names a fund of knowledge about a field of phenomena.

Which Conception of Education?

The question arises, then,

"Which concept of the term *education* ought we use in careful, disciplined discourse about educational phenomena?"

An adequate solution to this problem requires that each of the four concepts be evaluated with respect to a set of appropriate criteria. The appropriate set includes

(1) inclusiveness,
(2) exclusiveness,
(3) internal consistency,
(4) exhaustiveness,
(5) external relatedness and
(6) fruitfulness.

These criteria are generally recognized and accepted in the philosophy of science as relevant, conventional and adequate standards for evaluation of a concept that is to be used to identify a class of phenomena about which inquiry might be conducted.

The criterion of inclusiveness is used to determine whether a conception of education is sufficiently broad enough to include all of the cases and instances of educational phenomena that are related to each other in essential ways.

The criterion of exclusiveness is used to judge whether a concept of education excludes all of the cases or instances which ought to be excluded from the field of educational phenomena.

The criterion of internal consistency is used to judge whether a conception of education includes the necessary and sufficient distinguishing characteristics of an educational transaction so that all cases or instances that are identified as educational are consistent and clearly related to each other in essential ways.

The criterion of exhaustiveness relates closely to that of inclusiveness. It is used to judge whether a conception of education permits every instance or case that should be counted as a member of the field of educational phenomena is counted, or whether there are some cases which are left out and which should be included.

The criterion of external relatedness is used to judge whether a conception of education is sufficiently related to other concepts (such as schooling, studying, learning, teaching, coaching, tutoring, mentoring, counseling, curriculum, knowing, understanding and knowledge) to be useful in promoting clear and unambiguous discourse about educational phenomena.

The criterion of fruitfulness is used to judge whether the conception of education is generally useful in permitting unambiguous and clear discourse about educational phenomena and whether it promotes progress in developing and extending descriptions, characterizations, explanations, predictions, prescriptions and justifications of educational phenomena.

Education as the Process of Learning. One conception of the term *education* is to conceive of it as the process of learning (or the process of coming to know). An evaluation of the conception of the term *education* as the process of coming to know in relation to the six criteria reveals some serious deficiencies. Education as coming to know is an achievement concept. It includes successful instances, only, of coming to know, and it excludes unsuccessful

Figure 2.1a: Education as the Process of Learning

Education conceived as the learning process			
Phenomena included by the concept		**Phenomena excluded by the concept**	
Unguided unintentional learning	i.e. learning from accident and life experiences	**Guided intentional unsuccessful studying**	i.e. deliberately undertaking to learn something (but not succeeding) under the guidance of a teacher, mentor, coach, counselor, trainer or instructor
Unguided intentional learning	i.e. learning through deliberate trial & error and systematic experimentation		
Guided unintentional learning	i.e. learning through socialization, enculturation, conditioning, propagandizing, manipulation, advertising	**Effective teaching**	i.e. deliberately undertaking activities to guide someone in studying something with the intention that the student learn something and the student succeeds in learning

Figure 2.1b: Education as the Process of Learning

Education conceived as the learning process			
Phenomena included by the concept		**Phenomena excluded by the concept**	
Guided intentional learning	i.e. learning through the guidance of a teacher, mentor, coach, counselor, trainer, instructor	Ineffective teaching	i.e. deliberately undertaking activities to guide someone in studying something with the intention that the student learn something and the student does not succeed in learning
Guided intentional successful studying	i.e. trying to learn and succeeding under the guidance of a teacher, mentor, coach, counselor, trainer, instructor		

tries at coming to know. Also, it includes instances of coming to know in which no one tries, but nevertheless learns something. The learning is adventitious or accidental, or it is the result of manipulation, propagandizing or conditioning. Moreover, education as coming to know excludes teaching from the field of educational phenomena altogether. The conception, then, is too broad, too inclusive in some cases. And it is too narrow, too exclusive in other cases. If this conception were used to identify which phenomena were to be counted as educational phenomena and which were not, the activities of trying to learn (studying) and of trying to help someone to learn (teaching) could be excluded from the field or realm of educational phenomena. A concept which makes such exclusions as does education as coming to know has serious limitations in guiding inquiry and research, and it would produce a very limited range of discourse. (See Figure 2.1a and Figure 2.1b.)

Figure 2.2: Education as the Product of Learning

Education conceived as the product of learning	
Phenomena included by the concept	**Phenomena excluded by the concept**
Knowing, i.e. competence, knowledgeability, expertise, understanding	**The process of studying, i.e. deliberately undertaking to learn something under the guidance of a teacher, mentor, coach, counselor, trainer or instructor**
	The process of teaching, i.e. deliberately undertaking activities to guide someone in studying something with the intention that the student learn something
	The process of learning, i.e. the process of achieving knowing and understanding

Education as the Product of Learning. A second conception of the term *education* is to conceive of it as the product or outcome of the learning process. An evaluation of the conception of education as the product of coming to know, or knowing, in relation to the six criteria also reveals some serious difficulties. Education as knowing excludes the process of coming to know from instances that would count as belonging to the field of educational phenomena. It also excludes teaching from the field. A concept which excludes the process of coming to know, the activity of teaching and the process of trying to learn from the field or realm of educational phenomena is too exclusive in its implication. It would lead, again, to an extremely limited range of inquiry and discourse.

Education as Teaching. A third conception of the term *education* is to conceive of it as teaching. Teaching is acting in ways that are intended to help someone come to know something. An evaluation of the conception of education as teaching shows that it, also, is too narrow in its implication. It includes only the activity of teaching in the range of phenomena that would count as educational phenomena. It excludes coming to know (the learning process) and trying to come to know (the study process).

Figure 2.3: Education as Teaching

Education conceived as teaching	
Phenomena included by the concept	**Phenomena excluded by the concept**
The process of teaching, i.e. deliberately undertaking activities to guide someone in studying something with the intention that the student learn something	**The process of studying, i.e. deliberately undertaking to learn something under the guidance of a teacher, mentor, coach, counselor, trainer or instructor**
	The process of learning, i.e. the process of achieving knowing and understanding
	The product of learning, i.e. knowing, competence, knowledgeability, expertise, understanding

Education as Teaching and Studying. The remaining candidate from common usage is the conception of *education* as the process of teaching and studying something under guidance in some setting (physical, social cultural) with the intention that learning be achieved. With regard to inclusiveness, this conception counts the

Figure 2.4 Education as Teaching and Studying

Education conceived as teaching and studying	
Phenomena included by the concept	**Phenomena excluded by the concept**
The process of teaching, i.e. deliberately undertaking activities to guide someone in studying something with the intention that the student learn something	The process of unguided and unintentional learning, i.e. learning through random events, accidents and experience
The process of guided studying, i.e. deliberately undertaking (successfully and unsuccessfully) to learn something under the guidance of a teacher, mentor, coach, counselor, trainer or instructor	The process of unguided and intentional learning, i.e. learning through trial and error, systematic experimentation, research and inquiry
The process of guided intentional learning, i.e. deliberately learning something under the guidance of a teacher, mentor, coach, counselor, trainer or instructor	The process of guided and unintentional learning, i.e. learning through conditioning, manipulating, indoctrination, propagandizing, proselytizing, advertising, socialization and enculturation

following as members or instances of the field of educational phenomena:

    (1) unsuccessful attempts to learn under guidance,
    (2) successful attempts to learn under guidance,
    (3) unsuccessful attempts to help someone learn under guidance,
    (4) successful attempts to help someone learn under guidance.

Education as teaching and studying under guidance excludes the following from the field of educational phenomena: the process of learning which is

(1) unguided and unintentional on the part of the learner,
(2) unguided and intentional on the part of the learner,
(3) guided and unintentional on the part of the learner.

The exclusion of these three categories of learning from the field of educational phenomena is advantageous from the point of view of being able to distinguish the process of education from

(1) learning from random events and accidents (learning without guidance and without intention on the part of the learner),
(2) learning from unguided research, unguided inquiry and trial and error (learning without guidance, but with intention on the part of the learner),
(3) learning from conditioning, manipulating, indoctrinating, propagandizing, proselytizing, advertising, socialization and enculturation (processes that cause learning unintentionally on the part of the learner, but with guidance by someone other than the learner).

Although distinct from the general process of learning, the activity of research and the product of coming to know (i.e. knowing), education conceived as teaching and studying under guidance has an external relatedness to them. It also has a close relationship with enculturation, socialization and schooling.

Official and Unofficial Education. Some might argue that the concept of schooling (or official education) is the one that ought to be used to determine the limits of the field of educational phenomena. However, the concept of the term *schooling* is too exclusive in its implication. It discounts instances of education which occur outside of the setting of schools, academies, colleges, institutes, universities and the like. Schooling is teaching and guided intentional studying that takes place within official education, but education as teaching and studying under guidance includes all instances of teaching and studying, both official and unofficial. Thus education as teaching and studying under guidance is a broad enough concept to facilitate and extend discourse about education that occurs within

(1) families, churches, mosques, temples, youth organizations, adult groups, clubs, factories, farms, businesses, or

(2) among friends, workmates, casual acquaintances, relatives, peer groups, as well as

(3) within nursery schools, kindergartens, primary and elementary schools, secondary and high schools, colleges, universities, academies and institutes.

An example of unofficial education is the following scenario. A single parent mother (Sharon) buys herself a copy of the computer game *Minecraft*. Her two children beg her to play with them. She has never played before, and she initially struggles with playing the game. She finds it difficult, and she hates the thought of looking like a big fat dummy in front of her kids. Her children know how to play the game very well. Her son (Jason), who is obsessed with *Minecraft*, starts to explain to her how the game is played. They start playing the game. Jason becomes the teacher, and his mother, the student. When she makes mistakes in the game, he follows her moves and fixes what she has done wrong. When monsters attack her avatar, her son makes his avatar leap in front of hers and saves hers as she struggles to find a suitable weapon in her inventory. The mother gradually learns under the guidance and example of her son how to play the game well enough to be competitive with her children.

An example of official education is the following scenario. An instructor in an English language college explains to a class of students, who are studying English as a second language, how to use the possessive pronouns (*mine, yours, his, hers, its, ours, yours, theirs*). He gives examples of sentences that use the possessive pronouns. He then gives his students a set of study activities in which they substitute possessive nouns with possessive pronouns (*This is Ron's book. This is his book.*) The students complete the study activities. In the following week, the instructor gives the students a written test that requires them to substitute possessive nouns with possessive pronouns. In the test, the students demonstrate in writing that they can correctly substitute possessive nouns with possessive pronouns.

The concept of education as schooling (or official education) would confine the discourse to discussions, characterizations and analyses of schools, academies, institutes, colleges or universities.

Figure 2.5: Official and Unofficial Education

Education conceived as teaching & studying	
Official education	**Unofficial education**
The process of teaching and intentional guided studying something (with the intention that the student achieve some range of knowing) **with** ▪ certified teachers, ▪ enrolled students, ▪ certified administrators, ▪ specified place & hours for attendance ▪ specified content, ▪ specified learning goals, ▪ certification of achievement, ▪ laws, rules & regulations, ▪ sorting of students (age, ability. gender) ▪ payment for teaching & administrative services ▪ record keeping	The process of teaching and intentional guided studying something (with the intention that the student achieve some range of knowing) **without** any of the features of official education
For example, education that takes place in schools, academies, institutes, colleges, universities	For example, education that takes place within families and among peer groups, workmates, recreational groups, casual acquaintances

While these features of official education are almost always in evidence in any system of schooling, whether ancient or contemporary, they are not features that are essential to the process of education. They are the institutional aspects of official education, and they are incidental to the educational process, rather than being generic to it. That is, a transaction could be properly named *education* and have none of the structural features associated with official education. Unofficial education is teaching and guided studying without the structural features of official education.

The concept of education as teaching and studying under guidance with the intention to achieve learning, then, provides necessary and sufficient distinguishing characteristics to

(1) include all that belongs to the field of educational phenomena (and thus meets the criterion of appropriate inclusions),

(2) exclude all that does not belong to the field of educational phenomena (and thus meets the criterion of appropriate exclusions),

(3) connect all that belongs to the field of educational phenomena through a system of internal coherency (and thus meeting the criterion of internal consistency),

(4) exhaust the possibilities of instances that could be counted as part of the field of educational phenomena (and thus meeting the criterion of exhaustiveness),

(5) relate the field of educational phenomena to other phenomena outside of the field (e.g. enculturation, socialization, conditioning) and thus meeting the criterion of external relatedness and

(6) establish a fruitful basis for extending careful disciplined discourse about educational phenomena (and thus meeting the criterion of fruitfulness).

Therefore, in relation to the six criteria for evaluation of a suitable concept of education to use in inquiry about education, the concept of education as teaching and studying under guidance with the intention to achieve learning is the most appropriate one, and it is the one that ought to be followed in determining the limits of the field of educational phenomena.

Four Basic Components of Education

If the term *education* is used to identify the educational process as the process of teaching and studying under guidance something in some setting, then it becomes possible to identify the basic components of education. The components of something are the parts which constitute it, and the basic components are those parts which are fundamental to something being what it is. The components of education are the things that give education its form. Education, in the sense of teaching and studying under guidance, has four basic components. If any one of the four is missing, then education can not take place, or function. The four are:

(1) teacher,
(2) student,
(3) content and
(4) setting.

Teacher. All who attempt to help someone to learn something in some setting are teachers. With respect to deciding whether people are playing the role of teachers, it does not matter whether those who try to help in fact do things that do not help. People still are playing the role of teachers as long as they are acting with the intention to help or cause someone to learn something. In other words, teachers can at times be effective, and at other times, ineffective. People do not have to hold an officially certified position within a school, an academy, a college, an institute or a university to be teachers.

Each of us plays many roles in our day-to-day lives, e.g. friend, parent, son or daughter, brother or sister, customer, employee; and one of the roles is that of teacher. Thus, a teacher is, at times, a mother or father, an aunt or uncle, a friend or acquaintance, a policeman, shop clerk, physician or bartender. A teacher is always a person, not a machine, book, chart, computer, TV or some other physical object. The role of teacher is universal. It exists in all cultures and societies. It is one of the distinctive features of human kind.

Student. Anyone who deliberately tries to learn something under the guidance of someone else is a student, i.e. is playing the role of student. The concept of student belongs to the same family of concepts as pupil, learner, disciple and follower. Sometimes students (or pupils) may try to learn, but fail. This does not disqualify them as students. Students can be, at times, successful in their studies, and at other times, unsuccessful. As long as they try to learn, successfully or otherwise, they are students. It is not necessary that a person be enrolled in a school or college, university or academy, to be a student. A person can be a student in a train station, a taxi cab or on a street corner, in a business office, or in a family. A student is, at times, a friend, relative, postman, airline pilot, soldier, architect, adult or child. In our day-to-day existence, among the many roles that each of us assumes from time to time is that of student. We want to know something, and we place ourselves under the guidance of someone to be assisted in our studying and learning. The role of student exists universally in all societies and cultures.

Content. The something that is taught and studied is the content (also referred to with the terms *subject* and *subject matter*). The content is the fund of knowledge that is selected and arranged in some order for the purposes of teaching and studying.

It is worth recalling that a fund of knowledge (vs. a range of knowing) is a set of warranted assertions, or true statements. Content, taken as a fund of knowledge, then, is a set of true statements that is organized for the purposes of teaching and studying.

The content may be a fund of knowledge (i.e. a set of true statements) about how to roller skate or how to tie shoelaces. It may be the knowledge of Australian history (i.e. a set of true statements about past events in Australia) or sociology (i.e. a set of true statements about society) or physics (i.e. a set of true statements about physical entities and states of affairs). It may be the knowledge (i.e. the true statements) that making people suffer is bad or that honesty is the best policy. It may be the knowledge (i.e. true statements) about how to make valid inferences or how to inquire effectively. It may be the knowledge (i.e. true statements) about how to gain people's confidence or how to persuade them to buy a car. The content is a selection from all that is available from the total fund of knowledge produced by a culture (or cultures), and the selection is organized for the purposes of teaching and studying under guidance.

At least two persons, one acting as teacher and the other acting as student, transact with each other in relation to a content (a selection of knowledge from the culture) with the intention of extending the student's knowing (i.e. extending her or his realized cognitive ability to perform in a well informed and intelligent manner to achieve desired outcomes, intentions or goals).

People, acting as students, direct their activities towards developing their preconventional range of knowing into a conventional range of knowing in relation to a particular content (fund of knowledge or set of true statements).

Setting. Education always takes place as an integral part of a society and culture. Those who teach and study are members of a society and a culture. The content is a selection of knowledge available from their society and culture. The knowledge available within a culture includes knowledge about customs, beliefs, laws, social arrangements, economic systems, political systems, language usages and religious systems of the society. The set of relationships among the culture and the three components of teacher, student and content constitute the setting of education. We could characterize the setting in terms of cultural setting for education, and this would be characterizing it in the broadest and most inclusive terms possible. Or we could characterize the setting in more selective and exclusive terms. For example, we could characterize the setting of education only in terms of its political setting, or only its religious setting or only its economic setting, or its historical setting, its administrative setting or its institutional setting. The setting places the limits (physical, social and cultural) on the extent and range of teachers' and students' activities, content selections and intended learning outcomes for the students. The effect of the setting on the educational process can be constructive, destructive or reconstructive of the educational process.

Constructive Relationship. An example of a constructive effect of social and cultural setting upon the educational process was that of Australian indigenous societies before European settlement. The values and norms of the Australian indigenous societies and cultures were supportive of the educational process within their societies. The educational process took place primarily within the social settings of families and kinship groups. It was within family groups and kinship groups that children and youth learned about their social roles, their obligations to each other, their mores and norms, their beliefs and customs and their ways of achieving sustenance through hunting, gathering and processing of flora and fauna. The societies and cultures of the indigenous groups supported the educational processes of teaching and studying under guidance through unofficial education. The educational process supported the values and norms of the society, and the society supported the educational process.

Destructive Relationship. An example of a destructive effect of social and cultural setting upon the educational process was that of Australian indigenous society after British settlement. After the arrival of British settlers, Christian missionary groups established schools for Australian indigenous children. A number of indigenous families resisted placement of their children in missionary schools. The education offered in the missionary schools conflicted with their nomadic way of life as hunters and gatherers and their life views and mythologies. Students were compelled to speak English and punished for speaking their first indigenous language. From the British point of view, the norms and values of Australian indigenous societies had a destructive effect upon the educational process in missionary schools. Some Australian indigenous families refused to send their children to missionary schools, and when forced to attend missionary schools, some Australian indigenous children resisted by running away or absenting themselves frequently from the schools. The societies and cultures of the indigenous groups did not support the educational processes of teaching and studying under guidance through official education in missionary schools. Likewise, the educational process in those schools did not support the values and norms of indigenous societies.

Reconstructive Relationship. An example of a reconstructive effect of social and cultural setting upon the educational process was that of the denazification program pursued by the Allies at the conclusion of the Second World War. After the defeat of Nazi

Germany, the Western Allies, as part of the policy of denazification, reconstructed education within German schools with the intention of eradicating Nazi values, including those of anti-democracy, racial vilification and genocide. The values and norms of the Allies had a reconstructive effect upon the educational process.

The Importance of Cultural Point of View. Whether the relationship of societies and their cultures with the educational process is constructive, destructive or reconstructive depends upon the point of view that one takes in analyzing the relationship. That is to say, you must adopt the worldview of a reference community in order to determine whether the norms and values of that reference group are supportive of any specific educational process. The same educational process can be judged worthy of support or unworthy of support depending upon the values and norms of the

Figure 2.6: Effects of Social and Cultural Settings on the Educational Process

Effects of social and cultural setting on the educational process		
Constructive	**Destructive**	**Reconstructive**
The values and norms of the reference community support the educational process as it is currently functioning	The values and norms of the reference community oppose the educational process as it is currently functioning	The values and norms of the reference community support the reformation of the educational process

reference community. In the above examples, from the Nazi viewpoint, the denazification school program was destructive in that it was directed towards eradicating Nazi values from German school programs and replacing them with liberal democratic values. In the example of British missionary schools for indigenous

Australian children, from the missionaries' viewpoint, the school program was reconstructive. Its aim was to eradicate the values and norms that indigenous children held and replace them with Christian values as the missionaries understood them.

Two Basic Processes of Education

Education has both form and function. The form of education is its structure, and the four components of teacher, student, content and setting constitute the form of education. The function of education is it characteristic workings, operations or processes. A process is the functioning of a set of parts in a pattern of relationships. The functioning of a teacher and student in relation to some content and some setting constitutes the basic processes of education, viz. teaching and studying under guidance (and if all goes well, intentional learning under guidance).

Teaching. Any activity by a person which is intended to help a second person learn something counts as teaching. Paradoxically, this sometimes includes withholding action as well. The feature of intention is what distinguishes activities which count as teaching from activities in general. Teaching is not merely doing something from which someone else learns, however. Always, intention must be present for activities to be counted as teaching.

For example, a person may observe his friend drive a car, and from that set of observations learn the basics of operating a car. So, was the friend who did the driving, teaching? It depends upon whether he was driving with the intention to help his friend develop an understanding of how to drive. If so, he was teaching. If not, he was merely driving, and nothing more. The example illustrates the nature of teaching as an intentional activity. It also illustrates that teaching is not only done by school teachers in classrooms. It can occur in a house, with one's family; on the job, with one's work mates; in a restaurant, with one's friends. The range of activities which might count as teaching is broad and extensive.

Some examples will suggest just how broad. A preschool teacher is teaching when she or he arranges a set of toys early one morning with the intention that, after they arrive, the children will have practice in socializing with each other and developing a sense of cooperation and sharing. The teacher is teaching by arranging the learning resources within the environment. A farmer shows his hired hand how to operate a cream separator. He is teaching by demonstrating. A musician listens to a pianist play. He recommends ways to improve technical and interpretational aspects of the pianist's recital. He is teaching by listening, evaluating and recommending. A senior pilot rides along and observes a junior pilot do practice take-offs and landings. The senior pilot identifies correct procedures and errors, recommends things to anticipate and reminds the junior pilot about the essential checks to make for take-offs and landings. The senior pilot is teaching by observing, evaluating, directing, recommending and explaining.

It is the peculiar nature of teaching that you can not determine whether a person is teaching by merely observing the performances or conduct of the person. You must also know her or his intentions. Teaching is deliberate performance by a person in ways that she or he intends to help a second person (the student) learn something in some setting (physical, social and cultural).

There are at least two other senses of the term *teaching* which arise in common usage, and they deserve some defining, explicating and relating to the conception of *teaching* as intentionally trying to help someone learn something. They will be distinguished with subscripts. $Teaching_1$ is the sense of teaching which has just been distinguished. $Teaching_2$ is intentionally causing learning, and $teaching_3$ is causing learning.

An example of $teaching_2$ is an older sister showing a younger brother how to fly a kite and the brother practicing until he knows how to operate the kite by himself. $Teaching_1$ allows the distinction between effective teaching and ineffective teaching. $Teaching_2$ does not. Only effective performances count as instances of $teaching_2$. Another way to regard $teaching_2$ is to conceive of it as effective $teaching_1$. The conception of teaching as $teaching_2$ is implied in the statement,

(1) "If the children don't learn from a lesson, then what the
teacher was doing doesn't deserve to be called teaching,"
and in the statement,

(2) "I am waiting for the day to come when it is impossible for us to say that we have been teaching if our students have not learned from our teaching."

An example of teaching3 is a boy finding out that eating peanuts makes him break out in hives. One could say,

(3) "The experience of eating peanuts was teaching the boy with the allergy to avoid peanuts in his diet."

This third sense of teaching includes unintentional activities, and it removes a person who is offering guidance from the scene altogether. It is close in meaning to the concept of learning as coming to know unguided and unintentionally.

Figure 2.7: Three Common Usage Conceptions of Teaching

Three Common Usage Conceptions of the Term *Teaching*	
Teaching₁	Intentionally trying to cause learning
Teaching₂	Intentionally causing learning
Teaching₃	Causing learning

Of the three common usage conceptions, teaching1 is the most appropriate for use in furthering disciplined discourse and unambiguous, useful knowledge about education. Teaching2 makes the distinction between effective and ineffective teaching impossible because it functions as an achievement concept. It counts only effective performances, ones which cause learning, as teaching. Thus teaching2 is too narrow in its implication. It excludes instances of conduct that should be considered in relation to helping someone learn something. Teaching3 is too broad in its conception. It includes events and circumstances in which there is no person acting as teacher, and it blurs the distinction between teaching and studying under guidance. The concept of teaching1 is the one among the three which makes the essential distinctions that are necessary to facilitate and extend useful, disciplined discourse about the field of educational phenomena.

Studying. Teaching1 makes sense only in relation to the process of studying under guidance. At least four common usages of the term *studying* are distinguishable. One conception of *studying* (studying1) is undertaking to learn something under the guidance of someone else (i.e. under the guidance of a teacher). An example of studying in this sense is a young man studying a course in economics at university. He enrolls in a course at the university, attends classes, takes notes in lectures, completes the assigned readings, participates in tutorials and completes the assignments prescribed for the course. He is clearly undertaking to learn a selection from the fund of knowledge (i.e. true statements) named by the term *economics* under the guidance and direction of his instructors and tutors. His purpose is to master some conventional range of knowing about economics.

A second conception of *studying* (studying2) is undertaking to learn something without the guidance of someone else (sometimes we call this *self teaching*). An example of studying2 is a young woman who decides that she wants to learn to touch type. She borrows a book from the library about touch typing. She reads the instructions about how to position the fingers over the keyboard. She practices the exercises provided in the book. She practices until she can type without looking at the keyboard. She continues to practice to achieve accuracy and speed until she can type 50 words per minute with only 3 mistakes. Her purpose is to master some conventional range of knowing about touch typing.

A third conception of *studying* (studying3) is undertaking inquiry without guidance to verify new knowledge claims about some state of affairs. An example of studying3 is a team of medical researchers conducting inquiry to produce a vaccine which prevents melanoma. No one knows whether such a vaccine can be produced, thus there is no one who can teach the team. The team undertakes a series of laboratory experiments to develop a vaccine. The team organizes and conducts clinical trials to test the efficacy of the vaccine. The clinical trials show that the vaccine is effective 98% of the time with minimal harmful side effects. The team establishes new knowledge about how to prevent melanoma. The team's purpose is to verify new knowledge and create some range of postconventional knowing about disease prevention.

A fourth conception of *studying* (studying$_4$) is illustrated in the sentences:

(1) "The ship's captain was studying the horizon for any signs of the approaching hurricane;"
(2) "The veterinarian was studying the horse's leg for any signs of swelling or soreness;"
(3) "While questioning the suspect, the policeman was studying the suspect's speech, gestures and eyes for any signs of intoxication."

The meaning implied by this usage of *studying* is undertaking to learn something without guidance so as to verify or nullify a proposition. In the first sentence above (Sentence 1), the purpose of the captain's studying is to verify the proposition that the hurricane is within sight. In the second sentence (Sentence 2), the purpose of the veterinarian's studying is to verify the proposition that the horse's leg is sound. In the third sentence (Sentence 3), the purpose of the policeman's studying is to verify the proposition that the suspect is intoxicated.

So the fourth conception of *studying* (studying$_4$) is closely related to studying$_3$. The distinction is in the purpose of the studying. The purpose implied in studying$_3$ is to establish some new knowledge and some range of postconventional knowing. The purpose implied by studying$_4$ is to establish some knowledge about a particular matter (the knowledge is not necessarily new).

Of the four conceptions of *studying* the concept of studying$_1$ (studying under the guidance of someone) is the one that is most appropriate for use in systematic inquiry and discourse about education.

Teaching and Studying as Task Concepts. Studying$_1$ and teaching$_1$ are task concepts, rather than achievement concepts. Other task concepts are hunting and fishing. One goes fishing, but does not necessarily catch any fish. One goes hunting, but does not necessarily bag any game. One can conduct teaching (teaching$_1$) and yet no one learns from the teaching. And one can undertake studying$_1$, but not necessarily achieve the intended learning outcomes. Studying$_1$ implies trying to learn, and it includes both the successful and the unsuccessful attempts.

Figure 2.8: Four Meanings of Studying

Four Means of Studying	
Studying$_1$	Intentionally trying to learn something <u>under</u> the guidance of someone in some setting for the purpose of mastering some existing conventional knowing
Studying$_2$	Intentionally trying to learn something <u>without</u> the guidance of someone in some setting for the purpose of mastering some existing conventional knowing
Studying$_3$	Intentionally trying to learn something <u>without</u> the guidance of someone in some setting for the purpose of creating some new postconventional knowing
Studying$_4$	Intentionally trying to learn something <u>without</u> the guidance of someone in some setting for the purpose of verifying some proposition

In contrast, learning is an achievement concept. It implies only successful attempts at coming to know. There is no process of learning without the product of knowing. It is paradoxical and nonsensical to say,

"I learned, but I didn't learn."

But it makes perfectly good sense to say,

"I studied, but I didn't learn."

Deliberate guided learning is a subset of studying (studying$_1$). Any activity which a person intentionally undertakes to attempt to learn something counts as studying (studying₁). Thus studying (studying₁) can take place in schools or universities, colleges or institutes, but it can also occur in homes and churches, clubs and social gatherings, sporting events and parties, among friends, acquaintances and strangers. Examples of studying (studying₁) include:

(1) a young man practices bidding hands in the card game of contract bridge under the tutelage of a second person who explains and demonstrates a bidding system;

(2) a young boy works on perfecting his playing a piece on his guitar under the directions and suggestions of another more experienced guitar player;

(3) an adult man watches his mentor demonstrate how to upholster furniture with the intention of upholstering some of his old furniture;

(4) a young woman reads about marriage customs of traditional societies in West Africa under the guidance of her university anthropology tutor.

It can not be determined by observation alone whether a person is engaged in studying (studying₁). The intention of the person must also be known. Reading a book, sewing, listening to an explanation, kicking a football are nothing more than that, if the person performing the activity is not doing it with the intention to learn and if the person is not doing it in relation to someone else who has provided or is in the act of providing guidance.

Thus, in order that people's activities count as performances of studying (studying₁), they must:

(1) intend to learn something;

(2) intentionally and willingly place themselves into a relationship of being guided in their activities by someone; and

(3) follow the guidance and undertake appropriate guided practice.

These are the bare essentials of studying (studying₁).

***In* an Experience and *of* an Experience**. The distinctions of being *in an experience* and being *of an experience* relate to the process of studying under guidance (studying₁). People can be placed into circumstances in which someone else chooses to teach them. Those people are thereby *in* an experience. But if they choose not to cooperate, not to accept guidance, not to attend to the matters at hand and not to try to learn, then they are only *in* the experience. They are not *of* the experience. Someone is teaching, but the intended students are not playing the role of students and are not studying under guidance (studying₁). Without people playing the role of students, the process of education is nonexistent. As the old adage goes, "You can lead a horse to water, but you can't make it drink." Or, as the Chinese proverb goes, "Teachers open the door. You enter by yourself."

Once given the opportunity to study, should the intended students choose to play the role of students, undertake to learn, accept guidance, attend to the matters at hand and use the opportunities to study under guidance, then they are both *in* the experience and *of* the experience. They are studying (studying₁). There is no guarantee, of course, that the studying will be effective. One may try to learn and still not succeed in learning. Studying (studying₁) is transactive with teaching, not reactive to it.

An example of a reactive process is what happens in a chemical reaction. Hydrochloric acid is added to calcium carbonate at room temperature and normal atmospheric pressure, and the products are carbon dioxide, calcium chloride and water. When hydrochloric acid is added to calcium carbonate, the result is always the same. A reactive process produces an invariant result.

A transactive process does not have an invariant result. Teaching and studying are transactive processes. Teaching is a set of activities performed by a person with the intention to help another person learn. Studying under guidance is a set of activities performed by a person with the intention to learn. Both teachers and students transact with each other and with the content with the intention that the student learn. But the intentions are not always realized. Less than complete success is always possible. Many factors come into play in the transactions, e.g. the students' motivations, the level of difficulty of the learning task, the aspirations of the group of students involved in the learning task, the expertise of the teacher, the support (or lack of support or opposition) of the society and culture within which the educational transactions are taking place.

The Misleading Metaphor of Transference. Sometimes the educational process is described as a process of transference of knowledge, but this is an inaccurate and misleading metaphor. In transference, something changes location. People receive transfers in employment. They move from location *A* to location *B*. Location *A* is vacant, and *B* is occupied. Money is transferred from one bank to another. The account in the first bank is debited, and in the second bank, an account is credited.

Transference contrasts with education. In education, if guided studying and teaching are effective, the cognitive functioning of the student develops to a greater range (level, kind, form) of knowing, but the teacher's cognitive function is not diminished. In the development of the students' knowing, teachers lose none of their knowing, and the knowledge recorded in the content is not diminished in any way. Nothing is transferred or passed on from one location to another.

Thus transference is an inadequate characterization of the processes of teaching and guided studying. They are not processes of transference or passing on, but rather, they are processes of transaction. A development of a new range of knowing in one person (the student) proceeds through transactions with the content (the subject, subject matter or the fund of knowledge) and the range of knowing in another person (the teacher) without diminishing the original range of knowing of the teacher and without diminishing the content.

Education is a transactive process that is made up of the basic components of teacher, student, content and setting and the basic processes of teaching and studying under guidance.

Derivative Features of Education

Teacher, student, content and setting are the basic components of education. They constitute the form of education Teaching and studying under guidance are its basic processes. They constitute the function of education.

In addition, a set of features, which is derivative of the basic set of components and processes, is usually present in educational transactions. This derivative set includes at least twelve features. (See Figure 2.9.)

Figure 2.9: Derivative Features of Education

Derivative Features of Education	
Derivative features	*Connection of features with basic components & processes of education*
▪Language in education	▪Language of teachers ▪Language of students
▪Resources	▪Resources for teachers ▪Resources for students
▪Methods	▪Methods of teaching ▪Methods of studying
▪Styles	▪Styles of teaching ▪Styles of studying
▪Focus	▪Focus of teacher's attention ▪Focus of students' attention
▪Organization	▪Organization of teachers ▪Organization of students
▪Pace	▪Time span allowed for teaching ▪Time span allowed for studying
▪Sequence	▪Sequence established by teacher ▪Sequence established by students
▪Initiation	▪Initiation by teacher ▪Initiation by students ▪Mutual initiation
▪Intentions, purposes, goals	▪Intentions of teachers ▪Intentions of students ▪Intentions of third parties
▪Goal structures	▪Goal structures of teachers ▪Goals structures of students
▪Assessment & evaluation	▪Assessment & evaluation by teachers ▪Assessment & evaluation by students ▪Assessment & evaluation by third parties

Language in the Educational Process. The process of education, i.e. the process of teaching and guided studying, requires language for educational transactions to occur. In educational transactions, the language among teachers and students assumes characteristic forms, and it performs characteristic functions. The functions include:

- analyzing
- characterizing
- comparing
- contrasting
- describing
- defining
- demonstrating
- directing
- emphasizing
- evaluating
- exemplifying
- explaining
- explicating
- guiding
- illustrating
- justifying
- predicting
- prompting
- questioning
- recommending
- relating
- stating
- suggesting
- summarizing

The above list is not intended as an exhaustive list, but rather as a suggestion as to what can be looked for when observing and analyzing the language that takes place within the educational process among teachers and students.

The forms of language characteristic of educational transactions divide into ordinary and specialized. Ordinary language is that of everyday conversations. Specialized language occurs as systems or organizations of discourse. For example, mathematics, chemistry, zoology and hydrology constitute four separate systems of discourse, each with a distinctive viewpoint, a special set of terms, concepts, descriptions and explanatory principles. In the educational process, teachers and students transact using the specialized language of some set of discourse in order for students to extend their range of knowing.

In addition, the language that is used in teaching and guided studying is always some kind of language of some cultural community, e.g. English, Russian, French, Swahili, American Sign Language (ASL), Australian Sign Language (Auslan).

In multilingual societies where two or more different languages are spoken, the question of which language is to be used as the medium of instruction becomes an important and sometimes contentious issue. In past times, language groups have been forbidden to use their first language in schools, e.g. the English forbid the Scots to use Scottish Gaelic (after the Battle of Culloden in 1746 and during the Highland Clearances). American Indian students, in the late 19th to the mid 20th century, were forbidden to use their first language in U.S. Bureau of Indian Affairs boarding schools established for Indian students. Australian indigenous children were forbidden to use their first language in missionary schools in the late 19th to mid 20th century. After the defeat of France in the Franco-Prussian War (1870-71), the medium of instruction in schools in the newly acquired Imperial Territory of Alsace-Lorraine became the German language, and French was removed from the curriculum.

As a rule, the language that is used as the medium of instruction in official education is usually determined by the group which holds the dominant political power within a community, state or nation.

Resources in the Educational Process. Resources are the physical objects that are used in teaching and guided studying. The range of objects that can be used is extensive. Examples include pens, paper, films, books, desks, balls, engines, tools, shoes, cameras, computers, e-book readers, puzzles, workbooks, video players, photographs, diagrams, gymnasiums, playing fields, play equipment, laboratory equipment, TVs, etc. Resources can be distinguished as ones used by teachers, by students and by both. Resources can be effective or ineffective, extant or nonexistent and intrinsically bad or good.

Methods in the Educational Process. Methods are procedures that are followed in an activity. Procedures relate to ordering or arranging conduct into sets of patterns. In the educational process, there are both methods of teaching and methods of studying.

Examples of teaching methods include:

Partial List of Teaching Methods		
• answering questions • arranging resources • asking questions	• demonstrating procedures • evaluating performances	• modeling procedures • observing carefully

• assigning activities • assigning appropriate practice • assigning projects • defining terms	• explicating concepts • giving directions • giving examples • leading discussions • listening attentively	• organizing activities • playing games • playing roles • posing problems • providing advice • providing resources

There are methods of guided studying as well as those of teaching. These are procedures used for trying to learn something under guidance, i.e. they are procedures followed in playing the role of student. At times, the methods of guided studying are identical to those of teaching, and at times, they are different. Examples of study methods include

Partial List of Studying Methods		
• answering questions • asking questions • assigning projects • conducting experiments • conducting appropriate practice • conducting research • creating models • defining terms • demonstrating procedures • drawing diagrams • drawing pictures	• giving directions • leading discussions • listening attentively • making charts • making presentations • modeling procedures • observing carefully • organizing activities • paraphrasing texts • participating in discussions, • playing games	• reading resources • rehearsing procedures • rehearsing roles • selecting activities • selecting resources • solving problems • summarizing texts • undertaking activities • undertaking appropriate practice • undertaking projects

• evaluating performances • explicating concepts • finding resources • following directions • following guidance	• playing roles • posing problems • preparing reports • providing examples	• watching demonstrations • writing texts (notes, reports, essays, speeches, etc)

Methods of teaching and guided studying can be distinguished with respect to whether they are effective or ineffective, extant or nonexistent and intrinsically good or bad.

Styles in the Educational Process. Styles of teaching and guided studying are the manner in which a method is used or executed. Terms which characterize style include supportive, unsupportive, friendly, unfriendly, personable, aloof, kind, sarcastic, patient, impatient, abrupt, jaded, enthusiastic, concerned, disinterested, nervous, calm, confident, unconfident, stern, mocking, cruel, etc.

Styles relate closely to personality, and both student and teacher manifest styles with their methods. An identical method can be executed in different styles. The method of asking questions, for example, can be employed using a warm, supportive style, or an aloof, abrupt style.

Like methods, styles can be chosen, used and changed to suit the circumstances. Both teachers and students have it within their abilities to choose and use and change styles to suit a situation.

Also like methods, styles may be distinguished with respect to whether they are effective or ineffective, extant or nonexistent and intrinsically good or bad.

Focus of Attention. As human beings, we typically focus on one or a few aspects of our environment and experience at any one moment, and our attention typically moves from one thing to another fairly rapidly. This is especially so of children, but it is generally true of anyone at any age. It is through selective attention that we focus and discern those aspects of our experience that matter to us at the moment. Daydreaming is natural, and we drift in and out of focus on the people, activities, things and states of affairs which are immediately before us.

In characterizing possible methods and styles of teaching and guided studying, it is helpful to consider on what persons, entities, activities or states of affairs students might place their attention while engaged in education. At least five centers of focus are possible. Students may focus their attention on (1) teachers, (2) other students, (3) themselves, (4) resources or (5) situations. Or they may become completely distracted and focus on matters outside of what is happening immediately in the educational process.

Teacher Focused Activities. Teacher focused activities are those in which the teacher intends that the attention of the student or students be upon the teacher's performance.

Student Focused Activities. Student focused activities are those in which the teacher intends that the attention of the students be upon the performances of another student or other students.

Self Focused Activities. Self focused activities are ones in which the teacher intends the student to be focused upon her or his own performances.

Resource Focused Activities. Resource focused activities are those in which the teacher intends that the attention of the student or students be upon the resources provided for study, e.g. pictures, diagrams, photographs, computer programs, books, question sets, videos, etc.

Situation Focused Activities. Situation focused activities are ones in which the teacher intends the student or students to be focused upon a set of circumstances, phenomena, events or state of affairs (e.g. the things that might be observed on a field trip to a factory, a farm, a beach, a forest or a market).

Figure 2.10: Some Possibilities of Student Focus in Education

Focus intended by teacher	*Examples*
▪**Teacher focused activities**	**Students are intended to pay attention to a teacher** ▪ defining the concept of nationalism,

	▪ demonstrating how to factor quadratic equations, ▪ modeling the fingering of a chord on the guitar
▪**Student focused activities**	**Students are intended to watch & listen to a student** ▪ delivering a report, ▪ playing the violin, ▪ reciting a poem, ▪ integrating a function, ▪ demonstrating an electric motor the student has made
▪**Self focused activities**	**A student is intended to focus on her or his own performance as she or he** ▪ practices touch typing, ▪ fingers notes on the flute, ▪ practices bead welding, ▪ writes an original short play
▪**Resource focused activities**	**A set of students is intended to** ▪ watch a video about tropical cyclones, ▪ add an acid to a base and watch for a change in the indicator color, ▪ read a text and write answers to comprehension questions
▪**Situation focused activities**	**A set of students is intended to** ▪ visit a pig farm and note steps in pig breeding & husbandry, ▪ visit a water purification plant & note the steps in water purification ▪ visit a ginger processing factory & note the steps in ginger processing ▪ visit a bee farm & note the steps in bee husbandry ▪ visit the beach, collect plastic and measure the amount of plastic per square meter in the sand on the beach ▪ breed silk moths, keep records of time taken to hatch eggs, weight gain of the larvae, time taken to form the pupae, formation of the cocoon & the time taken for the moths to emerge from their cocoons

Apart from the intention of the teacher with regard to the focus of student attention, students of course choose to focus their attention on whatever they wish, regardless of what teachers are intending. Sometimes their focus is on study tasks, and sometimes it is on other things outside of the educational process altogether.

Organization of Teachers, Students and Study Tasks or Activities. In the educational process, teachers may be organized as individuals, operating independently of each other, or as groups or teams of teachers working in connection with each other to some greater or lesser degree of cooperation and consultation.

Likewise students may be organized
(1) as individuals studying independently or studying with each other,
(2) in small groups or
(3) studying with each other as one large group.

Organization as Individuals. Organization of students as individuals gives the flexibility for each student to be studying something unique to each individual student and to be using a set of resources different from all other students. On the other hand, if a group of students is observed working individually, it does not necessarily imply that each student is working on some learning task that is unique to that particular student. The learning task that each student is working on must be examined to determine its uniqueness.

Organization in Small Groups. Organization of students in small groups gives the flexibility for different groups of students to be using different sets of resources and to be undertaking different study activities and tasks at the same time. On the other hand, if students are observed working in small groups, it does not necessarily imply that each group is working on some learning task that is unique to that particular group. The learning task that each group is working on must be examined to determine its uniqueness.

Organization in Whole Group. Organization of students into a whole group provides the opportunity for all students to be focused on the same study resources and study activities at the same time. On the other hand, if students are observed working as a whole, it does not necessarily imply that each student is working on the same learning task as all of the others in the whole group. The learning task that each member of the group is working on must be examined to determine whether all students are working on the same task.

Students may be organized at various times to suit various circumstances. They may be organized according to various criteria, e.g. age, ability, gender, previous experiences, interests, achievement, availability of resources, etc.

Regardless of how students might be organized, they may be

Figure 2.11: Organization of Students and Study Activities or Tasks in the Educational Process

Organization of students	*Study tasks or activities*
▪**Students organized as individuals**	Study task or activity can be ▪ the same for all students ▪ the same for some of the other students ▪ unique to the individual ▪ initiated by teacher, student or both parties
▪**Students organized as small groups**	Study task or activity can be ▪ the same for all students in other groups ▪ the same for students in the same group but different from other groups ▪ unique to the individual ▪ initiated by teacher, student or both parties
▪**Students organized as one large group**	Study task or activity can be ▪ the same for all students ▪ the same for some students and different for others ▪ unique to the individual ▪ initiated by teacher, student or both parties

engaged in

(1) the same study activities simultaneously, or

(2) various activities simultaneously, or

(3) an activity unique to the individual student

. The nature of the study task or activity is not necessarily tied to the grouping of the students. For example, students can be organized as individuals and be engaged in the same study activity. They can be organized in small groups and be engaged in the same study activity. They can be organized as a whole class, and each student can be engaged in an activity that is unique to each individual student. (See Figure 2.11.)

Pace of Teaching and Studying. The pace of teaching and studying is the time frame in which students are expected to achieve a set of intended learning outcomes. Some outcomes can be achieved within a few minutes. Others take a few days. Others take a few months, or even a year or several years. Teachers might specify the pace at which something is taught and studied. Students might specify the pace. The pace might be mutually established by teachers and students in cooperation with each other. Or the pace might be established by interested third parties, e.g. the administration of a school district, state departments of education, administrators of universities, publishers of educational materials, funding bodies, etc.

Sequence of Teaching and Studying. The sequence is the order in which acts of teaching and studying take place within a given time frame. The sequence can be determined by the teacher, by the students, by mutual agreement between teacher and students or by interested third parties.

An example of a sequence determined by a teacher is the scenario in which a teacher has pupils in Year 1 (or Grade 1) (average age of 6 years old) trace over simple three-letter words, then join the dots for the same set of words presented in line-dot form, then write one missing letter in the same set of words with a single missing letter, then write the last two missing letters in the same set of words, then write the three letters of each of the words after hearing them spoken.

An example of a sequence determined by a student is the scenario in which a ten-year old boy goes to his first piano lesson, shows the piano teacher a piece of sheet music that he wants to learn to play, and the teacher shows him where to place his fingers for his left hand and his right hand on the piano for the notes on the sheet music, gives him guidance and practice in wrist position, finger placement, rhythm and tempo and helps him until he can play the piece to his satisfaction.

An example of a sequence established by a third party is the administration of a school district prescribing that secondary school mathematics be studied in this order: (1) introductory algebra, (2) geometry, (3) advanced algebra, (4) trigonometry, (5) calculus.

Initiation of Study Activities. Study activities are any activities that students undertake with the intention of extending their range of knowing. Study activities or tasks can be initiated by

    (1) the teacher or teachers,

    (2) the student or students,

    (3) some third party, or

    (4) a combination of initiatives from teachers, students and/or some third party.

Teacher Initiated Activities. In official education, an example of a teacher initiated study task is the case of a Year 11 secondary school teacher telling the class that they will be reading, analyzing and interpreting the novel *Moby-Dick* by Herman Melville. In unofficial education, an example of a teacher initiated activity is a situation in which a father tells his son that he wants to show him how to clean the air filter on the motor of the lawn mower.

Student Initiated Activities. In official education, an example of a student initiated study task is the case of a student (a girl) bringing in some tadpoles in a jar and saying that she would like to make a study of the life cycle of frogs. Other students agree that it is a great idea, and the class proceeds to conduct a study of frogs. In unofficial education, an example of a student initiated study task is the situation in which a child asks another child to show him how to skip rope. The other child says okay and shows the first child how to do it.

Third Party Initiated Activities. In official education, an example of a third party initiated study task is the legislative requirement to allocate 20 hours of study in Year 10 (10th Grade) about the dangers of alcohol abuse and abuse of other substances such as tobacco, marijuana, cocaine, methamphetamine and heroin.

Teacher and Student Initiated Activities. In official education, an example of a mutually initiated (i.e. initiated by teacher and student) study task is the case in which a teacher assigns a research project to the students, but does not specify what is to be researched. Each student decides upon what it is that she or he wishes to research and consults with the teacher about how to conduct the research and report the results of the research.

In unofficial education, an example of a mutually initiated study task is the scenario in which a boy asks his mother to teach him to cook, and she says, all right, let's start with making a loaf of fruit bread. He says that sounds great.

Again, the initiation of the study task or activity is not necessarily linked to the way that the students are organized as individuals, or in small groups or in a large whole group.

Timing of Organization. The organization of both teachers and students, of course, is fluid. It can be changed at anytime, and any particular organization can be effective or ineffective, extant or nonexistent and good or bad.

Intentions in the Educational Process. Within the educational process, there is always intention. Teachers, students and interested third parties (e.g. parents, administrators, funding bodies, law makers. philanthropists, etc.) all have the general intention that students will extend their range of knowing (i.e. a combination of levels, forms and kinds of knowing) in relation to something or some state of affairs. The concept of intention belongs to the family of concepts of aims, goals, objectives and intended outcomes. An educational intention, aim, goal or objective is a learning outcome that someone wants to achieve by means of using the process of teaching and guided studying.

Possible aims might include understanding how to
(1) drive a car safely and responsibly, or
(2) distinguish poisonous mushrooms from harmless ones, or
(3) resolve conflicts through negotiation and compromise.

We can conceive of a seemingly infinite number of learning outcomes. The outcomes will always be a selection from the possible levels, kinds and forms of knowing. A statement about an intended learning outcome will always be a specification of some range of knowing that a student expects, or is expected, to achieve.

In unofficial education, people rarely articulate, either in spoken or written language, their intended learning outcomes, but they, at times, do. A child will say that she or he wants to know how to tie shoe laces, snap fingers, play the piano, ride a bicycle, skip rope or bake a cake. Parents rarely say that they want their children to master speaking, reading and writing their native language, but their conduct in helping their children achieve these ranges of knowing provides sufficient evidence to infer confidently that they do. Also it is clear that parents want their children to develop attitudes and values that are consistent with the familial group. They rarely articulate these intentions, most probably because they take them to be self evident and totally unnecessary to specify and delineate.

In contrast, in official education, teachers, students, curriculum developers, administrators, funding bodies and regulatory agencies insist upon an articulation of intended learning outcomes. Those who fund official education generally want an accounting of how their money is spent and what results are achieved. For accountability to be achieved, for decisions to be made about the rational allocation of funds and for choices to be made about relevant resources for educational programs, clear statements of intended learning outcomes become imperative.

While the three terms *aims*, *goals* and *objectives* are very much synonyms in ordinary language, it has become a convention in professional literature about education (i.e. in educological discourse) to stipulate special meanings for the three terms.

It has become conventional to stipulate that the terms

(1) *aims* means intended learning outcomes that are stated in general terms and that are intended to be achieved in the long term, i.e. over many months, or possibly a year or several years,

(2) *goals* means intended learning outcomes that are stated in more specific terms and that are intended to be achieved in

the medium term, i.e. over a period of a few days, or possibly a few weeks, and

(3) *objectives* means intended learning outcomes that are to be achieved in the short term (possibly after one or two lessons) and that are stated in terms of what observable (i.e. senceivable) performances students must manifest in order to demonstrate the achievement of the intended learning outcome, under what conditions the students must perform and what set of criteria the performances must satisfy (see Robert Mager, 1990).

Figure 2.12: Aims, Goals and Objectives within Official Education

Aims	**Intended learning outcomes that are** ▪ to be achieved in the long term (many months or a year or several years) ▪ stated in general terms
Goals	**Intended learning outcomes that are** ▪ to be achieved in the medium term (over a period of a few days or possibly a few weeks) ▪ stated in more specific terms
Objectives	**Intended learning outcomes that are** ▪ to be achieved in the short term (after one or a few lessons) ▪ stated in terms of (1) the observable (senceivable) performances the student must manifest in order to demonstrate the achievement of the intended learning outcome (2) the conditions under which the student must perform (3) the set of criteria the performances must satisfy

Examples of Educational Aims. There are seemingly an infinite number of examples of statements of aims in official education. As a first example of aims in official education, we can look at what the Australian Curriculum, Assessment and Reporting Authority (ACARA, retrieved 2014, http://www.australiancurriculum.edu.au/mathematics/aims) states as aims appropriate for the Australian Year 10 (i.e. age 15) mathematics curriculum.

"The Australian Curriculum: Mathematics aims to ensure that students:

- are confident, creative users and communicators of mathematics, able to investigate, represent and interpret situations in their personal and work lives as active citizens
- develop an increasingly sophisticated understanding of mathematical concepts and fluency with processes, and are able to pose and solve problems and reason in *Number and Algebra, Measurement and Geometry, and Statistics and Probability*
- recognise [sic] connections between the areas of mathematics and other disciplines and appreciate mathematics as an accessible and enjoyable discipline to study."

As a second example of aims in official education, we can look at what ACARA (retrieved 2014) specifies as appropriate aims for Australian Year 10 science students (http://www.australiancurriculum.edu.au/Science/Aims):

"The Australian Curriculum: Science aims to ensure that students develop:

- an interest in science as a means of expanding their curiosity and willingness to explore, ask questions about and speculate on the changing world in which they live
- an understanding of the vision that science provides of the nature of living things, of the Earth and its place in the cosmos, and of the physical and chemical processes that explain the behaviour [sic] of all material things
- an understanding of the nature of scientific inquiry and the ability to use a range of scientific inquiry methods, including questioning; planning and conducting experiments and investigations based on ethical principles; collecting and analysing [sic] data; evaluating results; and drawing critical, evidence-based conclusions
- an ability to communicate scientific understanding and findings to a range of audiences, to justify ideas on the basis

of evidence, and to evaluate and debate scientific arguments and claims
- an ability to solve problems and make informed, evidence-based decisions about current and future applications of science while taking into account ethical and social implications of decisions
- an understanding of historical and cultural contributions to science as well as contemporary science issues and activities and an understanding of the diversity of careers related to science
- a solid foundation of knowledge of the biological, chemical, physical, Earth and space sciences, including being able to select and integrate the scientific knowledge and methods needed to explain and predict phenomena, to apply that understanding to new situations and events, and to appreciate the dynamic nature of science knowledge."

Statements of aims typically include verbs and verbal phrases such as *understand, appreciate, grasp the importance of, apply understanding to new situations, develop confidence with, develop problem solving abilities, develop an interest in* and the like. The statements also typically specify a time span of six months to a year or more for achievement of the intended learning outcomes.

Examples of Educational Goals. Some examples of educational goals are the following statements:

The student
- "explains the significance of particular people, places, groups, actions and events in the past in developing Australian identities and heritage."
- "explains the development of the principles of Australian democracy."
- "describes different cultural influences and their contribution to Australian identities."
- "explains how various beliefs and practices influence the ways in which people interact with, change and value their environment." (from *Stage 3 Units, Human Society & Its Environment K-6, Units of Work*, "Overview of Outcomes," Board of Studies, NSW Government, 2013, p. 114 http://k6.boardofstudies.nsw.edu.au/wps/wcm/connect/84278

, retrieved 2014).

Statements of goals typically include verbs such as *explain*, *describe*, *outline*, *summarize*, *identify*, *compare*, *contrast*, *solve*, *analyze*, *recognize* and the like. The statements also typically specify a time span of a few days to a few weeks or so for achievement of the intended learning outcomes.

Examples of Educational Objectives. Some examples of educational objectives are the following statements:
- The student, with textbook open and using a model of the heart, will correctly write a list of the effects, including at least two danger signals, of alcohol on the body.
- The student will write correctly the phrasal verbs *get out*, *check out*, *put up with*, *figure out*, *pick up*, *get on with* in a given written dialogue without the use of any reference materials.
- The student will correctly write answers to a set of given addition problems of two and three 3-digit numbers without assistance, calculator or reference material.

Statements of objectives typically begin with the phrase *The student* or *The learner*. The action verb used in the statement typically describes an action that is observable, e.g. *write*, *say*, *kick*, *point to*, *select*, *throw*, *assemble*, etc. The conditions under which the student must perform are specified (e.g. "without assistance, calculator or reference material"), as is the set of criteria the performance must satisfy (e.g. "correctly").

Summary of Intentions in the Educational Process. So, in summary, the intention of teachers and students (and interested third parties) in the educational process is that the students learn something. The learning of something is the extension of the students' range of knowing (levels, forms and kinds of knowing). Statements of intended learning outcomes are specifications of a range of knowing that someone wants students to achieve. Sometimes the intended learning outcomes are not stated at all. This is true for most of what takes place within unofficial education (i.e. education within families, peer groups, and the like). Within official education, intended learning outcomes are always specified. The specifications vary with respect to their detail, i.e. with respect to

- the range of knowing that is specified,
- the time frame that is envisaged for achievement of the intended learning outcome,
- the observable performances that are specified as evidence of achievement of the intended learning outcome,
- the conditions that are specified for the performances and
- the criteria that are specified for the performances.

Although the terms *aim*, *goals* and *objectives* are close synonyms in ordinary language, it has become a convention in educological discourse about intended learning outcomes that

(1) the term *aims* be used to mean intended learning outcomes which are
   - intended to be achieved in the long term, i.e. over many months, or possibly a year or several years, and
   - stated in general terms, i.e. using terms such as *develop an understanding of, develop an appreciation for, develop an extensive grasp of, develop a sound comprehension of,* etc.

(2) the term *goals* be used to mean intended learning outcomes which are
   - intended to be achieved in the medium term, i.e. over a period of a few days, or possibly a few weeks and
   - stated in more specific terms, i.e. using terms such as *explain, compare, contrast, analyze, recognize, list, describe, predict,* etc.

(3) the term *objectives* be used to mean intended learning outcomes which
   - specify what is to be achieved in the short term (possibly after one or two lessons),
   - describe in observable (i.e. senceivable) terms the performances students must manifest in order to demonstrate the achievement of the intended learning outcome,
   - state under what conditions the students must perform and
   - state what set of criteria the performances must satisfy.

Goal Structures in the Educational Process. Within official education, it is possible to structure educational goals for the students. That is, you can establish rules that govern how the goals can be achieved. Goal structures are distinguishable by the degree of dependence that one student has on other students in being able to achieve an intended learning outcome. There are at least three possible structures: individualized, competitive and cooperative (David W. Johnson and Robert T. Johnson, 1975).

Individualized Goal Structure. An individualized goal structure is a set of rules which stipulates that an individual student may achieve an intended learning outcome without transactions with other students. The student does not depend on other students in achieving the intended learning outcome. The educational goal is unique to the individual, and the individual may achieve the intended learning outcome regardless of what other students are studying or aiming to achieve.

Competitive Goal Structure. A competitive goal structure is a set of rules which stipulates that only one individual student can achieve an intended learning outcome to the exclusion of other students. All students are engaged in activities to achieve the same goal, but the first one to achieve the intended learning outcome at the specified criteria of excellence blocks all others from achieving the goal.

Cooperative Goal Structure. A cooperative goal structure is a set of rules which stipulates that an intended learning outcome can be achieved if, and only if, all students linked in the same group or team, achieve the goal simultaneously and together.

Assessment and Evaluation in the Educational Process. In the educational process, the central concern of teachers, students and interested third parties is that students learn something. In this context of expectations, assessment consists of the process of collecting evidence of students having learned something. Evaluation consists of the process of comparing the evidence with criteria (standards, rules or both) to make judgments about the degree to which cognitive achievement matches the criteria for excellence. The comparison of the evidence of achievement of learning with the criteria for achievement provides the basis to make a judgment about the degree to which students have achieved their intended learning outcomes. The achievement is usually reported as a rating (e.g. *A,B,C,D,F*) or a ranking (e.g. *1ˢᵗ, 2ⁿᵈ, 3ʳᵈ,* etc.) (Paul W. Taylor, 1961).

The results of the evaluation (i.e. the evaluation report) can then be used to

(1) make new plans for teaching and learning something (a preparative use),

(2) let students know how they are progressing in their learning so that they can adjust their studying methods and styles (a formative use),

(3) let students and third parties know the degree to which the students have achieved the intended learning outcomes (a summative use) (M Scriven, 1991).

Assessment and evaluation processes can be initiated and conducted by teachers or students or by both in collaboration with each other. The processes can also be initiated and conducted by third parties, such as school administrators, funding organizations, regulatory authorities or testing organizations.

Assessment and evaluation take place in both unofficial and official education. In unofficial education, it is rarely, if ever, documented. In official education, it is always documented, and usually in great detail.

Strategies in the Educational Process

All people who engage in the educational process can, and do, devise strategies for participating in education. Students devise strategies for studying. And teachers devise strategies for teaching. A strategy is a deliberate combination of language, resources, methods, styles, focus, organization, pace, sequence, initiation, intentions, goal structures and assessment & evaluation. Hilda Taba (1966) is attributed with being one of the first to promote the term *teaching strategy*. However, teaching strategies are only one-half of the picture. The other half is the set of strategies that students use in undertaking to learn something under guidance. Strategies in the educational process include both teaching strategies and studying strategies.

Many different combinations of derivative features of education are possible, thus many different strategies are available. Here are a few examples.

Figure 2.13: Strategies in the Educational Process

Derivative Features of Education	*Teaching Strategies*	*Studying Strategies*
▪ **Language in Education** ▪ **Resources** ▪ **Methods** ▪ **Styles** ▪ **Focus** ▪ **Organization** ▪ **Pace** ▪ **Sequence** ▪ **Initiation** ▪ **Intentions** ▪ **Goal Structures** ▪ **Assessment & Evaluation**	**Combinations of Derivative Features of Teaching**	**Combinations of Derivative Features of Studying**

Student Centered, Pupil Centered or Child Centered Education. One example of a teaching and studying strategy is student centered learning. The terms *student centered, pupil centered* and *child centered education* are names that have been given to this teaching and studying strategy. Other names given to it include *discovery learning* and *inquiry based learning.* Although the strategy is denoted by several names, the distinguishing characteristics of the strategy remain much the same. It is a strategy in which the teacher establishes a situation that allows, encourages, leads to and/or compels the students in their studies to declare and undertake:

- **initiation**, i.e. the students initiate the study activities based on their own interests,
- **intentions**, i.e. the students nominate their own intended learning outcomes,
- **goal structures**, i.e. the students establish their own competitive, cooperative or individualized goal structures,
- **methods**, i.e. the students choose their own study methods,
- **focus of attention**, i.e. the students focus on states of affairs or matters that interest them,
- **organization**, i.e. the students organize themselves in one large group, several small groups and/or as individuals,
- **pace**, i.e. the students establish the time frame within and the speed at which they intend to achieve the intended learning outcomes,
- **sequence**, i.e. the students decide on the order in which problems will be addressed, questions will be asked and answered, activities will be undertaken or concepts and principles will be studied,
- **resources**, i.e. the students find and/or develop resources that are relevant to their studies
- **assessment and evaluation**, i.e. the students devise their own ways and means of demonstrating the achievement of their intended learning outcomes.

In this configuration, i.e. this teaching and studying strategy, the teaching methods used by teachers include listening actively, clarifying ideas, providing advice, giving guidance, evaluating, organizing, monitoring progress, keeping records, etc. The teacher is still, of course, teaching and therefore using a combination of derivative features of the educational process. Proponents of this teaching strategy (or variations of this strategy) have included John Dewey (1916), William Heard Kilpatrick (1918), Carl Rogers (1969), Jean Piaget (1926, 1948, 1953, 1971), Lev Vygotsky (1934), Jerome Bruner (1960, 1971), Idit Harel and Seymour Papert (1991) and Maria Montessori (1947a, b, 1949).

Direct Instruction. A second example of a teaching and studying strategy is direct instruction. The terms *direct instruction*, *systematic teaching* and *explicit teaching* are names that have been given to a teaching and studying strategy in which teachers declare and undertake their:

- **initiation**, i.e. the teacher initiates the study activities,
- **intentions**, i.e. the teacher prescribes or uses a prescribed set of intended learning outcomes for the students,
- **goal structures**, i.e. the teacher prescribes or uses a prescribed set of competitive, cooperative and/or individualized goal structures for the students,
- **methods**, i.e. the teacher chooses a set or follows a prescribed set of teaching methods such as defining, explicating, exemplifying, assigning guided practice, monitoring student progress, posing questions and problems, assessing and evaluating student achievement, and the like,
- **focus of attention**, i.e. the teacher prescribes or follows a prescribed set of arrangements to focus the students' attention on states of affairs or matters that the teacher judges to be relevant for the student to achieve the intended learning outcomes,
- **organization**, i.e. the teacher prescribes or follows a prescribed organization of students into a whole group, small groups or as individuals as deemed appropriate by the teacher to achieve the intended learning outcomes,
- **pace**, i.e. the teacher prescribes or follows a prescribed time frame within which the teacher intends the students to achieve the intended learning outcomes,
- **sequence**, i.e. the teacher prescribes or follows a prescribed order in which students will address problems, answer questions, study concepts and principles or develop skills,
- **resources**, i.e. the teacher prescribes or uses a prescribed set of resources that the teacher (or a third party) judges to be relevant to the students in their studies
- **assessment and evaluation**, i.e. the teacher prescribes or uses a prescribed set of ways and means of collecting evidence that demonstrates the students' achievement of the nominated intended learning outcomes in accordance with a criteria for cognitive performance.

Proponents, developers and/or researchers of this teaching and studying strategy (or variations of this strategy) have included Wesley Becker and Seigfried Engelmann (1995-96), Robert Slavin et al. (1996), Barak Rosenshine and Robert Stevens (1986) and Douglas W. Carnine et al. (2009).

Other Examples of Teaching and Studying Strategies. Other examples of teaching and studying strategies can be found in G. Fenstermacher and J. Soltis (2009), B. Joyce and M. Weil (2011) and R. Marzano et al. (1997). Fenstermacher and Soltis describe three teaching and studying strategies, which they name "the executive, the facilitator and the liberationist approaches to teaching." They provide examples of each teaching and studying strategy and invite the reader to identify the distinguishing characteristics of each strategy and the values implied by each strategy. Joyce and Weil give the name of "models of teaching" to teaching and studying strategies. They assign similar teaching and studying strategies to categories, which they name "families," e.g. "the information processing family," "the personal family," etc. They provide detailed characterizations, descriptions and examples of each member of a family (i.e. of a category) of teaching and studying strategies. Marzano et al., provide a step by step guide to planning a teaching and studying strategy that incorporates their views of best practice, e.g. establishing a community favorable to teaching and studying, encouraging the development of habits of mind (within students) favorable to teaching and studying and sequencing teaching and studying activities that are deemed to be favorable to maximizing the probabilities that students will achieve nominated intended learning outcomes.

Issues Arising from Teaching and Studying Strategies. A number of issues arise from spoken and written discourse about teaching and studying strategies.

Identification: One issue is the challenge of distinguishing one set of strategies from another. Different terms have historically been used to name the same strategy (a case of the same wine with different labels). And the converse is true. The same term has been used to name different strategies (a case of different wines with the same label). Resolution of this issue requires identification of the distinguishing characteristics of a particular teaching and studying strategy and the consistent application of an appropriate name for the strategy.

Use: A second issue is the question of which strategies are actually in use and which are not. For example, some teachers will claim that they are using child centered strategies because the students are organized into groups. Yet organization of students does not constitute all of the distinguishing characteristics of child centered teaching and studying strategies. Resolution of this issue requires clear conception and naming of different categories of teaching and studying, systematic observation of teaching and studying practices and sound categorization and delineation of teaching and studying strategies.

Evaluation: A third issue is the question of how to evaluate teaching and studying strategies. Teaching and studying strategies can be evaluated from at least two points of view. They can be evaluated for their intrinsic value and their extrinsic value.

When evaluated for their intrinsic value, teaching and studying strategies are judged good or bad, or relatively better or worse, to the extent that they match a set of criteria (standards and rules) based on a value system that constitutes a way of life for a group or community (either an extant community or an idealized community).

When evaluated for their extrinsic value, teaching and studying strategies are judged good or bad, or relatively better or worse, to the extent that they contribute to the achievement of some nominated outcome.

A teaching and studying strategy can be judged effective (extrinsically valuable), but it can be rejected because it is cruel (intrinsically bad). Likewise, a strategy can be judged democratic and respectful of individual rights (intrinsically valuable for a democratic society), but ineffective in achieving desired outcomes of mathematical proficiency (extrinsically bad). (See Figure 2.14.)

Summary

In summary, education is the process in which someone intentionally teaches and someone intentionally studies under guidance some content in some setting (physical, geographic, social and cultural). The four basic components of education are teacher, student (pupil), content and setting. The three basic func-

Figure 2.14: Issues with Teaching and Studying Strategies in the Educational Process

Identification of Strategies	*Use of Strategies*	*Evaluation of Strategies*
▪ Is the strategy clearly identified with distinguishing characteristics that delineate it from other strategies? ▪ Is the strategy clearly and unambiguously named?	▪ Is the strategy extant or non-extant, i.e. in use somewhere, either in official or unofficial education? ▪ To what extent has the use of the strategy been systematically observed and documented? ▪ What is the frequency of use of the strategy, in what circumstances and for what purposes?	▪ What intrinsic value does the strategy have, i.e. to what extent is it consistent with the communal values and way of life within it must function? ▪ What extrinsic value does the strategy have, i.e. to what extent is it effective in achieving a set of nominated intended learning outcomes?

tions of education are teaching, studying under guidance and (when all goes well) intentional guided learning. The outcome of the process of intentional guided learning is always the acquisition of some range of knowing (some combination of level, form and kind of knowing). A range of knowing constitutes understanding. There are at least twelve features of the educational process which are derivative of the four basic components of education. They are language, resources, methods, styles, focus, organization, pace, sequence, initiation, intentions, goal structures and assessment & evaluation. Strategies of teaching and studying are constituted from combinations of the twelve derivative features.

Chapter 3: Curriculum and Educational Phenomena

Now it is time to turn our attention to the questions of (1) where does curriculum fit into education, (2) how educology relates to curriculum and (3) what are the basic components of curriculum. The short answers to these questions are that (1) curriculum is an aspect of education, (2) part of the fund knowledge that is educology is the educology of curriculum and (3) any sound curriculum has at least eight basic components. It is appropriate to examine each of these questions and answers in more detail.

Where Does Curriculum Fit into Education?

The question arises as to where does curriculum fit into the field of educational phenomena? Appropriate treatment of this question necessitates consideration of the more fundamental question,

"What is curriculum?"

This second question requires some work in definition and analysis of ordinary language usage. We can restate the question by posing the questions,

"What other set of words can be used in place of the term *curriculum*?"

and

"To what do we point (denote) with the term *curriculum*?"

The activity of defining entails laying out the basic rules for using a term and inviting others to follow those rules. It is the activity of offering some set of words which has equivalent (or as nearly equivalent as is possible) meaning to the term being defined.

For example, if you choose to say that "curriculum is everything that happens [in school]" (Rita Tenorio, 2004, p. 81), this is equivalent to saying:

(1) I propose this rule for using the term *curriculum*: Use it in place of the set of words, "everything that happens in school;"

(2) I invite you to use this language rule.

An appropriate way to make the decision whether to accept this invitation is to consider the consequences of following the proposed language rule. Will using the rule (i.e. the definition), for example:

(1) Enable you to communicate more clearly?
(2) Describe what you want described?
(3) Help others to understand you?
(4) Create confusion?
(5) Dumbfound whoever hears you?

The factors relevant for consideration relate to the functions that you want a definition to perform. Although we can make definitions perform three functions for us (I. Scheffler, 1960), usually the call for *What is X* implicitly demands a common usage definition. You could, of course, prescribe the way in which you would like for everyone to use the term *curriculum*. This would be making the definition function programmatically. Or you could declare that you will use the term *curriculum* in an idiosyncratic way, regardless of how others use the term. This would be making the definition function stipulatively (I. Scheffler, 1960).

Either of these moves might be justified if the common usage meaning was found wanting or deficient. But should you decide that you wish to depart from the common usage meaning of the term *curriculum*, you have the obligation to report how people commonly use the term so as to evaluate its usage and identify its deficiencies, if any are extant.

Common usage meanings of terms are reported in dictionaries, so dictionaries are an appropriate starting point for a conceptual analysis of the term *curriculum*.

One dictionary reports that *curriculum* means the same as "set course of study" (*Australian Pocket Oxford Dictionary*, Melbourne: O.U.P., 1976). A second dictionary reports that the term *curriculum* means "the courses offered by an educational institution" (*Webster's New Collegiate Dictionary*, Springfield, Massachusetts: G. and C. Merriam, Co., 1973). A third reports that the term *curriculum* means the same as "the whole range of studies offered in a school, college, etc., or in a type of school" (*World Book Dictionary*, New York: Field Enterprises, 1974). In a more recent dictionary (http://www.thefreedictionary.com/curriculum, retrieved 2014) the term *curriculum* is defined as "all the courses of study offered by an educational institution" and "a group of related courses, often in a special field of study: the engineering curriculum."

Figure 3.1: Dictionary Definitions of the Term *Curriculum*

In ordinary language usage the term *curriculum* is used to mean	<ul><li>Set course of study</li><li>Courses offered by an educational institution</li><li>The whole range of studies offered in a school, college, etc., or in a type of school</li></ul>

This is a beginning for the conceptual analysis. Now we need to do some explication of key terms in the definitions: *set, course, study.* Something that is set is something that is fixed, settled, organized, established. The concept of the term *course* relates to something that is arranged, ordered, structured and/or sequenced. In short, it is a written plan. And the concepts of the terms *study* and *studies* relate to undertaking to learn something under guidance. Studying under guidance implies a teacher providing guidance and some content (i.e. some fund of knowledge) being taught and studied. That is to say, the way that the terms *study* and *studies* are functioning in these common usage definitions is in the sense of undertaking to learn something under the guidance of someone (a teacher).

The implications of the common usage definitions can be further clarified by term substitutions.

***First term substitution*:** By term substitution, the common usage definition,

"[set] [course] of [study],"

means the same as,

"[established] [written plan] of [undertaking to learn something under the guidance of a teacher],"

***Second term substitution*:** By term substitution, the common usage definition,

"the [courses] offered by an educational institution,"

means the same as,

"the [written plans for undertaking to learn something under the guidance of a teacher] offered by an educational institution."

Third term substitution: By term substitution, the common usage definition,

"the whole range of [studies] offered in a school, college, etc., or in a type of school,"

means the same as,

"the whole range of [written plans for undertaking to learn something under the guidance of a teacher] offered in a school, college, etc., or in a type of school."

The common sense of these reported definitions is that the term *curriculum* means the same as *a written plan for undertaking to learn something under the guidance of a teacher.* The entity which does the arranging is some educational institution, i.e. some organization that intends to make arrangements for teaching and studying something under guidance. Possibly this entity is a school, but the matter is left open: "… a school, college, etc., or in a type of school." In practice, curriculum documents are produced by teachers, schools, local school districts, county school districts, state school authorities, federal government authorities and commercial entities.

A plan for teaching and studying something under guidance differs from the activity of planning. It also differs from the actual activities of teaching and studying under guidance some content. A plan differs from the content that is taught and studied under guidance. And a plan differs from all of the transactions, events and experiences that take place in the lives of students while at school. Thus curriculum is not the act of planning. It is not the activities of teaching and studying under guidance. It is not the content that is taught and studied under guidance. It is not all the life experiences of students in schools. It is the plan (i.e. the arrangement) for integrating and coordinating teaching and studying activities in relation to some content with a view that students achieve some range of knowing (level, form and kind). Thus, common usage of the term *curriculum* follows the rule that says,

Use the term *curriculum* to point to (denote) a written plan for studying something under guidance from a teacher. As corollaries to the main rule,

(1) don't use the term *curriculum* to point to the activity of forming the plan (viz., planning),

(2) don't use the term *curriculum* to point to the activity of executing or implementing the plan (viz., teaching and studying under guidance),

(3) don't use the term *curriculum* to point to the something being taught and studied under guidance (i.e. the content or the fund of knowledge),

(4) don't use the term *curriculum* to point to life experiences encountered as a student in a school,

(5) don't use the term *curriculum* to point to the setting (physical, geographic, social, cultural, political, religious, etc.) in which the teaching and guided studying takes place.

A plan takes the form of a group of sentences. In practice, within official education, the sentences are always written. A curriculum, by implication, is the set of written sentences which forms a plan. The intention behind the plan is to order and coordinate the teaching and studying under guidance some content for the purpose of the student achieving some range of knowing (i.e. some level, form and kind of knowing).

In conclusion, an analysis of the three common usage definitions of the term *curriculum* implies that the term *curriculum* means the same as the set of words *a written plan for teaching and studying under guidance some content with the view in mind that the student will achieve some range of knowing*.

From the analysis of these three common usage meanings of the term *curriculum* emerges three clear choices.

(1) We can choose to adhere to common usage and use the term *curriculum* in the sense of a written plan for studying something under the guidance of a teacher with the view in mind that the student will achieve some range of knowing.

(2) Or we can choose to depart from common usage and prescribe how we would like everyone to use the term, i.e. make up another definition and make it function programmatically (I. Scheffler, 1960);

(3) Or we can say how we choose to use the term idiosyncratically, regardless of what dictionaries say or common usage indicates, i.e. we can construct a unique definition and make it function stipulatively (I. Scheffler, 1960).

Relevant to making the choice are the criteria for evaluating the adequacy of the common usage concept of the term *curriculum*.

The criteria are:
(1) inclusiveness,
(2) internal consistency,
(3) exhaustiveness,
(4) exclusiveness,
(5) external relatedness and
(6) fruitfulness.

These criteria are generally recognized and accepted in the philosophy of science as relevant, conventional and adequate standards for evaluation of a concept that is to be used to identify a class of phenomena about which inquiry might be conducted.

The criterion of inclusiveness is used to determine whether a conception of curriculum is sufficiently broad enough to include all of the cases and instances of curriculum that are related to each other in essential ways.

The criterion of exclusiveness is used to judge whether a concept of curriculum excludes all of the cases or instances which ought to be excluded from curriculum.

The criterion of internal consistency is used to judge whether a conception of curriculum includes the necessary and sufficient distinguishing characteristics of a curriculum so that all cases or instances that are identified as curriculum are consistent and clearly related to each other in essential ways.

The criterion of exhaustiveness relates closely to that of inclusiveness. It is used to judge whether a conception of curriculum permits every instance or case that should count as a member of curriculum be counted, or whether there are some cases which are left out and which should be included.

The criterion of external relatedness is used to judge whether a conception of curriculum is sufficiently related to other concepts (such as studying, learning, teaching, coaching, tutoring, mentoring, counseling, content and knowledge) to be useful in promoting clear and unambiguous discourse about curriculum.

The criterion of fruitfulness is used to judge whether the conception of curriculum is generally useful in permitting unambiguous and clear discourse about curriculum and whether it promotes progress in developing and extending descriptions, characterizations, explanations, predictions, prescriptions and justifications of curriculum.

The set of phenomena named by the common usage conception of *curriculum* is a plan (or set of plans) for studying something under the guidance of a teacher. A written plan is one of the derivative features of teaching and studying within the context of official education. Curriculum is a subset of official education, and official education is a subset of education.

In terms of the six criteria, the common usage sense of *curriculum* is adequate. It is a distinct feature of the field of educational phenomena. It does not conflate education with curriculum. It does not conflate learning as process nor learning as product with curriculum. It does not conflate all life experiences with curriculum. It does not restrict curriculum to topics, or concepts, or explanatory principles or funds of knowledge. It does not conflate curriculum with teaching strategies. It does not include too much. It does not exclude too much. It has internal consistency. It is exhaustive. It has external relatedness. And it is fruitful in that it provides a sound basis for extending useful, clear and accurate discourse about curriculum.

In relation to the six criteria for evaluation of the common usage concept of the term *curriculum*, it is justifiable to use the term *curriculum* to name written plans for undertaking to learn something under the guidance of a teacher, and it is justifiable to say that curriculum is written plans for undertaking to learn something under the guidance of a teacher.

The argument advanced in relation to the question of how do curriculum and education relate, then, is that education is a process of teaching and studying something in some setting. Educology is the fund of knowledge about education. Curriculum is an aspect or feature of education. The relationship of educology to curriculum, therefore, is the relationship of a fund of knowledge to an aspect of a field of phenomena. It is a relationship like that of zoology to vertebrates, or botany to angiosperms.

Figure 3.2: Relationship of Curriculum to Education and Educology

Funds of knowledge	Fields of phenomena	Aspects of fields of phenomena
Zoology	Animals	Invertebrates
Botany	Plants	Angiosperms
Educology	Education	Curriculum

Curriculum is a written plan or a set of written plans for undertaking to learn something under the guidance of a teacher. The educology of curriculum is knowledge (true statements) about the relationships of education and curriculum, i.e. knowledge about the relationship of the educational process to written plans for studying something under the guidance of a teacher.

The Educology of Curriculum

Educology is the fund of knowledge about education. The educological perspective treats the educational process as the dependent variable, and it examines how other factors or variables affect the educational process. In relation to curriculum, the fundamental question that can be posed from an educological perspective is,

"What are the effects of curriculum on education?"
This fundamental question implies a number of derivative questions, viz.,

(1) What are the meanings of terms used in discourse about curriculum and education and how does the use of those terms affect curriculum and education? This question is addressed by the analytic philosophical educology of curriculum.

Figure 3.3: Educology of Curriculum

The Educology of Curriculum	
Fundamental questions about the effects of curriculum on education	*Subfunds of educology which address the fundamental questions*
▪ What are the meanings of terms used in discourse about curriculum and how does the use of those terms affect curriculum and education?	▪ The analytic philosophical educology of curriculum
▪ What are good and bad (or relatively good and bad) effects of curriculum on education?	▪ The normative philosophical educology of curriculum
▪ What have been the effects of curriculum on education in past times, places, societies and cultures?	▪ The historical educology of curriculum
▪ What are extant effects of curriculum on education?	▪ The scientific educology of curriculum
▪ What practices in curriculum planning, development, implementation and evaluation are effective in achieving desired results or states of affairs in education?	▪ The praxiological educology of curriculum

(2) What are good and bad (or relatively good and bad) effects of curriculum on the educational process? This question is addressed by the normative philosophical educology of curriculum.

(3) How has curriculum affected education in the past? This question is addressed by the historical educology of curriculum.

(4) How does curriculum currently affect education in contemporary societies and cultures? This question is addressed by the scientific educology of curriculum.

(5) What practices for planning, developing, implementing and evaluating curriculum are effective in achieving desired results and/or states of affairs in education? This question is address by the praxiological educology of curriculum.

Answers to these five questions constitute the educology of curriculum, i.e. the fund of knowledge about how curriculum affects the educational process. The educology of curriculum is the fund of knowledge that provides a basis for making decisions about curriculum design, development, implementation and evaluation.

Components of a Curriculum

If we accept the common usage definition of curriculum as a written plan or a set of written plans for undertaking to learn something under the guidance of a teacher, then the fundamental questions that any adequate curriculum addresses are

(1) What should the students learn?
(2) Why should they learn it?
(3) What needs to be done to help them learn it?
(4) How do we find out whether they have learned it?

Writing a sound curriculum requires sound planning. The components which constitute a sound, comprehensive curriculum include the following elements:

(1) analysis of the situation
(2) specification of intended learning outcomes
(3) justification of intended learning outcomes
(4) allocation of time
(5) specification of content
(6) nomination of resources

(7) specification of learning opportunities

(8) assessment and evaluation

With which of these elements one might begin is up to one's experience, circumstances and judgment and perspective or point of reference. In designing a car, engineers might start with the power plant, the transmission, the chassis or the purpose of the car (e.g. racing, commuting, delivering small parcels, providing taxi services). But eventually, all of those components must be considered. So it is with a curriculum. One may begin with resources or time allocation or learning opportunities or a situational analysis. Eventually, all components must be considered, if the plan is to be sound, adequate and comprehensive.

Situational Analysis. A sound, comprehensive, well conceived curriculum includes an analysis of the students and the social and cultural milieu in which the intended teaching and studying are to take place. A situational analysis describes and characterizes the students, the social and cultural context for a curriculum and the reasons for a curriculum. An adequate, well rounded situational analysis for a curriculum

(1) examines the characteristics of the students, e.g. their age, their gender, their social and cultural origins, their motivations and aspirations and their current range of knowing,

(2) examines the social and cultural milieu in which the students must function at the moment and in the future,

(3) identifies the range of knowing that is desirable and/or necessary to function adequately in the short term, medium term and long term within the reference set of communities, societies and cultures,

(4) provides a sound justificatory argument (Paul W. Taylor, 1961) for why the prescribed range of knowing is desirable.

A situational analysis looks at the extent to which the students have progressed in their cognitive development and what progress is desirable for them to achieve in the short term, medium term and long term. The person or set of persons conducting the analysis always starts with a point of view or perspective. The perspective is grounded or referenced within the set of norms, values, expectations and culture of some set of individuals, groups, organizations, institutions, communities or societies.

In the film *Black Robe* (released in 1991), the story takes place in the year 1634 along the Saint Lawrence River in Canada. A young French Jesuit priest, Father LaForgue, is sent from Quebec to Huron country to bring the word of God and salvation to the Hurons. A band of Algonguins are appointed as his guides, protectors and providers. They come upon a band of Montagnais. "Are they [the French] intelligent?" a Montagnais asks. "No," responds one of the Algonquins. The Algonquins regard the Jesuit priest (and his countrymen) as unintelligent because he and his fellow Frenchmen have no hunting skills and no forest craft. They can't navigate through a forest by remembering the pattern of the trees. They can't pitch a camp or make a shelter from branches and bark. They can't make a fire from sticks and dry tender. They can't forage or fish effectively. They can't make tools from branches, rocks and bones. They can't make weapons such as spears, bows and arrows from the resources in the forest. They have none of the range of knowing that is requisite for surviving and thriving in the forest, mountain and lake country along the Saint Lawrence River. From the point of view of the Algonquins and the Montagnais, Father LaForgue and the French are like babies, helpless, foolish, stupid, indeed, a liability on indigenous communities. A situational analysis from the point of view of the Algonquins of the early 17th century would no doubt result in a curriculum that required learning hunting and foraging skills, tool and weapon making skills, skills of navigating through forests both day and night, kinship and familial obligations as men and women and all the rest of the range of knowing requisite for functioning competently in Algonquin society and culture of the early 17th century.

So a situational analysis is always conducted with a cultural point of view. Contemporary French curriculum developers write curriculum which they judge to be appropriate for French children, youth and adults living in France. Contemporary Australian military trainers write curriculum which they judge appropriate for training Australian military personnel to function adequately in the modern, contemporary Australian armed forces. Islamic curriculum developers write curriculum which they judge to be appropriate for believers to learn how to live consistently with the tenets of their faith. In the former Soviet Union, curriculum developers wrote curriculum which they judged to be appropriate for living in and contributing to life as a good soviet citizen in the USSR. Curriculum developers who embrace a society organized as a non-sectarian, religiously tolerant, liberal democracy will write a curriculum that promotes values, attitudes and skills consistent with their conception of a liberal democratic society.

Specification of Intended Learning Outcomes. A sound, comprehensive, well conceived curriculum includes a clear specification of intended learning outcomes. Intended learning outcomes, when well conceived, derive from a sound situational analysis, i.e. the specified intended learning outcomes are implied by the results of the situational analysis. The situational analysis and the intended learning outcomes have a coherency relationship.

The concept of the term *intended learning outcomes* can be clarified by explicating the key words in the term. An outcome is a result, consequent or product. An intended outcome is a result or consequent that is planned or deliberate. An intended learning outcome is the planned or deliberate result of a student having studied something under the guidance of a teacher. An intended learning outcome, then, is the deliberate or planned extension of a student's range of knowing (i.e. some combination of level, kind and form of knowing). Possible intended outcomes might include understanding how to

- calculate the molarity of a solution of hydrochloric acid,
- work collaboratively with others to achieve a mutually agreed upon goal,
- prepare a legal case for presentation in a criminal trial,
- lead a well balanced, healthy lifestyle that combines sensible nutrition, regular exercise and a positive outlook on life,
- play Dave Brubeck's *Take Five* on the saxophone with appropriate tempo, accurate technique and sound musical interpretation.

We can conceive of a seemingly infinite number of learning outcomes. The outcomes, when soundly conceived, will always be a selection from the possible levels, kinds and forms of knowing. A statement about an intended learning outcome will always be a specification of some range of knowing that a student expects, or is expected, to achieve.

Specification of intended learning outcomes has, over the years, taken a variety of forms. Here are some examples:
(1) to show students how to use a soldering iron;
(2) to develop the student's ability to solder a copper pipe joint;
(3) students will engage in the process soldering a number of pipe joints;
(4) students will solder a copper pipe joint that holds water under mains pressure.

Which of the four examples actually qualifies as a description of an intended learning outcome? The first example is a description of a teaching activity. "To show" is what a teacher would do in the educational process. So the first example, while offered by some curriculum developers as an intended learning outcome, does not qualify as such. It is not a learning outcome. It is a teaching activity.

The second example, "to develop the student's ability ...," is a description of a process in which students would be involved to achieve an intended learning outcome. Teaching, studying and the development of some cognition are the basic functions of the educational process. So, the second example, while offered by some curriculum developers as an intended learning outcome, does not qualify as such. It is not a learning outcome. It is a combination of processes, viz. teaching, studying and coming to know, and the combination of these three processes are the means to achieving an intended learning outcome.

The third example, "students will engage in ...," is a description of a study activity. It is part of the appropriate practice that students would undertake to master the skill of soldering copper pipe joints. So, the third example, again, while offered by some curriculum developers as an intended learning outcome, does not qualify as such. It is not a learning outcome. It is a study activity undertaken to achieve a learning outcome.

The fourth example, "students will solder ...," is a description of an intended learning outcome. It describes a range of knowing that is achieved by teaching and guided studying. The ability to solder joints which hold water under mains pressure is a range of knowing (i.e. procedural knowing in a physical form of knowing at the conventional level of knowing). (See Figure 3.4.)

Figure 3.4: Characteristic Educational Functions vs. Intended Educational Products

Process: Characteristic educational functions	**Product:** Intended educational outcomes
1. Teaching 2. Guided studying and 3. Developing knowing under guidance, i.e. learning (as process) under guidance	Intended consequences of teaching, guided studying and developing knowing, which is the same as ≡ Intended learning outcomes, which is the same as ≡ Intended range of knowing, which is the same as ≡ Intended knowing of some kind in some form at some level, which is the same as ≡ Intended understanding to some level and extent

Because the term *learning* names both process and product, it is easy to conflate the two. The first three examples must be ruled out as intended learning outcomes even though some curriculum developers might nominate them as intended learning outcomes. They can not be intended learning outcomes because they are not the consequences of the educational process. Rather, they are functions of the educational process. To confuse them with intended learning outcomes is to conflate process with product. Teaching, guided studying and the development of knowing under guidance are the characteristic functions of education. The intended products of education, in contrast, are the intended learning outcomes which someone (teachers, students, curriculum developers, interested third parties) chooses for the student to achieve by means of the educational process.

So, to avoid the mistake of conflating educational functions with educational products in specifying intended learning outcomes, it is important to follow these procedures:

(1) begin the statement of an intended learning outcome with the words, "The student ...;"

(2) always specify what range of knowing (kind, form, level) the students are intended to have attained as a result of successful teaching and studying;

(3) avoid describing educational functions in statements of intended learning outcomes, e.g. avoid phrases such as "to show the students ...," "to introduce the students to ...," "to develop an understanding of ...," "to expose students to ...."

The terms *intended learning outcomes*, *educational aims*, *educational goals* and *educational objectives* are near synonyms in ordinary language. However, it has become a convention in professional literature about education (i.e. in educological discourse) to stipulate special meanings for the terms *aim*, *goal* and *objectives*.

It has become an educological convention to stipulate that the term

(1) *aims* means intended learning outcomes that are stated in general terms and that are intended to be achieved in the long term, i.e. over many months, or possibly a year or several years,

(2) *goals* means intended learning outcomes that are stated in more specific terms and that are intended to be achieved in the medium term, i.e. over a period of a few days, or possibly a few weeks, and

(3) *objectives* means intended learning outcomes that are to be achieved in the short term (possibly after one or two lessons) and that are stated in terms of what observable (i.e. senceivable) performances students must manifest in order to demonstrate the achievement of the intended learning outcome, under what conditions the students must perform and what set of criteria the performances must satisfy (see Robert Mager, 1990).

Figure 3.5: Educational Aims, Goals and Objectives

Educational Aims	**Intended learning outcomes that are** ▪ to be achieved in the long term (many months or a year or several years) ▪ stated in general terms
Educational Goals	**Intended learning outcomes that are** ▪ to be achieved in the medium term (over a period of a few days or possibly a few weeks) ▪ stated in more specific terms
Educational Objectives	**Intended learning outcomes that are** ▪ to be achieved in the short term (after one or a few lessons) ▪ stated in terms of (1) the observable (senceivable) performances the student must manifest in order to demonstrate the achievement of the intended learning outcome (2) the conditions under which the student must perform (3) the set of criteria the performances must satisfy

Examples of Educational Aims. An example of a set of educational aims is the following.

"The Senior Secondary Australian Curriculum: Geography aims to develop students'

- knowledge and understanding of the nature, causes and consequences of natural and ecological hazards; the challenges affecting the sustainability of places; land cover transformations; and international integration in a range of spatial contexts
- understanding and application of the concepts of place, space, environment, interconnection, sustainability, scale and change through inquiries into geographical phenomena and issues
- capacity to be accomplished, critical users of geographical inquiry and skills, and have the ability to think and communicate geographically" (Canberra: Australian Curriculum, Assessment and Reporting Authority, 2013, http://www.australiancurriculum.edu.au/SeniorSecondary/ Humanities-andSocialSciences/Geography/Rationale Aims#Aims, retrieved 2014).

Statements of aims typically include verbs and verbal phrases such as *develop knowledge of, develop understanding of, develop an appreciation of, grasp the importance of, apply understanding to new situations, develop confidence with, develop problem solving abilities, develop capacity to* ... and the like. Statements of aims typically focus on processes of education rather than outcomes of education. For example, developing understanding is a process of education. Understanding is the outcome. Developing appreciation is a process of education. Appreciation is the outcome. Also, as already noted, educational aims are typically intended to be achieved within a time span of six months to a year or more.

Examples of Educational Goals. An example of a set of educational goals is the following.

"Unit 1: Natural and ecological hazards .... By the end of this unit, students will:

- understand that places and environments can be influenced by both natural and ecological hazards
- understand the complexity of human-environment interdependence in relation to natural and ecological hazards

- demonstrate knowledge of the concept or risk management
- understand and apply key geographical concepts – including place, space, environment, interconnection, sustainability, scale and change – as part of a geographical inquiry
- apply geographical inquiry and a range of skills, including spatial technologies and field work, to investigate natural and ecological hazards
- compare Australian and international risk management policies, procedures and practices
- evaluate Australian and international risk management policies, procedures and practices" (Canberra: Australian Curriculum, Assessment and Reporting Authority, 2013, http://www.australiancurriculum.edu.au/SeniorSecondary/ Humanities-and-Social-Sciences/Geography/Curriculum/ SeniorSecondary, retrieved 2014).

Statements of educational goals typically begin with the phrase, *the student*, or *the students*, or *the learner*. Statements of goals also typically include verbs such as *understand*, *apply*, *explain*, *describe*, *outline*, *summarize*, *identify*, *compare*, *contrast*, *solve*, *analyze*, *recognize* and the like.

Examples of Educational Objectives. As previously noted, educational objectives are typically expected to be achieved within a time span of a few days to a few weeks. An example of a set of educational objectives is the following.

The students will
- write, without any resources or assistance and within 50 minutes, a sound and well informed explanation of how places and environments can be influenced by both natural and ecological hazards;
- make an oral presentation, lasting no less than 20 minutes and no more than 25 minutes, which evaluates Australian and international risk management policies, procedures and practices;
- write and submit a well documented and referenced paper of no less than 10,000 and no more than 11,000 words which accurately and validly compares Australian with international risk management policies, procedures and practices;

- produce a 30 minute video which describes, illustrates and explains the complexity of human-environment interdependence in relation to natural and ecological hazards.

Statements of objectives conventionally begin with the phrase *The student* or *The learner* or *The pupil* or *The trainee.* The action verb used in the statement describes an action that is observable. Observable actions are senceivable ones, i.e. ones that can be detected by one of the five senses, viz. seeing, hearing, touching, tasting and smelling. Educational objectives also include a description of the conditions under which the observable action is to be performed, and they include an indication of the criteria (i.e. the standards and/or rules) for the observable action (Robert Mager, 1990; Jeffrey Cantor, 1992; R.M. Gagné, L. Briggs & W. Wager, 1992; N.E. Gronlund, 1991). (See Figure 3.6.)

Figure 3.6: Form of Educational Objectives

Component	Example
1. **Start with *The student* or *The pupil* or *The learner* or *The trainee***	*The student will*
2. **Describe the linguistic or physical performance**	*Write*
3. **Describe the conditions required for the performance**	*without any resources or assistance and within 50 minutes*
4. **Describe the criteria (the standards and/or rules) for the performance**	*a sound and well informed explanation of how places and environments can be influenced by both natural and ecological hazards*

Observable Indicators of Knowing and Understanding. In the educational process, the expectation of everyone involved, teachers, students and interested third parties, is that the students will extend their range of knowing (i.e. their understanding). Educational objectives address the problem posed by the question,

"How do we find out whether students have achieved the intended range of knowing?"

As previously argued, knowing is the realized ability to perform intelligently with respect to some state of affairs to achieve some desired result. Understanding is an extensive range of knowing (some combination of levels, kinds and forms of knowing). How do we determine whether someone knows something? Can we tell simply by looking at the person? Obviously not. Suppose we look at a person sitting at a bus stop. Do we know whether that person can speak Russian, do a double somersault in aerial skiing, solder a joint in a copper pipe, play the violin, or give a plausible explanation for the causes of the Korean War of 1950-53? Does the person know how to swim using the butterfly stroke? We need some indicators of the person's range of knowing. We establish the truth of the matter by observing the person doing something, e.g. speaking Russian, doing a double somersault on skis, soldering a joint in a copper pipe, playing the violin, giving an oral explanation of the causes of the Korean War, swimming using the butterfly stroke.

We need to observe with our five senses (i.e. senceive) performances that are indicators (or evidence) of people's knowing in order to infer that they indeed have mastered some range of knowing. The two kinds of performances that we can observe (i.e. senceive) are linguistic performances and physical performances. We are not able to observe (i.e. senceive) emotional performances, imaginal performances, physiological performances and conative performances. What we can do is infer from linguistic performances and physical performances to some degree of probability that the other four performances are taking place. Also, we can observe the products of linguistic and physical performances, e.g. an essay, a design for a bridge, a flight plan, a piece of blown glassware, a tongue-in-groove joint, a research report, a restored tooth.

Linguistic performances are described with verbs such as *write* (in some language with some symbol system, including Braille), *speak*, *sign with gestures* (as one does with American Sign Language or Australian Sign Language), *tap out code* (as one does with Morse code) and *read out loud*. Physical performances are described with verbs such as *move*, *make*, *produce*, *play* (as in play a musical instrument or play a game), *sing*, *dance*, *run*, *swim*, *jump*, *skip*, *kick*, *throw*, *construct*, *build*, *frown*, *smile*, *laugh*, *gesture*.

Linguistic Performances (*Written in Some Symbol System, including Braille and Mathematical Symbols*). Examples of written linguistic performances include:

Partial List of Written Linguistic Performances		
• write an account of ... • write an abbreviation for • write an analysis of • write an answer to a question • write an argument for or against • categorize in writing • draw a chart • classify in writing • compare in writing • contrast in writing • write a composition • write a definition	• write an explanation • design a flow chart • write a formula • identify in writing • write about an issue • write an interpretation • write a justification • write a list • write a name • write numbers and mathematical symbols • write an outline • write a paraphrase	• write a report • write sentences • write a short story • write about similarities and differences • write about a situation • write a solution to a problem • write a solution to a mathematical problem • write the steps of reasoning in the solution of a mathematical problem • write the musical notation for a song

• write a description	• draw or paint a representational picture	• write the words for a song
• draw a diagram		• write a speech
• discriminate in writing between or among	• write a paragraph	• write a summary
	• draw a pattern	• draw a table
	• predict in writing	• write about a topic
• write an equation	• write a project plan	
• write an essay	• write about a problem	• write the musical notation for a tune
• write an estimate		
• write an example	• write a procedure	• spell words by writing, etc.
• write an evaluation	• write a poem	
	• write a précis	
	• write a proof for a mathematical theorem	

Linguistic Performances (Spoken or Signed Using American Sign Language or Some Other Symbol System). Examples of spoken or signed linguistic performances include:

Partial List of Spoken or Signed Linguistic Performances
• give an oral account of something
• use American Sign Language to give an account of something
• say an abbreviation
• give an oral analysis
• use American Sign Language to give an analysis
• give an oral answer to a question
• use American Sign Language to answer
• give an oral argument
• use American Sign Language to give an argument
• orally categorize
• use American Sign Language to categorize
• orally classify
• use American Sign Language to classify
• orally compare and contrast

- use American Sign Language to compare and contrast
- orally compose a poem
- use American Sign Language to compose a poem
- orally compose a story
- use American Sign Language to compose a story
- orally compose a song
- orally compose a tune
- orally define
- use American Sign Language to define
- orally describe
- use American Sign Language to describe
- orally discern
- use American Sign Language to discern
- orally discriminate between
- use American Sign Language to discriminate between
- orally distinguish
- use American Sign Language to distinguish
- say an equation
- orally give an estimate
- orally give an example
- orally give an exposition
- orally evaluate
- orally explain
- orally give a formula
- orally make an identification
- speak about an issue
- orally make an interpretation
- orally present a justification
- orally make a list
- say a name
- say numbers and mathematical symbols
- orally make an outline
- orally paraphrase
- orally predict
- orally present a project plan
- speak about a problem
- orally describe a procedure

- recite a poem
- orally give a précis
- orally give a proof for a mathematical theorem
- orally present a report
- speak sentences
- orally present a short story
- speak about similarities and differences
- speak about a situation
- orally present a solution to a problem
- orally present a solution to a mathematical problem
- orally compose a song
- orally compose and present a speech
- orally spell words
- orally present a summary
- speak about a topic
- orally compose a tune
- pronounce words
- etc.

Linguistic Performances (Reading Out Loud). Examples of reading out loud include:

• read out loud a paragraph
• read out loud a play
• read out loud a poem
• read out loud a set of
  directions
	• read out loud a set of
	  written musical notes
	• read out loud a short story
	• read out loud a recipe
	• etc.

Physical Performances. Examples of physical performances include:

• catch a ball
• construct objects
• cook scrambled
  eggs
• create a model
	• ice skate
	• jump
	• kick
	• lift
	• operate
	  machinery
		• play ice hockey
		• play a role in a
		  drama
		• prepare a meal
		• run
		• sing

• dive from a diving board	• paint a house	• skip
• drive a vehicle	• pilot an aircraft	• smile
• frown	• pilot a boat	• snow ski
• gesture	• play basketball	• swim
• grimace	• play the flute	• throw
• hit	• play the guitar	• wave
		• etc.

Classification of Educational Aims, Goals and Objectives. The forms, levels and kinds of knowing can be used to classify and organize educational aims, goals and objectives. (See Critical Category 10, 11, 12, 13 and 14 in Chapter 1 to remind yourself of the levels, forms and kinds of knowing and how they relate to the three levels of understanding.) To organize intended learning outcomes for a curriculum plan, it is a matter of choosing the level, kind and form of knowing that you want students to achieve. The possibilities are shown in Figure 3.7.

Level 3, or postconventional knowing is not included in Figure 3.7 because postconventional knowing can not be taught and studied under guidance. It can only be adapted, innovated or created by someone. Also procedural adaptive, procedural innovative and procedural creative knowing are not included in Figure 3.7. These three kinds of knowing are at the postconventional level of knowing. They can not be taught and studied under guidance. They can only be adapted, innovated or created. Of course, once established, they can become conventional knowing, and once they become conventional knowing, then they can be taught and studied under guidance as Level 2, conventional, procedural protocolic knowing.

Suppose you want Year 1 or First Grade pupils to write the letters *W, M, U* and *N* in their capital form with correct orientation, size and shape. The intended learning outcome can be properly stated in this way:

"Pupils will write the capitalized letters *W, M, U* and *N* in correct shape, orientation and size on lined paper."

This intended learning outcome is an ***A-7-a*** educational objective. It is knowing at the Level 1 or the preconventional level

Figure 3.7: Possible Combinations of Levels, Kinds and Forms of Knowing

C-1-a	C-1-b	C-1-c	C-1-d	C-1-e	C-1-f
C-2-a	C-2-b	C-2-c	C-2-d	C-2-e	C-2-f
C-3-a	C-3-b	C-3-c	C-3-d	C-3-e	C-3-f
C-4-a	C-4-b	C-4-c	C-4-d	C-4-e	C-4-f
C-5-a	C-5-b	C-5-c	C-5-d	C-5-e	C-5-f
C-6-a	C-6-b	C-6-c	C-6-d	C-6-e	C-6-f
C-7-a	C-7-b	C-7-c	C-7-d	C-7-e	C-7-f
B-1-a	B-1-b	B-1-c	B-1-d	B-1-e	B-1-f
B-2-a	B-2-b	B-2-c	B-2-d	B-2-e	B-2-f
B-3-a	B-3-b	B-3-c	B-3-d	B-3-e	B-3-f
B-4-a	B-4-b	B-4-c	B-4-d	B-4-e	B-4-f
B-5-a	B-5-b	B-5-c	B-5-d	B-5-e	B-5-f
B-6-a	B-6-b	B-6-c	B-6-d	B-6-e	B-6-f
B-7-a	B-7-b	B-7-c	B-7-d	B-7-e	B-7-f
A-1-a	A-1-b	A-1-c	A-1-d	A-1-e	A-1-f
A-2-a	A-2-b	A-2-c	A-2-d	A-2-e	A-2-f
A-3-a	A-3-b	A-3-c	A-3-d	A-3-e	A-3-f
A-4-a	A-4-b	A-4-c	A-4-d	A-4-e	A-4-f
A-5-a	A-5-b	A-5-c	A-5-d	A-5-e	A-5-f
A-6-a	A-6-b	A-6-c	A-6-d	A-6-e	A-6-f
A-7-a	A-7-b	A-7-c	A-7-d	A-7-e	A-7-f

A = Level 1, preconventional level of knowing, beginner or novice level

B = Level 2, conventional level of knowing at the intermediate level

C = Level 3, conventional level of knowing at the expert level

1 = Qualitative recognitive knowing
2 = Qualitative acquaintive knowing
3 = Qualitative appreciative knowing
4 = Quantitative instantive knowing
5 = Quantitative theoretical knowing
6 = Quantitative criterial knowing
7 = Procedural protocolic knowing

a = Linquistic knowing
b = Emotional knowing
c = Imaginal knowing
d = Physiological knowing
e = Physical knowing
f = Conative knowing

of knowing (*A*). It is a procedural protocolic kind of knowing (*7*). And it is a linguistic written form of knowing (*a*).

Now suppose that you want a group of Year 9 or 9th Grade students to list three contributing causes to the commencement of the Second World War. The intended learning outcome can be properly stated in this way:

"Students will correctly list in writing without the aid of any resources three contributing causes to the commencement of the Second World War."

This intended learning outcome is a *B-4-a* educational objective. It is knowing at the Level 2 or conventional intermediate level of knowing (*B*). It is a quantitative instantive kind of knowing (*4*). And it is a linguistic written form of knowing (*a*).

Suppose that you want a group of university students to use a spectrograph competently to identify the elements in a compound. The intended learning outcome can be properly stated in this way:

"Students will analyze an unknown compound with a spectrograph and correctly identify in writing the elements in the compound that are indicated by the spectrographic analysis."

This intended learning outcome actually combines two outcomes, as indicated by the two verbs, *analyze* and *identify*. So, for the sake of clarity, it is better to state the two outcomes separately, i.e.

First Outcome: "Students will analyze an unknown compound with a spectrograph."

and

Second Outcome: "Students will correctly identify in writing the elements in an unknown compound that are indicated by a spectrographic analysis."

The first outcome is a ***B-7-e*** educational objective. It is knowing at the Level 2 or conventional intermediate level of knowing (***B***). It is a procedural protocolic kind of knowing (***7***). And it is a physical form of knowing (***e***).

The second outcome is a ***B-5-a*** educational objective. It is knowing at the Level 2 or conventional intermediate level of knowing (***B***). It is a quantitative theoretical kind of knowing (***5***). And it is a linguistic form of knowing (***a***).

An effective technique for keeping track of educational objectives for a curriculum is to create a data base for the objectives. The essential information for each item in the data base includes

(1) an identifying number for the objective, e.g. *001, 002*, etc.
(2) level of knowing
(3) kind of knowing
(4) form of knowing
(5) range of knowing identifier
(6) related topic, concept, subject matter or content
(7) statement of educational objective

An example of how an individual record might appear in the database of educational objectives is illustrated in Figure 3.8.

Once a collection of educational objectives has been developed, the objectives can be mapped in relation to the range of knowing. For example, with educational objectives that have been assigned with the identifying numbers 001, 002, 003, 004 and 005,

Figure 3.8: Database Fields for Educational Objectives

Identifying number for the objective	001
Level of knowing	Conventional intermediate
Kind of knowing	Procedural protocolic
Form of knowing	Linguistic
Range of knowing identifier (from Figure 3.7)	B-7-a
Related topic, concept, subject matter or content	The author, title, subject database in a school library
Statement of educational objective	For an assigned subject, all Year 7 (7th Grade) students will locate and write a list of six relevant authors and titles from the author, title, subject database of the school library

Figure 3.9: Educational Objectives Mapped onto the Range of Knowing

C-1-a	C-1-b	C-1-c	C-1-d	C-1-e	C-1-f
C-2-a	C-2-b	C-2-c	C-2-d	C-2-e	C-2-f
C-3-a	C-3-b	C-3-c	C-3-d	C-3-e	C-3-f
C-4-a	C-4-b	C-4-c	C-4-d	C-4-e	C-4-f
C-5-a	C-5-b	C-5-c	C-5-d	C-5-e	C-5-f
C-6-a	C-6-b	C-6-c	C-6-d	C-6-e	C-6-f
C-7-a	C-7-b	C-7-c	C-7-d	C-7-e	C-7-f
B-1-a	B-1-b	B-1-c	B-1-d	B-1-e	B-1-f
B-2-a	B-2-b	B-2-c	B-2-d	B-2-e	B-2-f
B-3-a	B-3-b	B-3-c	B-3-d	B-3-e	B-3-f
B-4-a *003*	B-4-b	B-4-c	B-4-d	B-4-e	B-4-f
B-5-a *005*	B-5-b	B-5-c	B-5-d	B-5-e	B-5-f
B-6-a	B-6-b	B-6-c	B-6-d	B-6-e	B-6-f
B-7-a *001*	B-7-b	B-7-c	B-7-d	B-7-e *004*	B-7-f
A-1-a	A-1-b	A-1-c	A-1-d	A-1-e	A-1-f
A-2-a	A-2-b	A-2-c	A-2-d	A-2-e	A-2-f
A-3-a	A-3-b	A-3-c	A-3-d	A-3-e	A-3-f
A-4-a	A-4-b	A-4-c	A-4-d	A-4-e	A-4-f
A-5-a	A-5-b	A-5-c	A-5-d	A-5-e	A-5-f
A-6-a	A-6-b	A-6-c	A-6-d	A-6-e	A-6-f
A-7-a *002*	A-7-b	A-7-c	A-7-d	A-7-e	A-7-f

and identified with the range of knowing of B-7-a, A-7-a, B-4- a, B-7-d & B-5-a, i.e.

001 with a ***B-7-a*** range of knowing,
002 with an ***A-7-a*** range of knowing,
003 with a ***B-4-a*** range of knowing,
004 with a ***B-7-e*** range of knowing and
005 with a ***B-5-a*** range of knowing,

the five educational objectives can be mapped on the range of knowing as illustrated in Figure 3.9.

With the mapping of educational objectives, the curriculum developer can achieve a good visual sense of the range of knowing that the educational objectives specify. It provides a valuable set of information for making decisions about whether to extend the set of educational objectives or to be satisfied with them as they are.

Justification of Intended Learning Outcomes. Closely related to the task of specifying intended learning outcomes is that of developing justification for those intended outcomes. It is not requisite in the process of curriculum development to move in a sequence from situational analysis to specification of intended learning outcomes to justification of the outcomes. However, within the curriculum development process, the question as to why some outcomes are better than others must eventually be addressed. Justification is a process of developing a sound justificatory argument, i.e. a valid normative argument which supports a state of affairs on the basis of a set of sound values. To develop an argument competently requires criterial quantitative knowing. The basic form of the justificatory argument is that an intended learning outcome is good because it is coherent (i.e. logically consistent) with a set of desirable values. This is the process of value verification. The set of desirable values are justified in terms of being coherent with a higher set of values. This part of the argument is value validation. The higher set of values is justified as being good in terms of it constituting a way of life to which the author of the argument is committed. The way of life to which the author of the argument is committed is justified on the basis of it being one which the author has chosen, on a rational basis, free from intimidation, threat or coercion, from a set of known and well considered alternatives (Paul W. Taylor, 1961).

What are some examples of justificatory arguments for intended learning outcomes? One common and quite familiar one is that funds of knowledge which are offered in schools should be studied because understanding them enhances employment prospects. Suppose that this position is accepted and that it is offered as justification for a set of intended learning outcomes specified in a curriculum. The employment argument goes something like this. The set of intended learning outcomes specified for the curriculum is worthwhile to achieve because attainment of them will enhance the employability of the students in their adult lives. (This step in the argument is the one of value verification; the intended learning outcomes are justified in terms of a wider value, that of employability.) By implication, employment is desirable. Why? It might be argued that employment is good because it contributes to the production of all the goods and services which a society collectively requires, that everyone is obliged to engage in gainful employment to contribute his or her fair share of the workload, and that a personal income is necessary to buy the necessities and the luxuries of life. (This is the step of value validation in the argument; the value of employment is justified in terms of a wider set of values, viz. production, fairness, income, access to the necessities of life, access to the luxuries of life.) By implication, this set of values is desirable. How might the set be justified? It might be argued that it is through holding this set of values that one can attain happiness, and that happiness through material well being is an ultimate value, a way of life that is superior to alternative ways of living. (This step in the argument is value vindication; it is justification of the set of values of production, fairness and consumption in terms of a way of life, viz. happiness through consumption and material well being.) This is one example of a justificatory argument for a set of intended learning outcomes. From this argument is derived the rule to judge intended learning outcomes to be worthwhile to the extent that they ultimately contribute to a person's happiness through material well being.

Of course, no argument goes without it detractors. Our world is one of competing sets of values and ways of living. It can be argued that while employment is in some ways desirable, it must be kept in proportion to other worthwhile things in human existence. Generating income through employment is not the only thing in life. In fact, employment is more a necessary evil than an unmitigated good. Employment, after all, is wage for labor, a serving of someone else's interests rather than pursuing one's own genuine, authentically chosen interests. The good life is the one in which you are at liberty to pursue and to develop your own interests in accordance with authentic choices from well known, critically evaluated and readily available alternatives. Suppose one accepts this position and offers it as justification for the intended learning outcomes of a curriculum. How might the argument proceed?

The first step is value verification. The set of intended learning outcomes specified for a curriculum may have value for enhancing employability, but that is of a secondary or lesser value. The intended learning outcomes have primary value for enabling students to identify and pursue their own self interests.

The next step in the argument is value validation. This is justification of the wider value of self interest in terms of a set of higher values. An argument can first be made against employment, then an argument can be developed for self interest. First, employment is undesirable on the grounds of wastefulness and self destructiveness. That is, in a highly industrialized and automated economic system, not everyone can be employed nor need they be employed. Automation and robotics reduce the need for human labor, and to seek to attain full employment is wasteful of human beings. Moreover, it is ultimately self destructive if full employment is to be achieved by unending economic expansion. A modern production system is too efficient to permit it to produce as much as possible. It depletes nonrenewable resources and pollutes the renewable ones. It produces far more than a society should reasonably consume. When consumption becomes valued as the primary (or perhaps, only) means of achieving the good life, the combination of efficient production and unbridled consumption results in waste of colossal proportions. Gluttony, intemperance, selfishness, waste and rapaciousness, if unchecked, ultimately result in destruction of environment, of fellow human beings and finally of self. Certainly, no one should predicate self esteem and personal happiness upon how much one irrationally produces, unreasonably earns or mindlessly consumes and squanders. A far more desirable alternative is rational production. Rational production is limited to the capacity of resources to renew themselves and the demands of rational consumption. Such consumption is frugal, moderated, confined to reasonable needs, averse to excess. An efficient, highly automated economic system reduces the time required for human beings to be engaged in production and distribution. It gives us time on our hands. A worthwhile use of that time is the development of self interests, not the interests chosen for us by others. The highest self interest is to develop those qualities which enable us to live in ways that are befitting of human beings. What are those ways? An inkling of what constitutes those ways can be gained from an example which, paradoxically, appears to be nonhuman. In the old television series, "Lassie" (1954-73, CBS) the dog was presented to the audience as, not almost, but entirely human in function. She consistently exhibited mindfulness, purposefulness, reasonableness, virtuous-ness (including charitability, generosity, kindness, courageous-ness), and the ability to conceive meaning with symbols (use language). The Lassie of that series, although in a nonhumanoid biological form, exemplified to a large extent what is entailed in leading a life which is befitting of human beings, viz., having cognition and acting reasonably and morally in relation to that cognition. To inquire, to learn, to reason and to live one's life in relation to those three processes form the basis for treating one's self in ways that are befitting of a human being. (At this point in your argument, you have completed the process of value validation, i.e. you have justified your rejection of employment and your appeal for the pursuit of self interests in terms of a higher set of values, viz. learning, inquiring, reasoning, rational and moral action. Next in the justificatory argument comes value vindication, i.e. justification of the higher set of values by appealing to a way of life.)

If inquiring, learning, reasoning and taking rational and moral action are worthwhile, then why? What justification can be offered for them? You might argue, at this point, that these are means to happiness, and happiness through rational action is an ultimate value, a way of life which is superior to alternative ways of living. In this way of life, the primary values are open and free inquiry, sound evidential and criterial argumentation, resolution of conflict through reasonable and rational discourse, mindful and authentic action based on reflection and intelligent inquiry, a due regard for the interests of self and the rights of others and a disposition to inquire in order to know what truths can be known and to use those truths for personal and collective benefit. This way of life prizes frugality in consumption and abhors waste. It begrudges time required for human labor in production and distribution. It tolerates wage for labor or fee for service as a necessary evil, a sacrifice of part of one's time away from inquiry because a machine can not do the job required for the material well being of the society. Employment is time taken away from time better spent at pursuing one's interests as a human being. In terms of this way of life, happiness through rational action, intended learning outcomes are judged worthwhile to the extent that they enhance a student's willingness and ability

    (1) to inquire systematically and carefully,

    (2) to respect evidential and criterial arguments,

    (3) to use appropriate means to collect necessary and sufficient evidence for resolution of problems and for formulation of constructive, reasonable actions in relation to authentically chosen intentions and purposes and

    (4) to pursue one's worthwhile goals with intelligence and responsibility, with a sense of self determination, and with due regard for the concerns and rights of others as well as self.

This, then, is a second example of a justificatory argument. To develop a sound justificatory argument for your intended learning outcomes, you must develop it in terms of value verification, value validation and value vindication, culminating in a rational choice of a way of life to which you are authentically and rationally committed (Paul W. Taylor, 1961). Developing a sound justificatory argument goes far beyond quoting government department documents, laws or regulations or religious literature. It requires ultimately that you identify and explicate the way of life which you can authentically and genuinely recommend on the basis of rational choice. This requires that you personally engage in the reasoning process and not rely upon what someone else or some document tells you to value. In these matters, your own reason must be your guide.

Just when to develop a justification for a set of intended learning outcomes in the process of curriculum development is a matter of personal preference. It can be the first task, some task in the middle or the last task of curriculum development. But it should never be ignored or set aside in the too difficult basket. It ultimately gives the *raison d'être* for the entire curriculum.

Allocation of Time. A sound curriculum includes an allocation of time for achievement of the intended learning outcomes. An adequate allocation of time includes a specification of the total time to allow for students to achieve the intended learning outcomes and also an indication of the pace at which the learning is intended to occur. An example of an allocation is 200 hours of face-to-face learning opportunities with a teacher or teachers. An example of a specification of pacing is one hour per day in a five-day week over a time span of 40 weeks (a total of 200 hours).

When to include the time factor in the process of developing a curriculum is a matter of professional judgment and personal preference. It can be done at the beginning, at the end or some-where in the middle of the planning process. Starting with the time allocation before specifying intended learning outcomes may give a sense of what is possible for the students to achieve within given time constraints, and it may therefore give guidance to the specifi-cation of intended learning outcomes.

There is never an unlimited amount of time for the teaching and guided study of something, and often the amount of time is specified by school administrators, regulations or legislated policies. Within a school program, time allocated to the teaching and guided study of one content is time taken away from the teaching and guided study of another content. It is important, therefore, to have an accurate estimate of the time which will be required for students to achieve the intended learning outcomes.

Factors to take into account in developing time estimates include the capabilities of the students (as evidenced by their previous progress and achievement), the degree of their motivation, the inevitable interruptions of day to day school life that take students away from allocated time, the time students lose from illness (and the time it takes to make up for lost ground) and the time it takes for students to make up for learning gains that have atrophied from lack of practice during long holiday periods.

Specification of Content. An obviously important component of a curriculum is the specification of content. Specification of content can take place at any time in the curriculum planning process, i.e. at the beginning, middle or end. It is a matter of professional judgment and preference. But for any curriculum to be adequate, a specification of content needs to be included. Furthermore, for the curriculum to be coherent, the content needs to be logically connected with the intended learning outcomes, and, indeed, with all other components of the curriculum.

In the section, Critical Category 4, and in the section, Content, where an explication was presented of content as one of the four components of education, it has been argued that content is best regarded as funds of knowledge that are selected and organized for the purposes of teaching and studying under guidance.

Knowledge (as opposed to knowing) is a true statement or a set of true statements. Examples of knowledge include the following true statements.

(1) Leonardo Pisano Bigollo (c. 1170-1250), also known as Fibonacci, introduced the Hindu and Arabic numeral system into European mathematics with his book *Liber Abaci* (*Book of Calculation)* in 1202 A.D.

(2) One of the important properties of right triangles is that the square of its longest side (the hypotenuse) is equal to the sum of the squares of its two shorter sides.

(3) *The Tale of Two Cities*, published in 1859, is one of Charles Dickens' most famous and important novels.

A fund of knowledge is a collection of true statements. Examples of names for particular funds of knowledge include the following.

(1) geology
(2) physics
(3) anthropology

A fund of knowledge is most useful for teaching and studying under guidance when it is organized into a coherent set of descriptions, characterizations, explanations, predictions, justifications and prescriptions. Organization of knowledge for the purposes of teaching and guided studying is typically achieved with outlines (topic outlines and sentence outlines) or key concepts or key questions (sometimes called focus questions). Examples of each of these forms of organization are provided in Figures 3.10, 3.11, 3.12 and 3.13. The fourteen critical categories distinguished in Chapter 1 have an important bearing on the problems of selecting and arranging content for teaching and guided studying. The categories are important for at least two reasons. It is important to understand the categories from the point of view of keeping one's own thinking about content free of conflation and ambiguity. It is also important from the point of view of understanding how transactions with content are part of the normal functioning of the process of teaching and guided studying.

Confusion of Content, Disciplines and Funds of Knowledge. The funds of knowledge of physics, zoology and botany are sometimes called disciplines. This is misleading because all three funds share the same disciplines, viz. the rules, logical operations and procedures for making analytic, empirical and normative warranted assertions. They are distinct funds of knowledge, but they are not distinct disciplines. Their distinctiveness as funds derives from the field of phenomena (also called *object of knowledge*) which each fund describes, characterizes and explains, viz. physical matter (characterized by physics), animals (characterized by zoology) and plants (characterized by botany).

Related cases are those of sociology, psychology and anthropology. These three funds of knowledge share the same disciplines of analytic, empirical and normative rules, logical operations and procedures of inquiry. The three funds are not distinctive with respect to discipline, but they are distinctive with respect to the fields of phenomena which they describe and characterize. Each fund describes and characterizes a different field of phenomena, viz. society (characterized by sociology), mind (characterized by psychology) and humankind (characterized by anthropology).

Some funds of knowledge do not describe or characterize fields of phenomena at all. Logic and mathematics are two examples. These funds require analytic discipline to form them, and they describe, characterize and explain the meanings and necessary

Figure 3.10: Organization of Content by Topic Outline

Organization of Content by Topic Outline:

The United Nations (UN) since the end of the Cold War

1. The role and structure of the UN since the end of the Cold War
2. Nature of the relationship with major powers and alliances
3. Continuing efforts to promote disarmament and to prevent nuclear proliferation
4. The role and influence of the UN as an international peacekeeper in
   4.1. the Gulf War
   4.2. the former Yugoslavia
   4.3. Somalia (1993)
   4.4. Rwanda (1994)
   4.5. East Timor (1999-2001)
5. Challenges to peace facing the international community
   5.1. racism
   5.2. refugees
   5.3. child soldiers
   5.4. landmines
   5.5. poverty
   5.6. gender inequity
   5.7. war crimes
   5.8. illiteracy
   5.9. AIDS
   5.10. international terrorism

Figure 3.11: Organization of Content by Sentence Outline

Example of Organization of
Content by Sentence Outline:

Procedures for soldering a copper pipe to an elbow joint

1. Preparation

   1.1. Assure that the end of the pipe has been cut square (i.e. 90 degrees to the running length of the pipe.

   1.2. Assure that there are no rough edges or burrs on the cut edge of the pipe; if there are any, smooth them with a fine metal file or an emery paper.

   1.3. Clean the surfaces to be soldered on the pipe and the elbow joint thoroughly by sanding with a fine emery paper and wiping with a clean cloth.

   1.4. Apply flux to the surfaces to be soldered on both the pipe and the elbow.

   1.5. Push the end of the pipe into the sleeve of the elbow.

2. Soldering

   2.1. Heat the join of the pipe and the elbow until the flux melts; avoid overheating.

   2.2. Touch the solder wire to the hot surface and allow the solder to melt and run into the joint; apply the solder evenly, without gaps, all the way around the circumference of the pipe.

   2.3. Allow the joint to cool; take care to avoid touching the joint before it has cooled sufficiently.

Figure 3.12: Organization of Content by Concepts

Example of Organization of Content by Concepts:

1. The calculus
2. Change
   - 2.1. Limit
     - 2.1.1. Convergence of infinite sequences to a limit
     - 2.1.2. Convergence of series to a limit
     - 2.1.3. Maxima
     - 2.1.4. Minima
   - 2.2. Limit of a function
   - 2.3. Limit of a sequence
   - 2.4. Indeterminate form
   - 2.5. Orders of approximation
   - 2.6. (ε, δ) - definition of limit
3. Differential calculus
   - 3.1. Rates of change
   - 3.2. Slopes of curves
   - 3.3. Differentiation
   - 3.4. Inverse of integration
4. Integral calculus
   - 4.1. Accumulation of quantities
   - 4.2. Areas under curves
   - 4.3. Areas between curves
   - 4.4. Integration
   - 4.5. Inverse of differentiation

Figure 3.13: Organization of Content by Key Questions

Example of Organization of
Content by Key Questions:

What makes a good story?

1. How does a theme improve a story?
   1.1. What are some good themes for a story?
   1.2. What can you do to make the theme grow out of the story, rather than tell the readers what the theme is?
2. What are some good beginning lines for a story?
3. Who are the characters?
   3.1. What do they look like and what do they wear?
   3.2. When they speak, what do they sound like?
   3.3. What do they do and think?
   3.4. Who are their friends and enemies?
   3.5. What are their problems and challenges?

4. Where is the story set and when?
5. What style and tone of writing contributes to a good story?
   5.1. Why is showing rather than telling a more interesting way to write a story?
   5.2. Is it better to write in the present or past, in first or third person and in direct or indirect speech?
   5.3. Why is using simpler language usually better than using more complicated language?

6. What is the plot?
   6.1. What happens to the characters?
   6.2. What conflicts might add interest to the plot?
   6.3. What can be done to build up to a climax in the story?
   6.4. What do the characters do to resolve their conflicts?

7. What makes a good ending for the story?

implications of symbols, terms, concepts and propositions, rather than characterizing actual phenomena.

A sound, useful and fruitful system of classification of funds of knowledge has been offered by E. Steiner (1981), viz. physical, biological and hominological funds of knowledge. (Steiner uses the term *discipline* in the sense of *fund of knowledge.*) Physical knowledge describes, characterizes, analyzes and explains phenomena within the physical world. Examples of such funds include physics, chemistry, hydrology, climatology, meteorology, and geology. Biological knowledge describes, characterizes, analyzes and explains phenomena within the living world. Examples of such funds include biology, zoology, botany, ornithology, ichthyology and virology. Hominological knowledge describes, characterizes, analyzes and explains human beings. Examples of such funds include anthropology, sociology, economics, political science, linguistics and educology.

Perspectives of Different Funds of Knowledge. Each fund of knowledge provides its own perspective on a field of phenomena or state of affairs. The distinguishing feature of a perspective is the field of phenomena or state of affairs that is treated as the dependent variable. The fund of knowledge that is sociology, for example, analyzes and characterizes society and examines variables that affect the structure and function of society. Social stratification, social class, social caste, social mobility and social norms are central concerns in sociological discourse. The fund of knowledge that is economics, as a second example of perspective in a fund of knowledge, analyzes and characterizes the ways and means that goods and services are produced and distributed. The production, distribution and consumption of goods and services in an exchange economy are the central concerns of economics, and other factors are analyzed in relation to how they affect the production and distribution of goods and services.

Thus, the same set of phenomena can be characterized from many different perspectives. A young man, for example, can be characterized from the perspective of chemistry. The chemical processes taking place within the body of the young man can be analyzed and characterized. He can be characterized from the perspective of sociology. His social identity, social roles, social class, social status and social interactions can be analyzed and characterized sociologically. He can be characterized from the perspective of anthropology. His values, way of life, world view and his enculturated view of what is normal and his general world view can be analyzed and characterized anthropologically. There can be discourse from many different perspectives (i.e. from the point of view of many different funds of knowledge) about the man, but regardless of the discourse about him, he remains the same man.

Figure 3.14: Funds of Knowledge Organized in Relation to Object of Knowledge

Organization of Funds of Knowledge by Object of Knowledge			
Object of knowledge	Physical world	Living organisms	Human beings
Category of fund of knowledge	Physical knowledge	Biological knowledge	Homino-logical knowledge
Examples of members of this category of knowledge	Chemistry Climatology Geology Meteorology Physics	Biology Botany Ornithology Virology Zoology	Economics Educology Linguistics Psychology Sociology

Interdisciplinary Studies and Funds of Knowledge. In discourse about content and subject matter, there is often conflation of the categories of
- funds of knowledge,
- discipline of inquiry,
- field of phenomena and

• perspective of a fund of knowledge.

The term *discipline* is used in ordinary language to denote simultaneously a fund of knowledge, the rules used to verify a statement, a field of phenomena and the perspective of a fund of knowledge. So the term *discipline* is commonly used in such a way that it conflates four distinct categories.

That which is given the name of *interdisciplinary studies* is the study under guidance of different funds of knowledge to describe, characterize, analyze and explain the same set of phenomena. For example, the field of phenomena denoted by the term *sustainable development* might be studied from the points of view of economics, sociology, psychology, political science, agronomy, climatology, meteorology, ecology, demographics and ethics. The field of phenomena denoted by the term *human development* might be studied from the points of view of educology, psychology, sociology and anthropology. The field of phenomena denoted by the term *urban planning* might be studied from the points of view of demography, ecology, psychology, sociology, economics and political science.

Content, Subjects and Subject Matter. In primary and secondary schools, it is common to use the terms *subject* and *subject matter* to identify categories of content. For example, all of the items listed in Figure 3.15 are identified as subjects in the curriculum of various schools.

Each of the subject names in Figure 3.15 is commonly found in lists of school subjects offered by primary and secondary school systems. However, the subject names do not name the same category of objects. The subject names refer to at least three categories, viz. fund of knowledge, field of phenomena and range of knowing. For example, the term *chemistry* names a fund of knowledge about the ways that elements combine to form compounds and the ways compounds decompose to form elements. The term *health education* names a process of teaching and studying under guidance the concept of health and ways and means of achieving and maintaining health. The term *reading* names a range of knowing, i.e. seeing (or touching, in the case of using Braille) a set of symbols and conceiving the denotative and connotative meaning of the symbols.

Figure 3.15: Examples of School Subjects

Algebra	History	Physical Activity
Art	Health Education	Sports Studies
Business	Home Economics	Physical
Chemistry	Human Society	Education
Child Studies	& Its	Physics
Commerce	Environment	Reading
Computer Skills	Information &	Science
Craft	Communication	Sewing
Creative Arts	Technology	Social Science
Creative Writing	Information &	Spanish
Dance	Software	Spelling
Design &	Technology	Studies of Society
Technology	Industrial	& Environment
Digital Techno-	Technology	Technical
logies	Language Arts	Drawing
Drama	Marine &	Technology
English	Aquaculture	Tennis
Literature	Technology	Textiles Techno-
Food Technology	Mathematics	logy
French	Media Arts	Touch Typing
Geography	Music	Visual Arts
Geometry	Natural Science	Visual Design
Graphics Techno-	Personal	Visual &
logy	Development	Performing Arts
Handwriting	Photographic &	Vietnamese
	Digital Media	

The fact that names of subjects refer to these three categories indicates that the term *subject* is used ambiguously in discourse about education. It is commonly used to conflate the categories of fund of knowledge, field of phenomena and range of knowing.

The situation is further complicated by the fact that some terms used for subject names are used to denote two categories simultaneously, e.g. the term *technology* is commonly used to denote simultaneously (1) knowledge about effective practices for achieving some state of affairs and (2) computer hardware and other electronic devices. (See Figure 3.16.)

Figure 3.16: School Subjects Organized in Relation to Fund of Knowledge, Field of Phenomena and Range of Knowing

Fund of Knowledge	Field of Phenomena	Range of Knowing
Algebra	Business	Art
Chemistry	Child Studies	Computer Skills
Digital Techno-	Commerce	Craft
logies	Drama	Creative Arts
Geography	English Literature	Creative Writing
Geometry	French	Dance
History	Health Education	Design
Home Economics	Human Society &	Handwriting
Information &	Its Environment	Language Arts
Communication	Music	Media Arts
Technology	Personal Develop-	Reading
Information	ment	Sewing
&Software	Photographic &	Spelling
Technology	Digital Media	Technical Drawing
Industrial	Physical Activity	Tennis
Technology	Physical Education	Touch Typing
Marine &	Spanish	Visual Arts
Aquaculture	Sports Studies	Visual Design
Technology	Studies of Society	Visual & Perform-
Mathematics	& Environment	ing Arts
Natural Science	Technology	
Physics	Tennis	
Science	Vietnamese	
Social Science		
Food Technology		
Graphics Tech-		
nology		
Textiles		
Technology		

The Confusion Caused by Using the Categories of Knowledge, Skills and Attitudes. Another source of confusion in discourse about content is the use of the categories of knowledge, skills and attitudes. These three categories are frequently used in statements about content and curriculum.

First, there is the confusion caused by using the term *knowledge* without distinguishing between true statements and cognitive function. The double meaning of the term *knowledge* was described, analyzed and explicated in Critical Category10 in Chapter 1. It was noted in Critical Category 10 that the term *knowledge* has a least two common usage meanings. It is used to name true statements, and it is used to name cognitive function. Knowledge as true statements is located in books and other media for recorded warranted propositions. Knowledge as cognitive function, or knowing, is located in people, or more accurately, in the functioning of people.

This conflation is immediately dispelled by using the term *knowledge* for warranted assertions (i.e. true statements) and using the term *knowing* for cognitive function. If the term *knowledge* is being used in the sense of true statements, then asking what knowledge you want students to study is the equivalent of asking for the specification of content (i.e. the fund of knowledge) that should be included in a curriculum.

If the term *knowledge* is being used in the sense of cognitive function, then, rather than ask what knowledge you want students to learn, it is a much more clear approach to ask what range of knowing do you want students to achieve. This is obviously not a question about content. It is one about intended learning outcomes.

Second, there is the confusion caused by using the term *skill* in relation to choosing appropriate content to include in a curriculum. A skill is some level and form of the protocolic procedural kind of knowing. Rather than ask what skills you want students to learn, it is much more precise and clear to describe the level and form of procedural protocolic knowing that you want the students to achieve. The question of what skills students are to learn is not one about content. It is one about intended learning outcomes and, by implication, about the range of knowing that students are intended to achieve.

Third, there is the confusion caused by using the term *attitudes* in relation to choosing appropriate content to include in a curriculum. An attitude is some level and kind of the conative form of knowing. Rather than ask what attitudes you want students to learn, it is much more precise and clear to describe the level and kind of conative knowing that you want the students to achieve. The question of what attitudes students are to learn is not one about content. It is one about intended learning outcomes and, by implication, about the range of knowing that students are intended to achieve. (See Figure 3.17.)

Figure 3.17: Knowledge, Skills and Attitudes and Their Relationship to Content, Intended Learning Outcomes and Range of Knowing

$Knowledge_1$ true statements or warranted assertions	$Knowledge_1 =$ *Some content in a curriculum*	$Knowledge_1 =$ *Some fund of true statements*
$Knowledge_2$ cognitive function, i.e. some knowing	$Knowledge_2 =$ *Some intended learning outcome in a curriculum*	$Knowledge_2 =$ *A range of knowing, i.e. knowing of some level, form& kind*
Skill cognitive function, i.e. some knowing	Skill $=$ *Some intended learning outcome in a curriculum*	Skill $=$ *A range of knowing, i.e. procedural protocolic kind of knowing at some level and in some form*
Attitude cognitive function, i.e. some knowing	Attitude $=$ *Some intended learning outcome in a curriculum*	Attitude $=$ *A range of knowing, i.e. conative form of knowing at some level and of some kind*

If the terms *knowledge* (in the sense of knowing), *skills*, and *attitudes* are being used to select and organize content in a curriculum, they have very little use because none of them is a category that can be used to select and organize content. All three denote the range of knowing that a student might achieve. The term *knowledge* (in the sense of knowing) denotes the entire range of knowing in all of its levels, forms and kinds. The term *skill* denotes the procedural protocolic kind of knowing in some form at some level. The term *attitude* denotes the conative form of knowing of some kind and at some level.

Content and Curriculum. A final note to be made about content is to iterate that content is not curriculum. Content is a component or element of curriculum. Content is a fund of knowledge (i.e. a set of warranted assertions) that is organized for the purposes of teaching and studying under guidance. Commonly used ways to organize content is by means of topic outlines, sentence outlines, concepts, themes and focus (or key) questions. The amount of the content (the scope) and the order of the content (the sequence) are matters of professional judgment, taking into account the complexity of the content, the time available for teaching and studying under guidance, the motivation, interests and learning capabilities of the students, the resources available for teaching and studying under guidance and the intended learning outcomes.

Content is a fund of knowledge that is included in a plan for teaching and guided studying. The written plan is the curriculum. Content is part of the written plan. A sound, comprehensive plan specifies the fund of knowledge that should be taught and studied under guidance. The fund of knowledge that is specified is the content.

Content is not the knowledge (in the sense of knowing), skills and attitudes which the students are intended to learn. The use of the terms *knowledge*, *skills* and *attitudes* is an imprecise way to denote the intended learning outcomes, i.e. the range of knowing that is desirable for the students to achieve. A more precise and useful way to specify and organize intended learning outcomes is to conceive of them in terms of the level, kind and form of knowing (the range of knowing) that the students are intended to achieve.

Content (i.e. a fund of knowledge) is specified in a curriculum plan with the view in mind that teachers will help students, through studying under guidance, to achieve a range of knowing as a consequent of transacting with the content. The statement of intended learning outcomes prescribes the range of knowing that the students are intended to achieve.

Common use of the terms *subject* and *subject matter* (in school and university handbooks and catalogs) to denote content conflates three distinct categories, viz. fund of knowledge, field of phenomena and range of knowing. Sometimes this conflation is unavoidable because the English language is not developed to the extent that it has words that mean knowledge about each and every field of phenomena.

Thus a field of phenomena is named as a subject with the implication that what is being studied under guidance is knowledge about that field, e.g. the term *health education* is commonly used instead of *knowledge about health* for the name of a subject, with the implication that students will study under guidance some knowledge about health with a view to developing a range of knowing about health. And *physical education* is used as a name for a subject instead of *knowledge about physical activity* with the implication that students will study under guidance some knowledge about physical activity with the view in mind that they will develop some range of knowing about physical activity.

Likewise, a field of phenomena is named as a subject with the implication that what is being studied under guidance is knowledge, that when mastered, leads to a desired range of knowing. For example, the term *language arts* is used to name a subject instead of the name *knowledge about language* with the implication that students will study under guidance some knowledge about language with the view in mind that they will achieve some range of knowing about language. And *computer skills* is used as a subject name instead of the name *knowledge about computer use* with the implication that students will study under guidance some knowledge about computer use with the view in mind that they will achieve some range of knowing about computer use.

Nomination of Resources. Resources are the physical objects that are used in teaching and guided studying. The range of objects that can be used is extensive. Examples include pens, paper, films, books, e-book readers, desks, balls, engines, tools, shoes, cameras, computers, puzzles, video players, photographs, diagrams, playing fields, play equipment, gymnasiums, laboratory equipment, etc.

Resources can be distinguished as ones used by teachers, by students and by both. Resources can be effective or ineffective, extant or nonexistent and intrinsically bad or good.

For a curriculum (i.e. a written plan for the teaching and guided studying of some content to achieve some set of intended learning outcomes) to be sound and comprehensive, it should include the nomination of a set of relevant resources which teachers and students can use in the process of teaching and studying under guidance. For a curriculum to be coherent, the learning resources must be relevant, appropriate and sufficient for use by students in guided study activities. In other words, the resources should contribute to the students' efforts to achieve the range of knowing that is specified by the intended learning outcomes of the curriculum.

Specification of Learning Opportunities. Within the context of teaching and studying under guidance some content in some setting, learning opportunities are situations that are provided for students to study with the view in mind of achieving some new range of knowing or extending some existing range of knowing.

For a curriculum (i.e. a written plan for the teaching and guided studying of some content to achieve some set of intended learning outcomes) to be sound and comprehensive, it should include a specification of recommended learning opportunities. Learning opportunities consist of some configuration of

- language
- resources
- methods
- styles
- focus
- organization
- pace
- sequence
- initiation
- intentions
- goal structures
- assessment and evaluation.

These have already been described, analyzed and explicated in Derivative Features of Education in Chapter 2.

For a curriculum to be coherent, the learning opportunities must provide relevant, appropriate and sufficient guided study activities for the students to achieve the range of knowing that is specified by the intended learning outcomes of the curriculum.

Assessment and Evaluation. For a curriculum (i.e. a written plan for the teaching and guided studying of some content to achieve some set of intended learning outcomes) to be sound and comprehensive, it should include a specification of what should be evaluated, how it should be evaluated and what uses should be made of the evaluation report.

If, for example, an intended learning outcome is

"The student will calculate the molarity of a solution of nitric acid,"

then the thing that should be evaluated is the student's ability to calculate molarity of a solution of nitric acid. The assessment task must be coherent with the intended learning outcome. The assessment task must require the student to calculate the molarity of a given solution of nitric acid to the degree and under the conditions specified in the intended learning outcome.

In other words, there needs to be a clear logical connection between the intended learning outcome and the assessment task.

Evaluation. The term *evaluation* suffers from the process-product confusion. That is, in discourse that uses the term *evaluation*, it is common to hear or read the term used to name the process of coming to a value judgment (all the things you weigh up in your mind before making up your mind about the worth or value of something). The term is also used to name the result of making up your mind, i.e. the report of your judgment, e.g.

- Adequate, Inadequate
- Okay, Not Okay
- Excellent, Good, Satisfactory, Unsatisfactory
- 1st, 2nd, 3rd, etc.
- A, B, C, D, F and so forth.

The process-product confusion generated by the ambiguity of the term *evaluation* can easily be resolved by using the term *evaluation process* to mean the process of making a value judgment, and by using the term *evaluation report* to mean the result of the evaluation process, viz. the report of the value judgment.

In the evaluation process, there the person doing the evaluation, the *evaluator*, and there is the thing being evaluated, the *evaluatum*. The purpose of an evaluation is to answer the question, "What is the worth of the evaluatum?" The plural of *evaluatum* is *evaluata*.

With respect to curriculum, what things can be an evaluatum? The curriculum, itself (i.e. a written plan for the teaching and guided studying of some content to achieve some set of intended learning outcomes), can be evaluated. Any and all of the components of the curriculum can be evaluated, e.g. the plan for the learning opportunities, the plan for the learning resources or the plan for the intended learning outcomes. The degree to which the culture of a school supports implementation of the curriculum can be evaluated. Teachers can be evaluated with respect to how well they implement the curriculum. Students can be evaluated with respect to how well they achieve the intended learning outcomes specified in the curriculum. Indeed, any aspect of the educational process can be selected as an evaluatum.

Assessment. In discourse about education and curriculum, the term *assessment*, like the term *evaluation*, suffers from the process-product confusion. The term *assessment* is used to name the process for producing an evaluatum. The term *assessment* is also used to name the product of the process, viz. the evaluatum, itself. Consider the following sentence in which the term *assessment* is used.

- Sentence 1. "In the course, there will be three [assessments], viz. writing a research paper, completing a multiple-choice test and completing a final examination."

Substitute the phrase *processes for producing an evaluatum* for the term *assessment*, and the meaning of Sentence 1 is not changed.

- Sentence1. "In the course, there will be three [*processes for producing an evaluatum*], viz. writing a research paper, completing a multiple-choice test and completing a final examination."

Sentence 1 is an example of the use of *assessment* in the sense of *the process for producing an evaluatum*. In Sentence 1, the prescribed processes for producing the evaluata are writing a research paper, completing a test and completing an examination. The products of the writing and the completing are the evaluata. The evaluata produced are the written research paper, the completed multiple-choice test and the completed final examination. The evaluata are the items that are to be evaluated. Now consider this sentence.

- Sentence 2. "The [assessment] for the course will consist of an original written piece of music and the performance of the music on your choice of instrument."

Substitute the term *evaluata* (the plural for *evaluatum*) for the term *assessment* in Sentence 2, and the meaning of the sentence is not changed.

- Sentence 2. "The [*evaluata*] for the course will consist of an original written piece of music and the performance of the music on your choice of instrument."

Sentence 2 illustrates the term *assessment* being used in the sense of the evaluatum, itself, rather than the processes for producing the evaluatum. The evaluata specified in Sentence 2 are an original written piece of music and a performance of the music. They are the items to be evaluated.

When the term *assessment* is being used in the sense of *the process for producing an evaluatum*, it is common to find assessment discussed in terms of the processes of testing and measuring. The discourse commonly includes the nomination, analysis and explanation of rating scales, scoring systems, tests of various forms (multiple-choice, matching, short answer, fill-in, open essay, etc.), procedures for systematic observation and other forms of rating, scaling and measuring.

Evaluators. Evaluators are those who give the value judgment about the worth of some evaluatum. In relation to curriculum and the educational process, teachers, students and third parties can be (and are) evaluators. Teachers and students engage in the process of evaluation while participating in the educational process. In addition, third parties, such as parents, funding bodies, administrators and regulatory authorities conduct evaluations of teachers, students and other aspects of education, such as the curriculum. Evaluation is conducted for a variety of purposes, such as finding out whether money has been well spent or where to allocate funds and resources in the future or whether teachers and students are fulfilling their responsibilities or what resources should purchased, or whether pupils and students are happy with their learning environment and their learning opportunities, etc.

The Logical Steps of Evaluation. The logic of evaluation (Paul W. Taylor, 1961, pp. 9-10) is the steps in reasoning to a conclusion about the degree to which something is worthwhile. Someone, acting as evaluator, decides to evaluate something and

(1) selects a set of criteria (standards, rules or a combination of both),
(2) clarifies the criteria,
(3) chooses a category or class for comparison with the evaluatum,
(4) identifies the characteristics of the evaluatum that make it good, bad or both,
(5) draws a conclusion about the extent to which the evaluatum matches the criteria,
(6) answers the question, "What is the value of the evaluatum?"

An evaluator perhaps will not proceed through these steps in this order of 1 through 6, but for evaluators to conduct a sound, valid, fair evaluation, they must eventually complete all of these steps in some order.

Selection of Criteria. Criteria that can be used in the evaluation process can be either standards, rules or a combination of the two. Rules are statements with which the characteristics of the evaluatum must comply. There is no degree of compliance. Either the characteristics of the evaluatum correspond with the rule, or they do not.

When the criteria are rules, the evaluation report takes the form of a rating (never a ranking), e.g.

• Satisfactory or Unsatisfactory,
• Pass or Fail,
• Successful or Unsuccessful,
• Yes or No.

As an example, universities do not award a B.A. (failed). Either a student is granted a B.A. because all of the requirements (the rules) for the B.A. have been satisfied, or they have not. Thus, either the student is awarded a B.A. or not.

Suppose the evaluatum is an essay written by a student. Examples of criteria which are rules include:

(1) the essay must be written by the student, not by someone else;

(2) the essay must be at least 1,250 words and no longer than 1,500 words;

(3) the essay must include a bibliography of all of the references used in the essay;

(4) the bibliography must have a minimum of six references;

(5) the essay must be written in the words composed by the student (i.e. not plagiarized and not written by a third party);

(6) all quotations must be identified and correctly attributed with standard bibliographical notation as prescribed in the assignment instructions;

(7) all ideas presented from references either as summaries or as key concepts or propositions must be attributed with standard bibliographical notation as prescribed in the assignment instructions.

If the evaluatum (i.e. the essay) does not correspond with these seven rules, then it is given a rating of "Fail." If the evaluatum corresponds with these seven rules, then it is given a rating of "Pass."

When the criteria are standards, the evaluation report takes the form of either a grading or a ranking. Standards permit a judgment about the degree to which an evaluatum corresponds with the standard, e.g. to a high degree, a medium degree, or a low degree or to no degree at all. The evaluation report can take the form or either a grading or a ranking. A grading is an assignment of the evaluatum to a set of rating categories, e.g.

- A, B, C, D, F, or
- High Distinction, Distinction, Good, Satisfactory, Unsatisfactory, or
- 4, 3, 2, 1, or
- 9, 8, 7, 6, 5, 4, 3, 2, 1, or
- Band 1, Band 2, Band 3, Band 4, Band 5, Band 6 and so forth, or
- Competent or Not Competent.

A ranking is the assignment of an ordinal place in relation to other cases that are being evaluated, e.g.

- 1st, 2nd, 3rd, 4th, … Nth" or
- 99th percentile, 98th percentile, 97th percentile," etc.

Suppose again that the evaluatum is an essay written by a student. Examples of criteria that are standards include:

(1) the essay stays focused on the nominated topic;
(2) the essay presents a sound logical argument which leads to a set of conclusions that are coherent with the major premises of the essay;
(3) sound, necessary and sufficient evidence is presented to support the propositions put forward in the essay;
(4) the essay takes into account a variety of views about the issue that is addressed; and
(5) the essay is balanced, fair and reasonable in its viewpoint.

The essay can meet each of the criteria to some degree, and thus a judgment can be made about whether the essay satisfies each of the criteria to a very high degree, to a high degree, to a moderate degree, to a low degree or to no degree at all.

Clarification of the Criteria. Once the criteria have been nominated, then each criterion needs to be clarified. Clarification is a process of defining and explicating keys words in a criterion and generating examples which satisfy the criterion. Suppose the evaluatum is still an essay written by a student. One step in clarification of the criteria would be to write an exemplary essay which meets the criteria. The exemplary essay can then be used as an ideal to compare against each student's essay. Logically, clarification of criteria

"consists in a set of statements to the effect that if an object O has characteristics C, it fulfills a certain standard S to a certain degree D ...." (Paul W. Taylor, 1961, p. 10).

A Category or Class for Comparison with the Evaluatum. The evaluation process requires that a relevant category or class is selected for comparison with the evaluatum. For example, with a student's essay, a relevant category of comparison may be all essays written on the same topic and under the same conditions by 26 students in the same Year 11 (11th Grade) class. Or the relevant category of comparison may be all essays written on the same topic and under the same conditions by all Year 11 students in the same school. Or the relevant category of comparison may be all essays written on the same topic and under the same conditions by all Year 11 students in the same school district, or in the same state, territory or province, or nationwide or internationally.

Identification of the Characteristics of the Evaluatum that Make it Good, Bad or Both. This is the stage of the evaluation process in which the evaluatum is scored, marked, graded or ranked. For example, in scoring the essay mentioned in previous examples, the reference rating system for scoring an essay may look something like that in Figure 3.18.

Figure 3.18: Example of a Rating System for Scoring an Essay

Criteria: Rules and Standards for Evaluating the Essay	
Rules*: Rate the essay for each rule with "Yes" or "No"*	
1. The essay is written by the student, not by someone else.	Yes or No
2. The essay is at least 1,250 words and no longer than 1,500 words.	Yes or No
3. The essay includes a bibliography of all of the references used in the essay.	Yes or No
4. The bibliography has a minimum of six references.	Yes or No
5. The essay is written in words composed by the student (i.e. not plagiarized and not written by a third party).	Yes or No
6. All quotations are identified and correctly attributed with standard bibliographical notation as prescribed in the instructions.	Yes or No
7. All ideas presented from references, either as summaries or as key concepts or propositions, are attributed with standard bibliographical notation as prescribed in the assignment instructions.	Yes or No

8. The essay has a title page with the student's name.	1 mark

If rules 1 - 7 are "Yes" then assign 1 mark for the title page with the student's name and apply the standards. If there is at least one "No," assign "1 out of 25" marks for the essay. The essay has not qualified to have standards applied.

Standards:
Rate the essay on a scale of 4 – 0 for each standard.

1. The essay stays focused on the nominated topic.	4 - Always 3 - Mostly 2 - Somewhat 1 - Occasionally 0 - Not all
2. The essay develops a sound logical argument which leads to a set of conclusions that are coherent with the major premises of the essay.	4 - Always 3 - Mostly 2 - Somewhat 1 - Occasionally 0 - Not all
3. The essay presents sound, necessary and sufficient evidence to support the propositions put forward in the essay.	4 - Always 3 - Mostly 2 - Somewhat 1 - Occasionally 0 - Not all
4. The essay takes into account a variety of views about the issue that is addressed.	4 - Always 3 - Mostly 2 - Somewhat 1 - Occasionally 0 - Not all
5. The essay is balanced, fair and reasonable in its viewpoint.	4 - Always 3 - Mostly 2 - Somewhat 1 - Occasionally 0 - Not all
6. The essay is written in good, idiomatic English using correct spelling, correct punctuation, correct grammar, correct word usage and full sentences.	4 - Always 3 - Mostly 2 - Somewhat 1 - Occasionally 0 - Not all

Total the number of points given for each standard and record a mark of N out of a possible 25 marks for the essay (24 for the standards plus 1 for the title page with student's name).

If the evaluatum is being ranked, then all instances of the evaluatum should be ranked from first to last. For example, in the case of the essays, if ranking is being used, then each essay in the relevant group of comparison needs to be ranked in relation to its score, i.e. the highest score is 1st, the next highest is 2nd, etc .

Conclusion about the Extent to which the Evaluatum Matches the Criteria. After comparing the extent to which an evaluatum corresponds with the criteria (the rules, the standards or both), then it is time to draw a conclusion about the worth of the evaluatum.

Answers to the Question, "What is the Value of the Evaluatum?" The value judgment is reported as either a ranking or a rating.

Report as Ranking. A ranking is reported in terms of 1st, 2nd, 3rd, … N^{th}, where N is the total number of members within a category of evaluata that have been ranked in relation to each other. The so called "grading on the curve" or "norm referenced grading" is reporting evaluation judgments as rankings. Rankings can be reported as numerical order, for example 6th of out of 25, or as percentile ranks, for example, 85th percentile (i.e. as good as or better than 85 percent of the total number of things being evaluated). Other forms of reporting evaluation judgments as rankings are standard scores such as Z scores and t scores. The Z score system is a way of reporting rank in which the 50th percentile is assigned a value of zero, the 26th percentile a value of minus one (one standard deviation below the mean), and the 84th percentile a value of plus one (one standard deviation above the mean). The t score system is a way of reporting rank in which the 50th percentile is assigned a value of 50, the 84th percentile a value of 60 and the 26th percentile a value of 40 (each standard deviation is assigned a value of 10). See Figure 3.19: Z Scores, t Scores and Percentile Ranks as Ways of Reporting Rankings. (Figure 3.19 is from http://en.wikipedia.org/wiki/Standard_score, retrieved 2014.) For more extensive explanations of percentiles, Z scores and t scores, look for the topic *standard score* in any introduction to statistics reference. Reports of evaluation judgments as rankings are appropriate for uses such as selection, promotion, demotion and prediction. Also, rankings are only possible in relation to criteria which are standards. Rankings are not possible in evaluations in re-

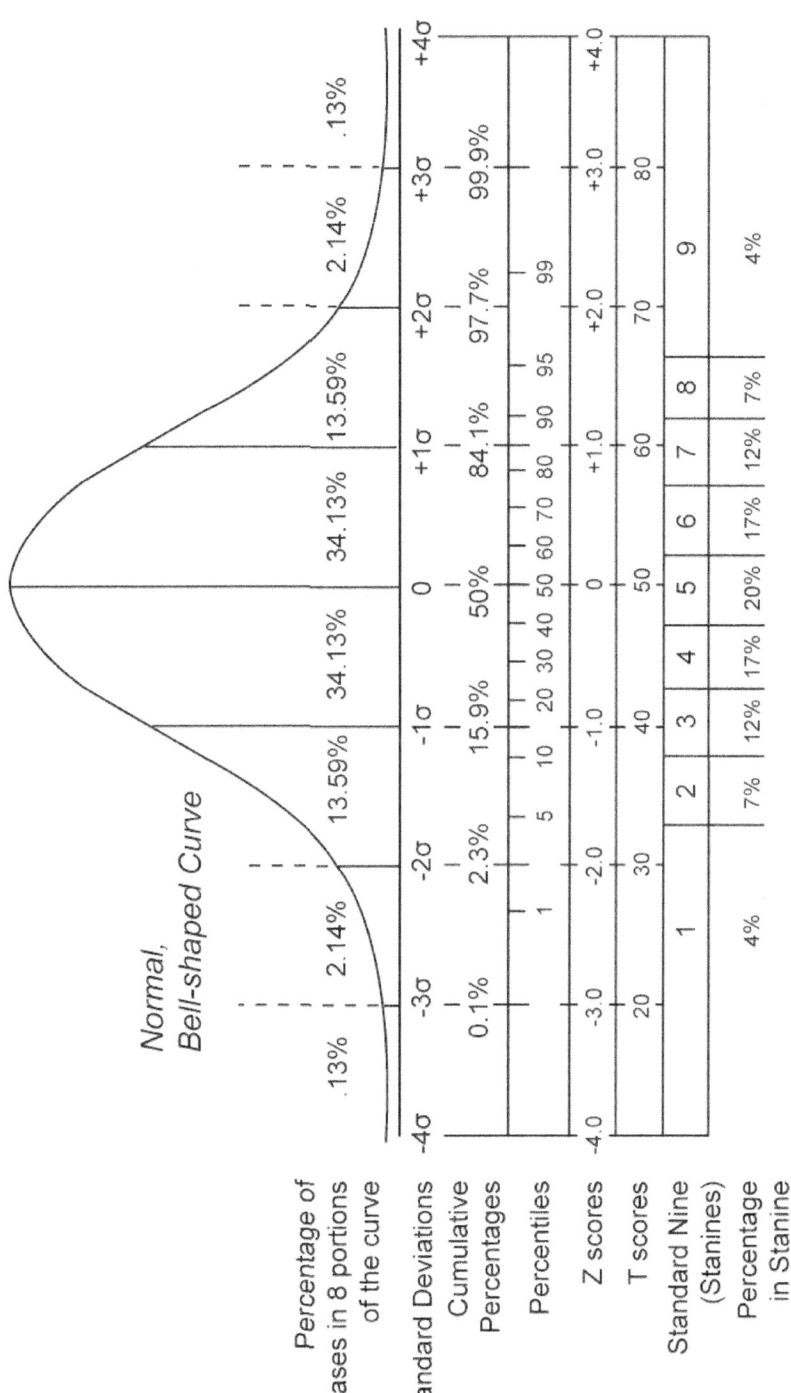

Normal, Bell-shaped Curve

Percentage of cases in 8 portions of the curve	.13%	2.14%	13.59%	34.13%	34.13%	13.59%	2.14%	.13%
Standard Deviations	-4σ	-3σ	-2σ	-1σ	0	+1σ	+2σ	+3σ	+4σ
Cumulative Percentages		0.1%	2.3%	15.9%	50%	84.1%	97.7%	99.9%	
Percentiles			1	5	10 20 30 40 50 60 70 80	90 95	99		
Z scores	-4.0	-3.0	-2.0	-1.0	0	+1.0	+2.0	+3.0	+4.0
T scores		20	30	40	50	60	70	80	
Standard Nine (Stanines)		1	2	3	4	5	6	7	8	9
Percentage in Stanine		4%	7%	12%	17%	20%	17%	12%	7%	4%

lation to criteria which are rules. The use of rules as criteria for evaluation produces ratings, not rankings.

Ratings. Ratings are reports of value judgments as categories of excellence. Examples of ratings are:
- Satisfactory and Unsatisfactory
- Distinction, Credit, Pass, Fail
- A, B, C, D, F
- Okay or Not Okay
- Pass or Fail

Ratings that Represent Rankings. Ratings (i.e. gradings) can be used to represent a range of rankings. For example, an evaluatum of each member of a group can be ranked, then grades assigned to the different ranges within the rankings, for example
- $+2\sigma \leq A$, i.e. a grade of A represents a range which is equal to or greater than two standard deviations (σ) above the mean,
- $+1\sigma \leq B < +2\sigma$, i.e. a grade of B represents a range which is equal to or greater than one and less than two standard deviations (σ) above the mean,
- $-1\sigma \leq C < +1\sigma$, i.e. a grade of C represents a range which is equal to or greater than one standard deviation (σ) below the mean and less than one standard deviation (σ) above the mean,
- $-2\sigma \leq D < -1\sigma$, i.e. a grade of D represents a range which is equal to or greater than two standard deviations below the mean (σ) and less than one standard deviation (σ) below the mean,
- $F < -2\sigma$, i.e. a grade of F represents a range which exceeds in the negative direction two standard deviations (σ) below the mean.

Ratings that Represent Competence or Degrees of Achievement. Ratings can also be used without rankings, e.g. they can be used to report the degree to which an evaluatum has satisfied a standard or whether the evaluatum has met a rule. Reporting evaluation judgments as ratings that meet standards and/or rules are most appropriate for evaluation report uses such as reporting or certifying competence.

An example of a rating which represents competence is a driver's license. The possession of a driver's license is certification of a level of competence. If the applicant does not meet the requirements (rules) for the license, no license is issued. There is no license that displays the words *Driver's License (Failed)*. The same applies for an airplane pilot's license or a medical practitioner's license or a solicitor's license to practice law. In these examples, the rating system used to report achievement is of only one category, viz. licensed.

So called *criterion referenced evaluation*, is the evaluation process in which the evaluation report is made as a rating in relation to a set of rules and/or standards. It is a paradox to call one evaluation process *criterion referenced* and another *norm referenced* because the evaluation process always requires a set of criteria (either rules, standards or both) for judging whether an evaluatum meets the criteria. The point of distinction between so called *criterion referenced* and *norm referenced* evaluation is the way in which the value judgment is reported, i.e. as a rating of an evaluatum against a set of criteria, or as a ranking of all instances of an evaluatum against a set of criteria.

An evaluation reported as a rating answers the question,
"To what degree does an evaluatum satisfy a set of criteria?"
An evaluation reported as a ranking answers the question,
"Who has been best, who has been second best, who has been third best, etc. at producing an evaluatum which satisfies a set of criteria?"

So called *competency based evaluation* is an evaluation process in which a set of rules are used for the evaluation. When the evaluatum satisfies all of the requirements (i.e. the rules), then the evaluation judgment can be made as a single rating, viz. competent (or achieved).

The evaluation process that uses rules for criteria and reports achievement of intended learning outcomes as *achieved* or *not achieved* has applications for learning for mastery (or mastery learning) strategies and competency based learning strategies. The terms *learning for mastery* and *mastery learning* are attributed to Benjamin Bloom (1968, 1974). Competency based learning strategies have been embraced by the military and by providers of technical and vocational education. Mastery learning and competency based learning strategies embrace the action plan of clearly delineating intended learning outcomes that can be evidenced by some set of observable behaviors and establishing a set of rules that when satisfied are evidence of achievement of the intended learning outcomes. Students are given appropriate, necessary and sufficient practice to achieve the intended learning outcomes. If students do not achieve the intended learning outcomes at their first attempt, they are given additional learning opportunities and time until they do achieve the outcomes. When the intended learning outcomes are achieved, the students are given a rating of "competent," or "achieved" or "mastered" or "certified." There is no ranking of achievement.

Uses of Evaluation Reports. Once the evaluation product is established, i.e. the value judgment is expressed or reported, then the report of the value judgment can be used to take some action. At least three uses, or actions, are possible (B.S. Bloom et al., 1971; M. Scriven, 1967, 1991):

(1) preparative uses,
(2) formative uses,
(3) summative uses

Using an evaluation report preparatively is to use it to plan a course of action, i.e. to make arrangements to do something or achieve something. For example, the evaluation report can be used to formulate a curriculum, to write a syllabus, to produce a unit plan or to articulate a set of lesson plans. The evaluation report can be used to formulate intended learning outcomes, produce learning resources or construct assessment plans. Teachers can use an evaluation report preparatively to plan a new unit for teaching and studying something, revise an existing plan for teaching and studying something or plan for further teaching and studying of concepts and skills already studied, but not yet mastered. Curriculum developers can use an evaluation report preparatively to devise a new curriculum or improve an existing curriculum.

Using an evaluation report formatively is to use it to improve some state of affairs that is currently in play and ongoing. For example, an evaluation report can be used formatively to assist teachers to improve their performance as teachers and to help students to improve their cognitive performance while engaged in some unit of study. Teachers can use an evaluation report formatively to improve ongoing classroom organization, goal structures, teaching methods and styles, etc. Students can use an evaluation report formatively to improve current study habits, sets of skills, a research report, etc. Curriculum developers can use an evaluation report formatively to make adjustments and improvements to a curriculum currently being implemented. The purpose of using an evaluation report formatively is to provide information that is intended to help someone improve her or his performance.

Using an evaluation report summatively is to use it to report a final result. Teachers can use an evaluation report summatively as a final evaluation report, e.g. to certify competence or to certify a degree of achievement in some range of knowing. Students can use an evaluation report summatively as proof of achievement (or some degree of achievement) and competence (or some degree of competence). Curriculum developers can use an evaluation report summatively as confirmation or disaffirmation that a curriculum has been effective to some degree in achieving intended learning outcomes or other desired states of affairs. An evaluation report can be used summatively to select applicants for another course (e.g. selection of high school students to university or to technical and further education courses), to promote applicants to a higher level of employment or to certify competence.

It seems to be a common misconception in discourse about curriculum, assessment and evaluation that there are preparative, formative and summative forms of evaluation. There are no preparative, formative and summative forms of evaluation. The misconception that there are forms of evaluation arises from conflating three distinct categories: (1) forms of evaluation, (2) forms of assessment and (3) uses of evaluation.

A form is a structure or organization. The form of the evaluation process is its logical structure, i.e. the six steps that are logically necessary in the evaluation process to produce a sound, valid and fair evaluation report. There are also forms of assessment. Some examples of forms of assessment include:
• diagram and label test
• essay (extended essay)
• essay (short essay)

- fill-in test
- matching test
- multiple-choice test
- oral examination
- oral report
- performance (with prescribed elements and circumstances)
- problem set or problem test
- project (completion and written and/or oral presentation)
- research report
- short-answer test
- systematic observation
- true-false test
- unobtrusive measures and observations, etc.

Any of these forms of assessment may be used to produce an evaluatum. The evaluatum can then be evaluated. From the evaluation, an evaluation report can be produced, i.e. a rating, a ranking or a combination of the two. Any evaluation report may be used preparatively, formatively or summatively. Indeed, the same evaluation report may be used, at different times, preparatively, formatively or summatively. It is not the form of the assessment process or the assessment product that determines whether an evaluation report (a rating, a ranking, or a combination) is used preparatively, formatively or summatively. It is the use of the evaluation report that is the determining factor. It is a serious fallacy and a total misconception to speak and/or write about preparative, formative or summative forms of assessment or evaluation. There are never forms of preparative, formative or summative assessment or evaluation. The evaluation process has form (the six steps in making an evaluation). Assessments, as both process and product, have form. Evaluation reports have forms (ratings, rankings or a combination). And evaluation reports have uses, viz. preparative, formative or summative uses. But evaluation reports never have preparative, formative or summative forms.

Important Decisions about Assessment and Evaluation. In relation to assessment and evaluation, important and vital decisions that must be made in writing a curriculum are those of

(1) how to make the assessments and evaluations coherent with the intended learning outcomes, i.e. how to make them valid,

(2) how to make the assessments and evaluations reliable, i.e. how to make them consistent,

(3) how to make the assessments and evaluations fair, i.e. provide just and equitable opportunities for the evaluatum to meet the criteria,

(4) at what stage in the instruction cycle should the assessments and evaluations occur and

(5) what uses should be made of the evaluation reports.

In relation to students, the central purpose of assessment and evaluation in a curriculum is to provide evidence of what degree students have achieved the intended learning outcomes, thus it is vital that coherency be achieved between intended learning outcomes and the processes of assessment and evaluation.

Summary of Curriculum and Education

In Chapter 3 the relationship between education and curriculum has been analyzed and characterized. Ordinary language analysis has shown that the term *education* is used to denote at least five things, viz. the process of learning, the product of learning, teaching, teaching and studying under guidance and knowledge about education. Education in the sense of teaching and studying under guidance is the conception of education that has been chosen as the basis for analysis in this work. It has been chosen because it allows consideration of the basic components of education, viz. teacher, student, content and setting, the basic processes of education, viz. teaching, studying under guidance and, if all goes well, learning from studying under guidance. Education in the sense of teaching and studying under guidance also allows consideration of curriculum.

Ordinary language analysis has shown that the term *curriculum* is used to denote a written plan for studying something under guidance from a teacher. Components of a sound, comprehensive curriculum include

(1) analysis of the situation,

(2) specification of intended learning outcomes,

(3) justification of intended learning outcomes,

(4) allocation of time,
(5) specification of content,
(6) nomination of resources,
(7) specification of learning opportunities and
(8) assessment and evaluation.

In a sound curriculum plan, there is logical consistency (coherency) among all components of the curriculum. This logical consistency is sometimes described as *alignment* in discourse about curriculum. Alignment is a familiar concept in geometry. Points are aligned when they lie in the intersection formed by two planes. In the discourse of curriculum, the term *alignment* is being used metaphorically. It makes sense only if one conceives of *alignment* as a logical consistency, i.e. a coherency among all the components of a curriculum.

A curriculum is always formulated within official education (but almost never, if ever, within unofficial education). Selections are made by someone (e.g. teachers, students, third parties, or some combination of the three) of some content to be studied under guidance. The content is some fund of knowledge, i.e. some set of warranted assertions organized for the purposes of teaching and studying under guidance. The intended outcome of the students' study is the students' development of some range of knowing. The range of knowing consists of some combination of

(1) some level of knowing (preconventional, conventional),
(2) some form of knowing (linguistic, physical, physiological, emotional, imaginal, conative) and
(3) some kind of knowing (qualitative, quantitative, procedural).

Of the content (i.e. the funds of knowledge), at least as many funds of knowledge are possible to select as there are fields of phenomena that can be distinguished. This is probably an indeterminate number, but all funds of knowledge will be knowledge about (1) physical phenomena, (2) organic phenomena, (3) human phenomena or (4) some combination of the three. The exceptions are mathematics and logic. Both are funds of knowledge about the logical relationships of concepts and propositions, rather than about phenomena. Within any fund of knowledge, there can be distinguished a few major subfunds. For example, for a field of phenomena named F, at least the following five subfunds of knowledge about F can be distinguished:

(1) the analytic philosophy of F, i.e. knowledge about the denotative and connotative meaning of terms and sentences used to describe, characterize and analyze F;

(2) the normative philosophy of F, i.e. knowledge about good and bad, or better and worse states of affairs in relation to F;

(3) the history of F, i.e. knowledge about past states of affairs of F;

(4) the science of F, i.e. knowledge about extant states of affairs of F;

(5) the praxiology of F, i.e. knowledge about effective practices to achieve desirable states of affairs of F.

A curriculum, conceived as a written plan for studying something under guidance from a teacher, is the basis for writing a syllabus, or a set of syllabi. A syllabus is the basis for writing a unit plan, or a set of unit plans. A unit plan is the basis for writing a set of lesson plans.

An appropriate name for knowledge about curriculum is the educology of curriculum. The educology of curriculum consists of at least five subfunds of knowledge, viz.

(1) the analytic philosophical educology of curriculum, i.e. knowledge about the denotative and connotative meaning of terms and sentences used to describe, characterize and analyze the effects of curriculum on education;

(2) the normative philosophical educology of curriculum, knowledge about good and bad, or better and worse states of affairs in relation to education and curriculum;

(3) the historical educology of curriculum, i.e. knowledge about past effects of curriculum on education;

(4) the scientific educology of curriculum, i.e. knowledge about extant effects of curriculum on education;

(5) the praxiological educology of curriculum, i.e. knowledge about effective practices to achieve desirable states of affairs in and for education through curriculum.

The educology of curriculum provides a fund of knowledge that can serve as the basis for making decisions about curriculum design, development, implementation and evaluation.

Chapter 4: Issues Arising from Discourse about Curriculum

Issues, controversies, challenges, problems and questions belong to the same family of concepts. The term *issue* denotes a question, the answer to which is unclear or disputed. Discourse about curriculum is replete with issues. This state of affairs will always be the case because of the questions which are inherent in formulating a curriculum, viz.

(1) what should be taught and studied under guidance?
(2) who should do the teaching and who should do the studying?
(3) why should it be taught and studied?
(4) how should it be taught and studied?
(5) when should it be taught and studied?
(6) where should it be taught and studied?
(7) what should be the results of having taught and studied something?
(8) how can it be established that the desired results have been achieved?
(9) what needs to be done to improve a curriculum?
(10) how should a curriculum be funded and resourced and by whom?
(11) who should control a curriculum and how?

Some issues in discourse about curriculum arise from ambiguous and misconceived language used in the discourse about curriculum and education. Other issues arise because of rival sets of values and perspectives.

Issues Arising from Ambiguities in Discourse

Some issues arise from ambiguous and misconceived language in discourse about curriculum. The English language is not developed well enough conceptually to avoid many of the ambiguities. It has already been noted that the term *education* has at least five meanings in ordinary language usage. The term *teaching* has at least three. The term *study* has at least four. And so it goes. The following are some issues which arise from ambiguities in discourse about curriculum.

The Ambiguity of the Concepts of *Subjects*, *Subject Matter* and *Disciplines*. The issue here is the set of questions,

"What constitutes a subject in the curriculum?"

"What constitutes subject matter in the curriculum?" and

"What constitutes a discipline in the curriculum?"

The term *subject* is commonly used to denote the historical or traditional names of courses studied in schools such as *art, geography, wood working, French, computer studies* and *physical education*. These are common and well known names for those things people commonly point to with the term *subjects* in the curriculum of a school. It has already been noted in Chapter 3 (Specification of Content) that there is considerable confusion created by using the terms *subject* and *subject matter* to identify selections of content to be taught and studied under guidance. The confusion is aggravated by the insistence of some to use the terms *subject* and *discipline* as synonyms. Content selections based on subjects will most probably be confused and somewhat misguided until it is clearly understood that the concepts of *subjects* and *subject matter* include the denotation and conflation of

(1) funds of knowledge,

(2) fields of phenomena,

(3) range of knowing and

(4) disciplines for producing knowledge.

The use of the terms *subject* and *subject matter* are strongly entrenched in ordinary language usage, so the conflation of the four distinct categories of funds of knowledge, fields of phenomena, range of knowing and disciplines for producing knowledge is likely to continue for some time to come simply because of old habits and historical inertia.

As a step forward, one of the most promising systems available to us for organizing all content as funds of knowledge is the one proposed by E. Steiner (1981), viz. physical knowledge, biological knowledge and hominological knowledge. In this system of organization, the field of phenomena is used to distinguish each of the three funds of knowledge.

Each of the funds of knowledge requires the use of a set of disciplines in the activity of inquiry to establish the knowledge. The rules followed in the verification of statements are the discipline of the inquiry. The product of successful inquiry about some field of phenomena is verified answers. Verified answers are verified statements. Verified statements are statements that are true, and true statements are knowledge. Knowledge about states of affairs in the field of physical phenomena is physical knowledge, e.g. physics, chemistry, hydrology, geology. Knowledge about states of affairs in the field of living phenomena is biological knowledge, e.g. biology, zoology, virology, ornithology. Knowledge about states of affairs in the field of human phenomena is hominological knowledge, e.g. sociology, anthropology, educology, psychology.

Within each of these three funds of knowledge, questions which are inherently important to address are

(1) what are the meanings and implications of the terms and sentences used in discourse about the field of phenomena (a question addressed by analytic philosophy);

(2) what are good and bad states of affairs in the field of phenomena (a question addressed by normative philosophy);

(3) what past states of affairs have existed in the field of phenomena (a question addressed by history);

(4) what states of affairs are presently extant in the field of phenomena (a question addressed by science);

(5) what practices are effective in achieving desired states of affairs in the field of phenomena (a question addressed by praxiology) (T. Kotarbiński, 1965).

A fund of knowledge is the outcome of forming verified statements about some field of phenomena by asking questions and making statements about education and adducing necessary and sufficient evidence from the field of phenomena. The rules of verification (i.e. the principles of verification) and procedures for collecting evidence are the discipline for forming the knowledge. At least five disciplines (i.e. principles of verification) can be distinguished for establishing publicly verifiable knowledge, viz.

(1) the principle of introspection$_1$;

(2) the principle of introspection$_2$;

(3) the principle of extrospection;

(4) the principle of deduction (necessity reasoning);

(5) the principle of evaluation (normative reasoning) (see Critical Category 7 above).

An empirical$_1$ statement requires the use of the principle of introspection$_1$ to verify it. An empirical$_2$ statement requires the use of the principle of introspection$_2$ to verify it. An empirical$_3$ statement requires the use of the principle of extrospection to verify it. An analytic statement requires the use of the principle of deduction (necessity reasoning) to verify it. A normative statement requires the use of the principle of evaluation (normative reasoning) to verify it.

The field of phenomena which is characterized by a fund of knowledge does not determine the discipline for the fund of knowledge. Rather, it is the kind of statement in a fund of knowledge that determines the relevant discipline to be used for verification of the statement. A fund of knowledge can be made of any or all of the five kinds of statements. Thus the establishment of a fund of knowledge may require the use of any or all of the kinds of disciplines.

The False Dichotomy of Theory vs. Practice. Sometimes in discourse about curriculum, the issue is raised, "Should the emphasis in teaching and guided studying be placed on theory or practice?" The very posing of this question is an illustration of confused thinking about curriculum. It is akin to asking the question, "In the process of breathing, should the emphasis be placed on inhaling or exhaling?" or the question, "In the function of the heart, should the emphasis be placed on expelling the blood from its chambers or receiving the blood into its chambers?"

One way to sort out the confusion is to think of theory as explanation and practice as some activity other than explaining. In the guided study and learning of some fund of knowledge, explanation (theory) and appropriate activity (practice) in relation to explanation complement each other. It is not a question of either explanation (theory) or appropriate activities (practice) connected with explanation that will contribute to the learning of some range of knowing, but rather both theory and practice must be included in the process of studying under guidance, if learning by the students is to be achieved.

A second way to sort out the confusion is to consider the distinctions of theory and practice in relation to uses of knowledge (i.e. funds of warranted assertions). At least three uses of knowledge can be distinguished: (1) theoretical use, (2) practical use and (3) productive use. (Aristotle is attributed with being the first to distinguish these categories. See R. McKeon, 1941, pp. 1032-1036.)

Theoretical uses of knowledge are those which are directed toward describing and explaining the way things are (and possibly predicting the way that they might be). Theoretical uses of knowledge, then, are descriptive, explanatory and predictive uses.

Practical uses of knowledge are those which are directed towards deciding what to do in a specific set of circumstances. Ought one marry or not? When confronted with a bully, ought one resist or surrender? Should one forgive the wrong that his friend has done him or not? Should one compromise his principles in this particular case or not? Confronted with the task of having to accept a number of unpleasant things in order to achieve a valued goal, what should one do? Practical uses of knowledge are those of deciding upon right courses of action and distinguishing them from wrong courses of action.

Productive uses of knowledge are those directed towards making something happen or constructing something. The product might be a useful one, or it might be an artistic one. Using knowledge to restore someone to health, to build a bridge or to repair a car are examples of productive uses of knowledge that end in a useful product or state of affairs. Using knowledge to compose a symphony, design a piece of sculpture or create a painting are examples of productive uses of knowledge that end in an artistic product or state of affairs. So there are the useful arts (medical practice, auto repair, civil engineering), and there are fine arts (composing music, sculpting, painting). Both require productive uses of knowledge.

In light of these three possible uses of knowledge, the question of whether content in a curriculum should include more or less theory relative to practice is misconceived, confused and incomplete. Relative to the three uses of knowledge, the question

should be one of whether content selections for a curriculum should be directed towards development of the student's abilities to use knowledge
> (1) theoretically (so that the student can describe, explain, anticipate and predict states of affairs),
> (2) practically (so that the student can decide upon right courses of action and avoid wrong courses of action),
> (3) productively (so that the student can produce either artistic states of affairs, useful states of affairs, or both) or
> (4) in some combination of theoretical, practical and productive ways.

In most circumstances, it is desirable to be well versed in all three uses.

Alignment of Curriculum, Pedagogy and Assessment. Bertrand Russell famously wrote that

> "The fact that an opinion has been widely held is no evidence whatever that it is not utterly absurd; indeed in view of the silliness of the majority of mankind, a widespread belief is more likely to be foolish than sensible (*Marriage and Morals*, 1929).

His remark applies to many situations and long standing practices, especially in the written discourse about curriculum and education. A case in point is the oft repeated contention in Australia (and especially in Queensland) that "research shows" that there needs to be an alignment of curriculum, pedagogy and assessment in order for effective education to occur. Queensland Education curriculum documents, school documents and even university course descriptions make this assertion and attribute it to Allan Luke (1999).

The assertion that there must be an alignment of curriculum, pedagogy and assessment is a classical case of Chinese Whispers. It is a misquote and a distortion of what Luke said in an opinion piece, not a research report.

People notoriously misquote the character Rick in the movie *Casablanca* (1942). They say that Rick said, "Play it again, Sam." But Rick never uttered these words. People misquote the character Harry Callahan in the movie *Dirty Harry* (1971). They say that Harry said, "Are you feeling lucky, Punk?" But Harry never uttered those words. People commonly attribute the statement, "Let them eat cake," to the unfortunate French queen, Marie Antoinette (guillotined in 1793 just short of her 38th birthday). Yet, there is no reliable historical record that verifies she ever uttered or wrote those words.

As it is with Rick and Harry and Marie Antoinette, so it is with Allan Luke. He is quoted as having written, "curriculum, pedagogy and assessment must be aligned for effective education," but he never did write those words. Here is one (there are many) example of a misquote and misinterpretation of Allan Luke:

"Dr Allan Luke, Professor of Education at Queensland
University of Technology, argues that the three key elements of
education i.e. curriculum, pedagogy and assessment, must be
aligned for effective education. Otherwise, there is dysfunction.
Further, he argues that if there is dysfunction in one area it
spreads to the others, and unless there is full alignment of these
systems, reform efforts will be hard to sell to practitioners."
(John Craig, 2007).

Michele Bruniges did a better job of quoting and interpreting Luke's remarks from his 1999 paper in her presentation to the Curriculum Corporation Conference in Brisbane in June 2005 (Michele Bruniges, 2005).

"Alan [sic] Luke argues that effective education reform
requires alignment of the three key message systems that exist
in education – curriculum, pedagogy and assessment. Unless
these systems are fully aligned, reform efforts will be hard to
sell to practitioners on the one hand, and will be dysfunctional
on the other" (Bruniges, 2005).

The most important phrase in the Bruniges quote is "key message systems."

What Luke wrote about the alignment of curriculum, pedagogy and assessment was

"The three message systems – curriculum, pedagogy,
assessment – need to be brought into proper alignment for us to
get desired educational results and outcomes" (Allan Luke,
1999, p. 4).

A message system is a system of discourse. It is a way of writing (and talking) about a set of entities or a state of affairs. Luke was arguing for coherency (i.e. logical consistency) among

(1) the discourse ("the message system") about curriculum,

(2) the discourse ("the message system") about pedagogy and

(3) the discourse ("the message system") about assessment.

This makes good sense. The written and spoken discourse about curriculum, pedagogy and assessment is frequently very messy, sloppy, ambiguous, conflated and nonsensical. For people engaged in the day to day task of guiding students in learning something worthwhile, badly written documents urging reform make little sense, offer unsound guidance and present useless distractions from the main game of teaching, studying and learning. It is common sense that documents that purport to be about curriculum, pedagogy and assessment should be using the same terms to talk about the same things in plain language. The language of the documents should be clear, simple and easy to read. The language should be noncontradictory. It should not conflate categories. It should make sense. This is the main message in Luke's paper (Allan Luke, 1999) with regard to curriculum, pedagogy and assessment. The discourse about them should be clear, consistent and sensible.

But Michele Bruniges moves from the admonition about clarity in discourse to the argument for "aligning assessment and curriculum." She writes:

"Luke's argument for alignment [of discourse] is a powerful one. If Australia is to achieve equitable, farreaching high-quality educational standards for all students, just as curriculum is reformed, so too must be the forms of assessment with which it is coupled. A key principle in aligning assessment and curriculum is that the assessment strategy selected must be appropriate to what it purports to measure or describe. The strategy needs to encompass a diagnostic capacity to inform further teacher [sic] and learning" (Michelle Bruniges, 2005).

This is a shift in argument from coherency in the discourse about curriculum, pedagogy and assessment to an argument for logical coherency among the components of a curriculum. And, as previously argued, a plan for assessment and evaluation is not outside of an adequately planned curriculum. On the contrary, it is a necessary component of a curriculum. And of course the plan for assessment and evaluation should be logically coherent with all the

other components of the curriculum, i.e. there necessarily must be coherency among
(1) the statement of intended learning outcomes,
(2) the statement of teaching and studying activities and strategies,
(3) the description of teaching and studying resources,
(4) the description of content to be taught and studied,
(5) the description of assessment and evaluation procedures (including the assessment procedures) for judging the degree to which students achieve intended learning outcomes.

Again, this is common sense. Who would argue for an incomplete, incoherent, contradictory, nonsensical curriculum?

And yet, the call for "an alignment of curriculum, pedagogy and assessment" is incoherent, contradictory and nonsensical, unless the authors of this assertion simply mean that it is desirable to have coherency among content, teaching strategies and assessment in a plan for the teaching and studying of some content. But to substitute the term *content* for the term *curriculum* is an inadequate conception of curriculum. From our previous analysis, we established that the term *curriculum* in ordinary discourse is used to denote a plan for the teaching and studying of some content with the intention that the students achieve some new range of knowing. Thus curriculum is not content. Rather it is a plan that includes specification of content.

A curriculum is a plan that provides the basis for a syllabus (or a set of syllabi). A syllabus is a plan that provides the basis for an instructional unit plan (or a set of unit plans). And an instructional unit plan provides the basis for a set of daily lesson plans. In other words, lesson plans are subsets of a unit plan. Unit plans are subsets of a syllabus. Syllabi are subsets of a curriculum.

The term *pedagogy* malfunctions in the English language. It is sometimes used to name the process of teaching, and it is sometimes used to name knowledge (warranted assertions) about the process of teaching. Let's focus on the first common usage meaning of the term *pedagogy*, viz. the process of teaching. Teaching includes all methods, approaches, strategies and social styles that a person might use in the process of guiding someone to learn something.

The term *assessment of learning* denotes the process of gathering evidence of a student's learning. The evidence of learning is the evaluatum. An evaluatum is the thing that is being evaluated, i.e. the thing about which a value judgment is to be made. The assessment process is the process of gathering or producing an evaluatum. The evaluatum may be (1) a performance by a student or (2) the product of a performance by a student. The assessment process provides the student the opportunity (1) to display a cognitive performance or (2) to present the product of a cognitive performance.

Assessment is a part of the evaluation process. The evaluation of a student's learning is the process of making a value judgment about the degree to which someone (a student) has achieved some intended range of knowing. The evaluation process is a process of reasoning that includes these steps:

(1) "Adoption of a standard or set of standards for evaluating (ranking or grading) the evaluatum."

(2) "Operational clarification of the standards. This consists in a set of statements to the effect that if an object O has characteristics C, it fulfills a certain standard S to a certain degree D; that if O has characteristics C', it fulfills S to a greater (lesser) degree D'; etc."

(3) "Specification of the class of comparison."

(4) "Determining the good-making and bad-making characteristics of the evaluatum. (In the case of value rankings this would ideally be done for every member of the class or comparison.)"

(5) "Deducing, from 2 and 4, the degree to which the evaluatum on the whole fulfills or fails to fulfill the standards. (In the case of value rankings this would ideally be done for every member of the class of comparison. The members would then be ranked in order according to the varying degrees to which they fulfilled or failed to fulfill the standards.)" (Quoted from Paul W. Taylor, 1961, pp. 9-10.)

An adequate curriculum includes plans for assessment and evaluation of student achievement that are consistent with the other components of the curriculum. To assert that assessment must be aligned with curriculum, is to say something like the part of the curriculum that makes plans for assessment and evaluation must be aligned (logically coherent) with plans for assessment and evaluation. Plans for assessment and evaluation must be aligned with plans for assessment and evaluation? What kind of tautological nonsense is that?

To make this clear, let's make some word substitution in the statement,

"Curriculum, pedagogy and assessment must be aligned for effective education."

Let the term *curriculum* mean the same as *plans for teaching and studying some content with some intended learning outcomes in mind and plans for evaluating student achievement of intended learning outcomes.*

Let the term *pedagogy* mean *plans for teaching.*

Let the term *assessment* mean *plans for gathering evidence of student achievement of intended learning outcomes.*

Let the term *aligned* mean *logically coherent*

Let the term *effective education* mean *teaching and studying that leads to student achievement of intended learning outcomes.*

Now, make the term substitutions in the original statement,

"Curriculum, pedagogy and assessment must be aligned for effective education."

The first term substitution produces the statement,

"[*Plans for teaching and studying some content with some intended learning outcomes in mind and plans for evaluating student achievement of intended learning outcomes*], pedagogy and assessment must be aligned for effective education."

The second term substitution produces the statement,

"[*Plans for teaching and studying some content with some intended learning outcomes in mind and plans for evaluating student achievement of intended learning outcomes*], [*plans for teaching*] and assessment must be aligned for effective education."

The third term substitution produces the statement,

"[*Plans for teaching and studying some content with some intended learning outcomes in mind and plans for evaluating student achievement of intended learning outcomes*], [*plans for teaching*] and [*plans for gathering evidence of student achievement of intended learning outcomes*] must be aligned for effective education."

The fourth term substitution produces the statement,

"[*Plans for teaching and studying some content with some intended learning outcomes in mind and plans for evaluating student achievement of intended learning outcomes*], [*plans for teaching*] and [*plans for gathering evidence of student achievement of intended learning outcomes*] must be [*logically coherent*] for effective education."

The fifth term substitution produces the statement,

"[*Plans for teaching and studying some content with some intended learning outcomes in mind and plans for evaluating student achievement of intended learning outcomes*], [*plans for teaching*] and [*plans for gathering evidence of student achievement of intended learning outcomes*] must be [*logically coherent*] for [*teaching and studying that leads to student achievement of intended learning outcomes*]."

The point of these term substitutions is to demonstrate that the statement,

"Curriculum, pedagogy and assessment must be aligned for effective education,"

is tautological nonsense. It amounts to saying that a plan for C (which already necessarily includes A and B) should include A and B. This is not a useful admonition or guideline for anything, and it certainly is not based on any kind of research.

It would be far more fruitful to say simply that a coherent curriculum plan probably improves the chances for education to be effective. A coherent curriculum plan is certainly necessary for accountability and for rational allocation of resources and effort. If we don't know what we want to achieve in an educational program, then we have no basis for allocating resources and effort to achieve it. And if we do know clearly what we want to achieve in an educational program, then we need some clear publicly verifiable evidence of our achievement. Otherwise we have no system of accountability and no clear way of knowing whether we are acting wisely and responsibly in allocation of resources and effort.

Back to the statement,

"Curriculum, pedagogy and assessment must be aligned for effective education."

It just doesn't make any sense, unless you conceive the term *curriculum* so narrowly that the term *curriculum* denotes only content and excludes plans for teaching activities and plans for assessment and evaluation of students' achievement of intended learning outcomes. But what sensible teacher, curriculum planner or educologist of curriculum would conceive the term *curriculum* so narrowly?

Yet the statement,

"Curriculum, pedagogy and assessment must be aligned for effective education"

is seemingly carved in stone in Education Queensland curriculum documents, educological publications and university curriculum courses (in Queensland). It is solemnly repeated as received truth and wisdom, even though it is such a silly and patently foolish statement.

Thus, we can end in the way we began, with the quote from Bertrand Russell.

"The fact that an opinion has been widely held is no evidence whatever that it is not utterly absurd; indeed in view of the silliness of the majority of mankind, a widespread belief is more likely to be foolish than sensible" (*Marriage and Morals*,1929).

There is No Curriculum. There is a group of educologists who argue that they have developed an educational program in which there is no curriculum. In 2001, Seymour Papert wrote

"During the last couple of years, I've been working in what's been one of the most moving and instructive educational experiences that I've had in my whole career. And this is working inside a state juvenile correctional facility, where children from age twelve upwards who've been sent there by courts -- they've done what would be considered a serious crime if it had been done by an adult. ... The governor of Maine, Angus King, who is a very progressive, forward-looking person, encouraged me to create a little project -- made it possible to create a little project where with just ten kids, we took them out of the regular school and they spent their time -- five hours a day -- doing project-based work."

"We used computers, we used MicroWorlds Logo, we used Legos. Some of them built airplanes, some of them built guitars. They worked on projects. And everybody who saw this was staggered at the difference of the energy that they showed there -- the kind of involvement, engagement -- compared with the lethargic, rebellious attitude in the classes. I think that this project that we could set up allowed some of them to get a new sense of themselves as learners -- that learning is something valuable, that setting yourself a goal and working to achieve it is something which some of them have never seen before in their lives. They've never known anybody who works over time for the achievement of some goal. So you can change their view of life."

"Well, first thing you have to do is to give up the idea of curriculum. Curriculum meaning you have to learn this on a given day. Replace it by a system where you learn this where you need it. So that means we're going to put kids in a position where they're going to use the knowledge that they're getting. So what I try to do is to develop kinds of activities that are rich in scientific, mathematical, and other contents like managerial skills and project skills, and which mesh with interests that particular kids might have" (retrieved 2014, http://www. edutopia.org/seymour-papert-project-based-learning).

The key phrase in the above quotation from Papert is

"Curriculum meaning you have to learn this on a given day." The common usage definition of the term *curriculum* does not mean this. Papert has stipulated a definition for the term *curriculum*, perhaps to highlight and emphasize the key aspects of project-based learning, viz. freedom for students to initiate the learning activities, to choose the content, to choose the intended learning outcomes, to determine the pace of the learning activities and to choose the resources. It may be true that Papert and his associates did not write a curriculum, and so there was no curriculum. But in principle, a curriculum for what Papert describes can be written, i.e. a plan can be written for undertaking to learn something under the guidance of a teacher using project-learning.

If we were to write a curriculum, with all of its key components, for project-learning as Papert describes it, then the components of the curriculum (the plan for teaching and learning something under guidance) might read something like the following.

(1) analysis of the situation – the students involved in the project are incarcerated; they have serious issues with rules, regulations and laws; they resent authority and regimentation; ironically they find themselves in a correctional facility; they are willing to pursue their own interests, but they rebel against anyone suggesting, recommending or directing them to undertake to learn something at a particular time, in a particular place and in a particular way.

(2) specification of intended learning outcomes – the students are given the freedom to select their own intended learning outcomes; in addition, the intentions underlying the curriculum are that

    (a) students will realize the value of learning;
    (b) the students will realize that they can perform as successful learners;
    (c) the students will realize the value of setting personal goals and working to achieve them;
    (d) the students will realize the value of being intrinsically motivated to pursue worthwhile self determined learning goals;
    (e) the students will develop skills of problem solving, including identifying a problem, hypothesizing a set of solutions, taking action to achieve a solution, testing solutions for their adequacy to resolve the problem, choosing the best solution and improving upon the best solution;
    (f) the students will feel empowered by their abilities to solve problems which they choose because of the personal importance and significance of the problems;
    (g) the students will take responsibility for the consequences of their choices.

(3) justification of intended learning outcomes – one of the most important things to achieve in life is to accept the consequences of one's choices in life; along with this, one

of the most important things to realize in life is that you can achieve a great deal of control over your life by becoming an effective problem solver of all sorts of problems; the problems can be ones that require a theoretical solution, or a practical solution or a productive solution, or a combination of the three; there is a general problem solving process that is best learned by engaging in problems that have significance and real life importance to you, the problem solver; improving your problem solving abilities gives you power over your life; you cease regarding yourself as a victim of circumstances, and you develop yourself into someone who can transform circumstances into opportunities to achieve worthwhile, authentically chosen goals; project-based learning is an excellent means to develop general problem solving skills which are applicable to all aspects of one's life.

(4) <u>allocation of time</u> − the amount of time spent on a project and the sequence of activities are determined by the individual student; the student chooses the time to commence work and to rest, the time to start one activity, then go on to another activity, the time to start, stop and start again; each student in a group (if there is a group) can be, and most probably will be, working at a different pace from all other students in the group.

(5) <u>specification of content</u> − each individual student is allowed the freedom to choose the problem and the related project; the individual student is allowed to choose the content that is relevant to the problem that the student has chosen to resolve; each student in a group (if there is a group) can be, and most probably will be, working with problems, projects and content that are different from all other students in the group.

(6) <u>nomination of resources</u> − the resources provided for students will include personal computers, computer software programs, including the MicroWorlds program and the Logo programming language, Lego construction toys, and any other resources that students might reasonably require to develop solutions for the problems

that they choose to address; students may develop resources of their own.

(7) specification of learning opportunities – students are allowed to establish their own competitive, cooperative or individualized goal structures, choose their own study methods, focus on states of affairs or matters that interest them, organize themselves in one large group, several small groups and/or as individuals, according to their own interests and inclinations.

(8) assessment and evaluation – students are allowed to devise their own ways and means of demonstrating the achievement of their intended learning outcomes.

In project-based learning, it is entirely feasible to write a curriculum, i.e. a plan for the teaching and learning of something under guidance using project-based learning opportunities. The plan incorporates a great deal of choice by students in initiating and executing learning activities related to their own interests. In the words of film maker, educational philanthropist and founder of Edutopia, George Lucas (1999?),

"Traditional education can be extremely isolating -- the curriculum is often abstract and not relevant to real life, teachers and students don't usually connect with resources and experts outside of the classroom, and many schools operate as if they were separate from their communities."

"Project-based learning, student teams working cooperatively, children connecting with passionate experts, and broader forms of assessment can dramatically improve student learning. New digital multimedia and telecommunications can support these practices and engage our students" (George Lucas, 1999?).

Curriculum is Everything that Happens in Schools. Some who engage in discourse about education and curriculum maintain that everything that happens in school counts as curriculum.

For example, La Escuela Fratney is an elementary public school serving Kindergarten through Grade 5 pupils. It derived its name from its location on Fratney Street in Milwaukee, Wisconsin. The school is situated in a culturally diverse region of Milwaukee, and it came into being in 1988 as the result of negotiations among neighborhood action groups and local political groups in Milwaukee. The school has distinguished itself through its bilingual (English and Spanish) program in which the medium of instruction is alternated between English and Spanish, its involvement of parents and community members in the governance and educational operations of the school, its advocacy for anti-racism and social justice, its whole language reading and writing programs (which include a collection of student authored books in the school library), a ten-minute early start schedule to allow a once-a-week early release for students and planning time for teachers and a program of mentoring students to encourage constructive behavior and positive attitudes. (Bob Peterson, 2007, in Apple and Beane, 2007).

Rita Tenorio was a founding member of La Escuela Fratney. She served as a teacher and principal of the school for over 30 years and retired in 2012 (Angela McManaman, 2012). Regarding the curriculum at La Escuela Fratney, Tenorio stated in an interview in 2004 that,

> "Curriculum is everything that happens. It's not just books and lesson plans. It's relationships, attitudes, feelings, interactions. If kids feel safe, if they feel inspired, if they feel motivated, if they feel capable and successful, they're going to learn important and positive things. But if those elements are not there, if they feel disrespected or neglected in school, they're learning from that too. But they're not necessarily learning the curriculum you think you're teaching them" (R. Tenorio, 2004, p. 81).

Tenorio iterates this conception of curriculum in 2010 with the statement

> "I want them [the pupils of La Escuela Fratney] to gain the knowledge to be successful in this [American] society. Beyond that, though, I want them to understand that they have the power to transform the society" (R. Tenorio, 2010, p. 91).

> "Remember that curriculum is 'everything that happens' at school. Your response or lack of response [to a racist or sexist remark] is just as much of a lesson as the morning math activity. Students will learn so much more if these issues are put on the table instead of under it" (R. Tenorio, 2010, p. 93).

The use of the term *curriculum* to mean *everything that happens at school* is an example of a programmatic use of the term (I. Scheffler, 1960). A programmatic definition is used in situations in which someone wants to use the schools to improve or reconstruct society in some way, usually to achieve a more nearly democratic society or a more nearly just society. This social reconstructionist view of schools has a long tradition and history, especially in the U.S.A. (see, for example, George Counts, 1932).

Since the school's inception, the leadership and staff at La Escuela Fratney have had an educational program in mind that is intended to empower pupils with a range of knowing that would enable them to combat racism and injustice and transform society into a social democracy as well as a political democracy. Thus they have specified a special meaning for the term *curriculum* which clearly departs from ordinary usage and which they believe supports their antiracist, antisexist, environmental protectionist and social justice programs. Their intention has been to alert their staff, students and interested third parties to their antiracist, antisexist, environmental conservationist and social justice values and school ethos. Their intention has also been to heighten teachers' sensitivities to the opportunities which arise from minute to minute to empower children with the range of knowing that can be used to transform society into a just society.

If we take the programmatic definition to its logical conclusion, the definition of *curriculum* as *everything that happens at school* quickly becomes an absurdity. The term *curriculum* becomes a synonym for *phenomena, happenings* and *occurrences*. Consider what happens at school. The atmospheric pressure fluctuates. Clouds come and go. Birds flutter and sing. Insects fly by and crawl around. Children cough and sneeze. Bacteria grow on the walls, ceilings and floors. Toilets are used and flushed. Grass produces sugar and carbon dioxide through photosynthesis. The sun rises and sets. The moon waxes and wanes. The rain falls and evaporates. All of these events happen at school, and if curriculum is everything that happens at school, then each of these phenomena is denoted by the term *curriculum*. Curriculum becomes indistinguishable from all phenomena.

By term substitution, the statement,

"[Curriculum] is everything that happens at school,"

becomes

"[Phenomena] are everything that happens at school,"
and there is no change in the meaning of the term. Curriculum as phenomena is not a useful concept for conducting inquiry about curriculum, for establishing knowledge about curriculum or for developing curriculum.

On the other hand, it is perfectly feasible to write a curriculum plan which incorporates the intended learning outcomes of empowerment of pupils with a range of knowing that would enable them to combat racism and injustice and transform society into a social democracy as well as a political democracy. It is also feasible to include in the plan provisions to engage students spontaneously, as and when appropriate circumstances arise, in analysis of issues of racism, sexism, ethnic bigotry, social bigotry, injustice, equity, political democracy, social democracy, environmental protection and any other important issues that arise from time to time. If one feels the need to assert that the term *curriculum* should be used to denote everything that happens in schools, then perhaps the curriculum has not been adequately written, i.e. has not been written inclusively enough in terms of what issues should be addressed, under what circumstances they should be addressed and how they should be addressed.

Curriculum is Experiences. Some who have engaged in discourse about education and curriculum have characterized curriculum as experiences. For example, Bill Page, a veteran American teacher, has chosen to make a number of stipulative definitions of the term *curriculum*. He has stipulated that the term *curriculum* denotes experiences, but he also has made nine additional stipulative definitions to differentiate among categories of experiences. He has written,

"The Question is, 'What are the kids learning in school?' The answer is, 'Whatever they are experiencing.' What is taught is not necessarily what is learned and what is learned is not the same for all of the kids in [the] same class, different classes or with different teachers. While experiences could be categorized and sub-categorized and listed in a variety of ways, here is a non-exhaustive, non-exclusive list of experiences-as-curriculum."

"Consider these categories of Curricula [sic]:"

"There is the official curriculum as written by the schools. It's in the book!"

"There is the actual curriculum. The experience of 'going to school.'"

"There is the taught curriculum. The teacher's twist on what the book says."

"There is the learned curriculum. What is taught is not what students learn."

"There is the tested curriculum. The fill-in-the-blank sampling of taught stuff."

"There is the hidden curriculum. It is going on every minute of every school day."

"There is the null curriculum. Important elements that should be taught but are not."

"There is the retained curriculum. What is remembered from what was taught?"

"There is the personal curriculum. Each individual has his or her own experiences."

"These are experiences that could stand alone, separately in the curriculum because of their impact and importance; including interpersonal skills, social, values, cultural, character experiences, and even lack of experiences. How shall we judge what is learned, what is taught and who or what did the teaching" (B. Page, 2008)?

Official Curriculum. The implication of the statements,

"There is the official curriculum as written by the schools. It's in the book!"

is that the term *official curriculum* should be used to denote what is in the book (i.e. the text book). That which is in the book is the content, i.e. knowledge arranged for the purposes of teaching and studying under guidance. The content is one of the components of a sound curriculum plan. By term substitution, the statement,

"There is the [official curriculum] as written by the schools,"
becomes

"There is the [content, i.e. the knowledge arranged for the purposes of teaching and studying under guidance] as written [or chosen] by the schools," and there is no change in meaning of the statement. The stipulative use of *official curriculum* to denote content relates to the ordinary sense of *curriculum* as a plan for the teaching and studying of some content under guidance in that the stipulative use denotes one component of the plan, i.e. the term *official curriculum* is being used to denote content.

Actual Curriculum. The implication of the statements,

"There is the actual curriculum. The experience of 'going to school,'"

is that the term *actual curriculum* denotes the experience of going to school. The experience of going to school, i.e. of attending school, is the set of experiences students have in and out of the classroom at school. By term substitution, the statement,

"There is the [actual curriculum],"

becomes

"There is the [experiences students have in and out of the classroom at school],"

and there is no change in meaning of the statement. The stipulative use of *actual curriculum* to denote life experiences inside and outside the classroom at school does not relate to the ordinary sense of *curriculum* as a plan for the teaching and studying of some content under guidance. Rather it relates to life's general experiences, and part of life's general experiences are those that one encounters both in and out of the classroom while attending school.

This stipulative use of *actual curriculum* is a synonym for *life experiences, inside and outside the classroom, at school.*

Taught Curriculum. The implication of the statements,

"There is the taught curriculum. The teacher's twist on what the book says,"

is that the term *taught curriculum* denotes the teachers' activities in undertaking to help students to learn some content in some setting. The teachers' activities are their teaching, including the methods and styles used in their teaching and their interpretation of content. By term substitution, the statement,

"There is the [taught curriculum],"

becomes

"There is the [teaching],"

and there is no change in meaning of the statement. The stipulative use of *taught curriculum* to denote teaching does not relate to the ordinary sense of *curriculum* as a plan for the teaching and studying of some content under guidance. Rather it relates to one of the basic functions of the educational process, viz. teaching. This stipulative use of *taught curriculum* is a synonym for *teaching.*

Learned Curriculum. The implication of the statements,

"There is the learned curriculum. What is taught is not what students learn,"

is that the term *learned curriculum* denotes the range of knowing achieved by the students from all of their learning experiences including guided intentional, unguided intentional, guided unintentional and unguided unintentional learning experiences. By term substitution, the statement,

"There is the [learned curriculum],"

becomes

"There is the [range of knowing achieved by the students from all of their learning experiences including guided intentional, unguided intentional, guided unintentional and unguided unintentional learning experiences],"

and there is no change in the meaning of the statement. The stipulative use of *learned curriculum* to denote the range of knowing achieved by the students from all of their learning experiences, including learning achieved from guided intentional, unguided intentional, guided unintentional and unguided unintentional learning experiences, does not relate to the ordinary sense of *curriculum* as a plan for teaching and studying of some content under guidance. Rather it relates to the process of learning and the product of learning.

The process of learning is the process of coming to know. The learning process, as previously noted (see Education as the Process of Learning in Chapter 2) can be guided and intentional, unguided and intentional, guided and unintentional and unguided and unintentional. Only guided and intentional learning takes place in the educational process. The other three conditions for the learning process take place outside of the educational process. Because they are outside of the educational process, there is, of course, no curriculum (in the sense of a plan for teaching and studying of some content under guidance) for them.

The product of learning is a range of knowing, i.e. a combination of kinds, levels and forms of knowing. A range of knowing can be achieved by any of the four conditions of the learning process. In a curriculum plan (a plan for the teaching and studying under guidance of some content in some setting), one of the important components is the specification of learning outcomes. It is a valid and obvious point that students can fail to achieve the specified intended learning outcomes or achieve the intended learning outcomes to some lesser degree than specified. It is also a valid point that all human beings are in a constant state of learning because of their day-to-day life experience. Most of this learning is taking place outside of learning experiences that are intentional on the part of the learner and guided by some person acting as teacher.

This stipulative use of *learned curriculum* is a synonym for *range of knowing achieved from all learning experiences, guided and unguided, intentional and unintentional.*

Tested Curriculum. The implication of the statements,

"There is the tested curriculum. The fill-in-the-blank sampling of taught stuff,"

is that the term *tested curriculum* denotes the assessment and evaluation of the range of knowing that is specified in the intended learning outcomes of a plan for the teaching and studying under guidance some content in some setting. By term substitution, the statement,

"There is the [tested curriculum],"

becomes

"There is the [assessment and evaluation of the range of knowing that is specified in the intended learning outcomes of a plan for the teaching and studying under guidance some content in some setting],"

and there is no change in the meaning of the statement. The stipulative use of *tested curriculum* to denote the assessment and evaluation of the range of knowing that is specified in the intended learning outcomes of a plan for the teaching and studying under guidance some content in some setting relates to the assessment and evaluation component of a curriculum plan (i.e. curriculum in the sense of a plan for the teaching and studying under guidance some content in some setting).

This stipulative use of *tested curriculum* is a synonym for *the assessment and evaluation of the range of knowing that is specified in the intended learning outcomes of a plan for the teaching and studying under guidance some content in some setting.*

Hidden Curriculum. The implication of the statements,

> "There is the hidden curriculum. It is going on every minute of every school day,"

is that the term *hidden curriculum* denotes the set of experiences that students encounter in and out of the classroom in their day-to-day life at school. By term substitution, the statement,

> "There is the [hidden curriculum],"

becomes

> "There is the [set of experiences in and out of the classroom that students encounter in the day-to-day life at school],"

and there is no change in the meaning of the statement. The stipulative use of *hidden curriculum* to denote the set of experiences that students encounter in and out of the classroom in the day-to-day life at school does not relate to the ordinary sense of curriculum as a plan for the teaching and guided studying of some content in some setting. Rather it relates to phenomena, happenings, occurrences and states of affairs.

This stipulative use of *hidden curriculum* is a near synonym for *phenomena* or *life experiences*, and this stipulative use of *hidden curriculum* is near in meaning to (if not the same) Page's stipulated meaning for *actual curriculum*, i.e. the experiences that one encounters inside and outside of the classroom at school.

Null Curriculum. The implication of the statements,

> "There is the null curriculum. Important elements that should be taught but are not"

is that the term *null curriculum* denotes the worthwhile content that is omitted in a plan for the teaching and studying under guidance of some content in some setting. By term substitution, the statement,

> "There is the [null curriculum],"

becomes

"There is the [worthwhile content that is omitted in a plan for the teaching and studying under guidance of some content in some setting],"

and there is no change in the meaning of the statement. The stipulative use of *null curriculum* to denote the set of worthwhile content that is omitted in a plan for the teaching and studying under guidance of some content in some setting relates to the content component of a curriculum in the sense of a plan for the teaching and studying under guidance of some content in some setting.

This stipulative use of *null curriculum* is a synonym for *omitted worthwhile content.*

Retained Curriculum. The implication of the statements,

"There is the retained curriculum. What is remembered from what was taught?"

is that the term *retained curriculum* denotes the range of knowing that is specified in the intended learning outcomes and that students retain in the long term. By term substitution, the statement,

"There is the [retained curriculum],"

becomes

"There is the [range of knowing that is specified in the intended learning outcomes and that students retain in the long term],"

and there is no change in the meaning of the statement. The stipulative use of *retained curriculum* to denote the range of knowing that is specified in the intended learning outcomes and that students retain in the long term relates to the intended learning outcome component of a curriculum in the sense of a plan for the teaching and studying under guidance of some content in some setting. The stipulative use of *retained curriculum* also relates to the range of knowing that students achieve as a result participating in the educational process.

This stipulative use of *retained curriculum* is a synonym for *range of knowing achieved from participating in the educational process.*

Personal Curriculum. The implication of the statements,

"There is the personal curriculum. Each individual has his or her own experiences."

and

"These are experiences that could stand alone, separately in the curriculum because of their impact and importance; including interpersonal skills, social, values, cultural, character experiences, and even lack of experiences,"

is that the term *personal curriculum* denotes the range of knowing that any person achieves in the process of growing up. By term substitution, the statement,

"There is the [personal curriculum],"

becomes

"There is the [range of knowing that any person achieves in the process of growing up],"

and there is no change in the meaning of the statement. The stipulative use of *personal curriculum* to denote the range of knowing that any person achieves in the process of growing up does not relate to a curriculum in the sense of a plan for the teaching and studying under guidance of some content in some setting. Rather it relates to the range of knowing that people achieve from all of their learning experiences, guided and unguided, intentional and unintentional, as they grow and mature.

This stipulative use of *personal curriculum* is a synonym for *range of knowing achieved from all of life's experiences.*

Unfortunately none of these stipulated definitions of curriculum-as-experiences contributes to clarification of discourse about curriculum in its ordinary sense of a plan for the teaching and guided studying of some content in some setting. On the contrary, most, if not all, of the stipulated definitions create confusion because they conflate distinct categories that are critical for clear and unambiguous discourse about education and curriculum. (see Chapter 1 above).

The Hidden Curriculum. An analysis has already been made of the way in which Bill Page (2008) has used the term *hidden curriculum*. The main issues associated with the hidden curriculum are the questions,

(1) "What is the hidden curriculum?" and

(2) "What role does the hidden curriculum play in promoting or impeding justice, fairness and equity in educational institutions?"

Philip Jackson (1968) is attributed with having introduced the term *hidden curriculum* into discourse about education and curriculum. He expressed the view that the educational process should be regarded more broadly than teaching and guided study, and that it should be conceived as the process of socialization as it functions within educational institutions such as schools, academies, institutes, colleges and universities.

Jackson's conception of *hidden curriculum* suffers the process-product confusion. The hidden curriculum is simultaneously characterized as what is learned and how it is learned within the social system of educational institutions. In other words, the term *hidden curriculum* is used to denote both

- the processes of learning that take place inside educational institutions but outside of official teaching and studying under guidance and without a curriculum in the sense of a written plan for the teaching and guided studying of some content in some setting, and
- the products of learning that result from the processes of learning, viz. the range of knowing, and especially the range of knowing that relates to social and cultural identity, social role, social and economic status, acceptance of social, political and economic status quo, norms, values, ethics, beliefs, aspirations, morality, distribution of power, wealth, and knowledge, justice, equity and fairness.

If the learning process is analyzed from the perspectives of intentional and unintentional learning on the part of the learner, and guided and unguided learning on the part of someone other than the learner, there are four possibilities for the learning process to take place outside of official education and without a written curriculum plan, viz.

- the learning process that is intentional on the part of the learner and guided by someone other than the learner (in unofficial education without a written curriculum plan),
- the learning process that is intentional and unguided (outside of education and without a written curriculum plan),

- the learning process that is unintentional and guided (outside of education and without a written curriculum plan),
- the learning process that is unintentional and unguided (outside of education and without a written curriculum plan).

See Figure 4.1.

Figure 4.1 Learning Processes and Products Denoted by the Term *Hidden Curriculum*

Term used to denote the corresponding learning process	Learning process denoted	Examples of learning process	Learning product denoted
Term: *successful official education*	Phenomena denoted by the term *successful official education*: Learning process • that takes place within educational institutions, • that is intentional by the learner & guided by someone other than the learner and • that has a written curriculum plan	E.g., deliberately undertaking to learn something (e.g. history, geography, English, etc.) and succeeding under the guidance of a certified teacher, tutor, mentor, coach, counselor, trainer or instructor and with a written curriculum plan	A range of knowing specified by a written curriculum plan in relation to the physical, biological & hominological fields of phenomena

Term: *hidden curriculum* First meaning	<u>Phenomena denoted by the term</u> *hidden curriculum*: Learning process • that takes place within educational institutions, • that is intentional by the learner & guided by someone other than the learner and • <u>that has no written curriculum plan</u>	E.g., deliberately undertaking to learn something (e.g. the institutional norms, values, ethics, rules, etc.) and succeeding under the guidance of a certified teacher, tutor, mentor, coach, counselor, trainer, instructor, sibling, peer or friend, etc. and <u>without a written curriculum plan</u>	A range of knowing <u>not specified by a written curriculum plan</u> in relation to the physical, biological & hominological fields of phenomena & especially social & cultural identity, social role, social & economic status, acceptance of social, political & economic status quo, norms, values, ethics, beliefs, aspirations, morality, distribution of power, wealth & knowledge, justice, equity & fairness

Term: *hidden curriculum* Second meaning	Phenomena denoted by the term *hidden curriculum*: Learning process • that takes place within educational institutions, • that is unintentional by the learner & guided by someone other than the learner and • that has no written curriculum plan	E.g., learning something (e.g. the institutional norms, values, ethics, rules, etc.) through socialization, encultura-tion, behavioral condition-ing, propa-gandizing, manipu-lation and advertising within the social setting of educational institutions without a written curriculum plan	A range of knowing not specified by a written curriculum plan in relation to the physical, biological & hominological fields of phenomena & especially social & cul-tural identity, social role, social & eco-nomic status, acceptance of social, politi-cal & econo-mic status quo, norms, values, ethics, beliefs, aspirations, morality, distribution of power, wealth & knowledge, justice, equity & fairness

| Term: *hidden curriculum* Third meaning | Phenomena denoted by the term *hidden curriculum*: Learning process • that takes place within educational institutions, • that is unintentional by the learner & unguided by someone other than the learner and • that has no written curriculum plan | E.g., learning something (e.g. the institutional norms, values, ethics, rules, etc.) from accident, random circumstances and life experiences within the social setting of educational institutions without a written curriculum plan | A range of knowing not specified by a written curriculum plan in relation to the physical, biological & hominological fields of phenomena & especially social & cultural identity, social role, social & economic status, acceptance of social, political & economic status quo, norms, values, ethics, beliefs, aspirations, morality, distribution of power, wealth & knowledge, justice, equity & fairness |

Term: *hidden curriculum* Fourth meaning	<u>Phenomena denoted by the term</u> *hidden curriculum*: Learning process • that takes place within educational institutions, • that is intentional by the learner & unguided by someone other than the learner and • <u>that has no written curriculum plan</u>	E.g., learning something (e.g. the institutional norms, values, ethics, rules, etc.) through deliberate trial & error and/or systematic reading and/or observation and/or experiment-ation and systematic analysis <u>without a written curriculum</u>	A range of knowing <u>not specified by a written curriculum plan</u> in relation to the physical, biological & hominological fields of phenomena & especially social & cul-tural identity, social role, social & eco-nomic status, acceptance of social, politi-cal & econo-mic status quo, norms, values, ethics, beliefs, aspirations, morality, distribution of power, wealth & knowledge, justice, equity & fairness

Many others have since elaborated upon Jackson's conception of the hidden curriculum. See, for example, Benson Snyder (1971) and Henry Giroux & David Purpel (1983). From sociological analyses of educational institutional life using the concept of the hidden curriculum, several observations have been put forward about what happens in schools, colleges and universities. It has been observed, for example, that students and teachers alike accept, without much thought, debate or hesitancy, a set of commonly shared norms, values, beliefs, expectations and rules of conduct, e.g. that failure to achieve intended learning outcomes is a personal responsibility of an individual student rather than a systematic deprivation imposed by low socio-economic status and oppressive political circumstances. It has been observed that the social system of educational institutions maintains divisions of social status and social class among students, and these divisions are not regarded by teachers or students as unfair, unjust or inequitable. For example, in secondary schools, the lower class students are assigned lower status trades subjects to study, and they readily accept these assignments. The upper class students are assigned higher status subjects that prepare them for entrance into universities, and they gladly accept these assignments. Neither students nor teachers see these arrangements to be unfair even though these arrangements are the result of systematic social and economic divisions within society. It has been observed that in societies which are divided by social and economic differences the same divisions of social and economic differences are reproduced in primary schools, secondary schools and tertiary educational institutions without any sense of unfairness or injustice (Henry Giroux and David Purpel, 1983).

The conception of the term *hidden curriculum* as

(1) *socialization within educational institutions* (a process) and

(2) *the range of knowing that results from socialization within educational institutions* (the product of the process)

does not relate at all to the ordinary conception of curriculum as a plan for the teaching and guided studying of some content in some setting. It is a confusing, misleading misnomer to use the term *hidden curriculum* to name (1) socialization within educational institutions and (2) the range of knowing resulting from socialization within educational institutions. But knowledge about the process and the product of socialization within educational institutions has direct relevance to the component of situational analysis in a curriculum plan. That is to say, part of a situational analysis within a curriculum plan should include consideration of the ways that socialization within educational institutions affects teachers and students and connects with the larger society and its norms and values. Such analyses would properly include considerations of, for example,

- the power relationship, as it exists or perhaps should exist, between teachers and students within educational institutions, judged from the perspective of social fairness, equity and justice,
- the norms, values and beliefs that teachers and students accept, or perhaps should accept, as appropriate for the social setting of educational institutions, judged from the perspective of social fairness, equity and justice,
- the extent to which prevailing economic, social and political divisions which exist in society are duplicated in the social interactions of educational institutions, judged from the perspective of social fairness, equity and justice. (See Henry Giroux & David Purpel, 1983, for an extensive analysis of the concept of hidden curriculum as the process and effects of socialization in educational institutions.)

Issues Arising from Competing Values and Perspectives

Aside from issues that arise from ambiguous discourse about education and curriculum, there are issues which emanate from beliefs, values and perspectives on what makes a good individual, a good life, a good society, a good culture, a good education and a good curriculum.

Curriculum from the Progressive Perspective. The historical context from which the progressive perspective on curriculum and education developed was a reaction to educational practices in schools in the late 19th and early 20th centuries. Publicly funded schools requiring compulsory attendance in Western Europe, the United Kingdom, Canada, the United States, Australia and New Zealand developed from the need for a literate and numerate population that could participate meaningfully in liberal democracies and contribute to the workforce needed in modern exchange economies. The early publicly funded primary schools were notorious for their inflexibility and harshness in dealing with children. The progressive perspective arose from a desire to reform prevailing practices of inflexibility and harshness and also from a reconceptualization of the educational process.

The foundations for the progressive perspective were laid in Europe in the early 18th and 19th centuries. Important figures included Jean-Jacques Rousseau (*Émile, or On Education*, 1762), Johann Heinrich Pestalozzi (*How Gertrude Teaches Her Children*, 1801), and his student, Friedrich Fröebel (originator of the concept of the kindergarten and author of *Die Menschenerziehung* [*The Education of Man*], 1826). They and their followers wrote of the desirability, indeed, the necessity to allow children to play and express their imagination, to pursue their natural inquisitiveness and curiosity spontaneously and to learn through transacting with their environment and drawing inferences from their experiences.

In the United States, the progressive perspective on curriculum and education developed momentum from the work of Colonel Francis Wayland Parker, a Civil War veteran and prominent school leader, speaker, author (*Talks on Teaching*, 1883; *The Practical Teacher*, 1884; *Talks on Pedagogies*, 1894) and inspiration for many progressive schools (e.g. the Francis W. Parker School, Chicago, Illinois, and the Francis W. Parker School, San Diego, California).

John Dewey further developed the influence of the progressive perspective through his work at the University of Chicago and Teachers College, Columbia University. Dewey extended his conception of pragmatism to its implications for education. His first major works, *Schools of Tomorrow* (1915) and *Democracy and Education* (1916), added to the momentum of progressivism that eventually precipitated the founding of the Progressive Education Association (1919). The PEA endured until 1955. Others who advanced the progressive perspective in the 1920s and 30s in the United States included William Heard Kilpatrick (notable for his advocacy of the project method of teaching and studying), Boyd H. Bode, John L. Childs, George Counts and

Vivian T. Thayer (along with John Dewey, a signatory to the first *Humanist Manfesto*, 1933).

After the Second World War, the progressive perspective in the United States was extended in the publications of George E. Axtelle, Ernest Bayles, H. Gordon Hullfish, Frederick C. Neff, R. Bruce Raup, William O. Stanley and Lawrence G.Thomas. In the remainder of the 20th century and the beginning of the 21st century, the name *progressivism* fell out of fashion, but its major distinguishing characteristics became integrated into teacher education courses, especially for early childhood and early primary education. Other names which have become fashionable in place of *progressivism* include *student centered education, pupil centered education, discovery learning, inquiry based learning, project based learning* and *the open classroom.* Although the perspective is denoted by several names, the distinguishing characteristics of the perspective remain much the same. From the progressive perspective, a curriculum plan is properly conceived of in the following terms.

(1) *Analysis of the Situation.* From the progressive perspective, the world is in a constant state of change. In fact, the only thing that is constant in anyone's life is change. What matters most is for us as human beings to learn to deal intelligently with the changing world. We learn how to deal with change effectively from our experience. Through reflecting upon an experience, analyzing it and coming to understand the meaning and significance of the experience, we learn how to deal with future experience more intelligently. In Dewey's words,

> "We thus reach a technical definition of education: it is that reconstruction or reorganization of experience which adds to the meaning of experience, and which increases the ability to direct the course of subsequent experience" (Dewey, 1916, p. 89).

The term *education* is thus taken to be a synonym for the term *learning process*, and the learning process proceeds from human beings having experiences, reflecting upon the meaning of those experiences and choosing to use what insights are gained from the experience to deal intelligently with future experiences. Through reflection and analysis of each or our experiences we develop an understanding of the experience. Consequently we develop over time a range of knowing that enables us to transact with future experience with understanding and intelligence. The learning process is a never ending cycle of experience, reflection, analysis, extension of understanding and dealing with new experiences. The social and political environment in which there is the greatest degree of freedom for experience is that of a social and political democracy. Learning through experience leads simultaneously to the development and growth of individuals and to the development and growth of a cooperative, democratic community.

We should accept children as they are, not as we want them to be or would like them to be. Children need to be allowed the freedom and responsibility to pursue their own interests and choose their own experiences from which to learn. Children are naturally curious, imaginative and playful. It is through their curiosity, imagination and playfulness that they transact with their environment, have experiences, reconstruct their experiences and deal with new experiences. The children's world is one of a never ending cycle of having experiences and learning from experiences and engaging in further experiences.

(2) *Specification of Intended Learning Outcomes.* Learners (i.e. children, pupils, students, etc.) should be accorded the freedom and responsibility to choose their own intended learning outcomes in accordance with their own individual interests. Teachers should act as advisers and guides, who ask questions for clarification and make suggests and recommendations, rather than act as bosses or supervisors, who give directives, enforce rules, coerce activities and impose sanctions.

(3) *Justification of Intended Learning Outcomes.* It is the learners' responsibility to choose intended learning outcomes that they authentically and genuinely want to achieve, according to their interests and needs. It is the teachers' responsibility to give advice, guidance and suggestions so as to assist learners in making responsible and authentic choices of intended learning outcomes.

(4) *Allocation of Time.* Learners are accorded the freedom and responsibility to determine the amount of time and the pace at which they wish to work towards achieving their intended learning outcomes. Teachers provide advice, guidance and suggestions about the amount of time and the pace. If there is a group of learners, then each learner may choose to work at her or his own pace. Or the learners may choose to work in pairs or in a small group. Or the learners may choose to work as a whole group in a team. How the learners choose to work is a matter for them to decide. The teachers' role is to provide advice, guidance and suggestions that are useful for learners to establish timetables, activities, conditions and goal structures conducive to learning what the students want to learn.

(5) *Specification of Content.* Learners should have the freedom and the responsibility to choose problems to solve or projects to develop, according to their current real life interests. The content (i.e. relevant fund of knowledge) is selected as a source to be used in the resolution of a problem or the development of a project. So, the problem chosen for resolution might be, for example,

- How do people in the community travel to work?
- How might parks and recreational areas be improved?
- Why are some people always acting like bullies and what can be done about it?
- Why are some people poor and others rich?
- Why do birds lay eggs and cats give live birth?
- Why do we need soldiers?
- Why do some people always want to fight and what can be done about it?
- Why are people mean to me and what can I do about it?

Obviously, there can be as many questions posed as there are stars in the sky, maybe more. The only limitations are the imaginations of the learners.

Projects might include, for example,

- cultivating a vegetable and fruit garden,
- selling the produce from the garden in the school store,
- running a school store and keeping accounts of revenues and expenditures,
- raising animals, such as chickens, lambs, goats, calves,
- planning and building a model city,
- forming a model government, writing a constitution, holding elections, formulating and voting on rules,

- designing and building a model bridge and testing it for its strength, etc.

Through the resolution of a range of problems and/or the execution of a series of projects, learners will naturally seek out the range of knowing in fine arts, craft and design and the knowledge of mathematics, history, geography, sociology, psychology, physics, biology, etc.

(6) *Nomination of Resources.* Resources that assist inquiry and support the implementation of projects are an absolute necessity. Resources can be located, collected and/or constructed by both learners and teachers. Resources are not confined to what might be collected, constructed and stored in the classroom. The community in which the learners live is a rich source of learning resources. Learning resources include the people who live in the community as well as the physical and biological environment of the community.

(7) *Specification of Learning Opportunities.* Children are naturally active, curious and playful, and they use their activity, curiosity and playfulness to transact with their environment and learn from their transactions. They accordingly should have the freedom and responsibility to select the learning activities that are attractive, interesting and relevant to them for solving the problems they want to solve or implementing the projects on which they want to work. The learning activities are learner chosen and learner directed. It is up to the learners to decide on the order in which problems will be addressed, questions will be asked and answered, activities will be undertaken or concepts and principles will be studied. The teachers' role is not to dictate, prescribe, direct, command, force or coerce, but rather to share, assist, advise, recommend, suggest, provide learning resources or indicate where learning resources might be found.

(8) *Assessment and Evaluation.* The learners have the freedom and responsibility to devise their own ways and means of demonstrating the achievement of their intended learning outcomes. The teachers' role is to share, assist, advise, recommend and suggest.

In addition to those already mentioned, proponents of some variation of the progressive perspective on curriculum include Ruth Bettelheim (2010), Jerome Bruner (1960, 1971), Idit Harel and Seymour Papert (1991), John Holt (1964, 1967), Herbert Kohl (1967, 1969), K.T. Margaret (1999), Maria Montessori (1947a, b, 1949), Jean Piaget (1926, 1948, 1953, 1971), Carl Rogers (1969), and Lev Vygotsky (1934).

Curriculum from the Social Reconstructionist Perspective. In the United States, the historical context from which the reconstructionist perspective developed began with the progressive school movement. George Counts and Theodore Brameld extended the notion that education not only was a process of reconstructing experience by the individual. It was also the means by which society could be reconstructed, reformed and improved. George Counts published his arguments for the reconstruction of society by means of education in *The American Road to Culture* (1930) and *Dare the Schools Build a New Social Order?* (1932). Harold Rugg extended the argument for social reconstruction in his publication, *Culture and Education in America* (1931). Isaac B. Berkson (1958), in *The Ideal and the Community*, argued for the use of schools to further ideals and reforms already afoot in society. Perhaps the most articulate and comprehensive of all those who have advocated for the social reconstructionist perspective was Theodore Brameld (1950, 1955, 1956, 1957), one of the signatories of the *Humanist Manifesto II* (1973). He argued that the schools had the responsibility, not just to follow social trends, but to take the initiative in advancing social reforms. Other advocates of some form of social reconstruction have included Paulo Freire (1970), Rita Tenorio (2004), Terry Burant, Linda Christensen, Kelley Dawson Salas and Stephanie Walters (2010) and Bob Peterson (2007). The *Rethinking Schools* organization, based in Milwaukee, Wisconsin, is an example of a contemporary group with a social reconstructionist perspective. Its mission statement (2014) declares that

> "*Rethinking Schools* is a nonprofit publisher and advocacy organization dedicated to sustaining and strengthening public education through social justice teaching and education activism. Our magazine, books, and other resources promote

equity and racial justice in the classroom. We encourage grassroots efforts in our schools and communities to enhance the learning and well being of our children, and to build broad democratic movements for social and environmental justice" (http://www.rethinkingschools.org/about/index.shtml).

(1) *Analysis of the Situation.* From the social reconstructionist perspective, it is an obvious fact that education, schools and individuals are significantly molded, for good and for bad, by society and culture. Sociology, psychology, anthropology, economics and political science have consistently substantiated this fact. The most desirable type of society and culture is a genuinely democratic one, i.e. socially and economically as well as politically democratic. Democratic societies allow the greatest degree of freedom for the exploration of individual interests, the formation and dissemination of knowledge and the open, unfettered discussion and expression of innovative ideas. Unfortunately, many societies which take pride in being democratic often fall short of being genuinely democratic. They are characterized by wide disparities in wealth, power and influence. They are marred by sexism, racism and violence. They suffer from ongoing corruption, injustice and inequity. They engage in censorship, invasion of privacy and violation of civil rights. One major purpose of official education is to provide opportunities for children and youth to develop a range of knowing that enables them to accommodate themselves to their society and to function effectively within their society. But accommodation to an unjust society merely perpetuates the injustices of the society. There is no improvement on the status quo, merely acceptance of it. A more important and worthy purpose of education is to enable children and youth to improve and reform their society and to transform it into a genuinely democratic society. As Theodore Brameld has commented about American society, for example,

> "Education has two major roles: to transmit culture and to modify culture. When American culture is in a state of crisis, the second of these roles – that of modifying and innovating – becomes more important" (Theodore Brameld, 1965, p. 75).

The social reconstructionist perspective agrees with the progressive perspective that the world is in a constant state of change. It differs from the progressive perspective about what matters most. What matters most is not for us as human beings to engage in systematic inquiry and learn how to deal intelligently with the changing world as it exists. What matters most is that we develop a well reasoned and articulated agenda for social reform, learn how to implement those reforms and commit ourselves to reformist action. We need to learn how to change and shape the world into a more desirable one. It is important that we learn how to eradicate social and economic injustices. For example, we need to learn how to resolve conflict peacefully and eliminate, or at the very least, minimize social ills such as racism, bullying, domestic violence, drug abuse, environmental pollution, child abuse, homophobia, ageism, sexism, poverty, etc.

Addressing social issues is a matter of urgency from the social reconstructionist perspective. When there are social injustices in play, there is no time to waste in working on eradicating them. The longer they are allowed to exist, the stronger their influence becomes, and the more damage they do to both individuals and communities. School should not be a preparation for life, but rather it should create opportunities to engage in resolving real life social issues for the advancement of democracy. The proper role of teachers is to persuade pupils and students democratically to discern current social issues, understand them, become well informed about them, take a value stand in relation to them and undertake effective action to resolve them.

(2) *Specification of Intended Learning Outcomes.* From the social reconstructionist perspective, the major desirable intended learning outcome is that students, out of their own free will, make well informed, authentic decisions to embrace the importance of taking effective action to resolve current social issues that in some way threaten to diminish and degrade the quality of their democratic society and culture. Along with this commitment to effective reformist action goes the commitment to learn how to conduct sound inquiry and solve problems based on relevant, necessary and sufficient evidence.

(3) *Justification of Intended Learning Outcomes.* From the social reconstructionist perspective, human beings have free will, and they also have an innate ability to reason morally and ethically. A democratic society and culture provides the best environment for the free expression of moral and ethical reasoning. However, within any society, including democratic ones, there are always anti-democratic forces at work. It is the proper role of official education, i.e. education in schools, colleges and universities, to provide an environment in which students may (1) come to understand the issues that are important, not only for the maintenance, but also for the advancement and extension of democracy and (2) develop the skill set necessary to take effective action to improve democracy. Within a society, those things which diminish some of us, ultimately diminish all of us. Racism and poverty, for example, are iniquities in a democratic society and culture, and it is important, not just to minimize them, but to eradicate them. The process of renewal and reformation is continuous and unending, and it is a process in which all ages can and should participate. The school is a proper and appropriate venue for renewal of values and social reformation to take place.

(4) *Allocation of Time.* As with the progressive viewpoint, the social reconstructionist perspective advocates that learners be accorded the freedom and responsibility to determine the amount of time and the pace at which they wish to work towards achieving their intended learning outcomes. Teachers provide advice, guidance and suggestions about the amount of time and the pace. If there is a group of learners, then each learner may choose to work at her or his own pace. Or the learners may choose to work in pairs or in a small group. Or the learners may choose to work as a whole group in a team. How the learners choose to work is a matter for them to decide. The teacher's role is to provide advice, guidance and suggestions that are useful for learners to establish timetables, activities, conditions and goal structures conducive to learning what the students need to learn to understand crucial social issues and take effective action to resolve them.

(5) *Specification of Content.* From the social reconstructionist perspective, the content should be organized around significant social issues. Some issues change with each generation. Some remain the same. The content should be selected and organized as issues arise. It is the task of the students to use their reasoning abilities and their inquiry skills to pose questions, collect evidence, form conclusions and take a moral stand. The social reconstructionist perspective maintains that values are not fixed for all time. As new circumstances arise, as they always do, then existing values must be reexamined, reevaluated and reinterpreted. This is the challenge for each generation. The proper role of the teacher is to take a well reasoned, well informed position and to challenge students to do the same, without intimidating them, coercing them or manipulating them.

(6) *Nomination of Resources.* As with the progressive perspective, the social reconstructionist perspective recognizes that resources which assist inquiry and support the implementation of projects are an absolute necessity. Resources can be located, collected and/or constructed by both learners and teachers. Resources are not confined to what might be collected, constructed and stored in the classroom. The community in which the learner lives is a rich source of learning resources. Learning resources include the people who live in the community as well as the physical and biological environment of the community.

(7) *Specification of Learning Opportunities.* As with the progressive perspective, the social reconstructionist perspective recognizes that children are naturally active, curious and playful, and they use their activity, curiosity and playfulness to transact with their environment and learn from their transactions. The teacher's proper role is to channel these natural dispositions into activities that result in students recognizing critical social issues, becoming well informed about them, taking a defensible viewpoint in relation to them and undertaking action to improve a situation. Teachers have the obligation to assist students to become aware of what they have unconditionally accepted in their personal value system and their social existence and to undertake well formed and sound inquiry about what should be accepted, why it should be accepted and what actions need to be taken to change themselves and society for the better.

From the social reconstructionist perspective, students should have the freedom and responsibility to select the learning activities that are attractive, interesting and relevant to them for investigating crucial issues and implementing relevant projects. The learning activities are learner chosen and learner directed. It is up to the learners to decide on the order in which problems will be addressed, questions will be asked and answered, activities will be undertaken or concepts and principles will be studied. The teachers' role is not to intimidate, dictate, prescribe, direct, command, force or coerce, but rather to persuade democratically, challenge, share, assist, advise, recommend, suggest, provide learning resources or indicate where learning resources might be found.

(8) *Assessment and Evaluation.* The learners have the freedom and responsibility to devise their own ways and means of demonstrating the achievement of their intended learning outcomes. An important part of the evaluation is the demonstration by students that they have authentically chosen, freely and without coercion or intimidation, a defensible position on a crucial social issue and that they have undertaken action to improve the situation relating to the social issue. The teacher's role in the evaluation process is to challenge, share, assist, advise, recommend and suggest.

Curriculum from the Essentialist Perspective. From the essentialist perspective, the proper role of school is to prepare children and youth to be socially and culturally competent in adult life. Preparation for cultural competence requires the study of funds of knowledge and the development of a range of knowing that are necessary to function competently within the context of adult society and culture.

The essentialist perspective has perhaps been in existence in some form or another since the beginning of civilization and schools.

In educological literature of the 20th century, one of the best articulations and justifications of the essentialist perspective was developed by the distinguished American educologist William C. Bagley (1934). During his career, Bagley worked as a teacher and principal in primary schools, served as founder and first Director of the School of Education at the University of Illinois (1908-1917) and held the position of Professor of Education at Teachers College, Columbia University (1917-1940). He was editor of the *Journal of the National Education Association* (1920-1925). He founded the Essentialistic Education Society (1938) and also the journal of *School and Society*, a publication which editorially supported the essentialist perspective (J. Wesley Null, 2003).

Bagley argued that there are certain funds of knowledge that all people should study, regardless of whether, as children, they have any initial interest in those funds. An understanding of those funds is crucial to functioning within democratic society and culture as an adult. It takes time and dedicated practice to master and appreciate the range of knowing that results from the study of funds of knowledge essential to understanding our society and culture. Children are too immature and inexperienced to understand what is important to learn, thus it is up to responsible, well educated adults (i.e. teachers, school administrators, curriculum developers, other well educated and well informed interested parties) to prescribe which funds of knowledge should be studied and learned. It is also the responsibility of well educated adults to initiate the learning opportunities and to evaluate the degree to which students achieve intended learning outcomes (William C. Bagley, 1934).

Other educologists of the 1930s and 1940s with similar views to those of William C. Bagley included Michael J. Demiashkevich (1935), Frederick S. Breed (1939), Henry C. Morrison (1924, 1926, 1943), Thomas Briggs, Ross L. Finney and Isaac L. Kandel (1930, 1933, 1943, 1955).

Proponents of essentialism in the 1950s and 1960s included William W. Brickman, editor of *School and Society* (1953-76), and cofounder of the Comparative Education Society (1956), James D. Koerner (1963, 1968), Hyman G. Rickover (1959, 1962, 1963), Arthur Bestor (1953) and Mortimer B. Smith (1954), cofounder of the Council for Basic Education (1956).

Advocates of the essentialist viewpoint in the 1970s, 80s, 90s and the early 2000s included Paul Copperman (1978), Theodore R. Sizer (1984, 1992, 1997), whose work established the basis for the Coalition of Essential Schools (1984), and Eric D. Hirsch (1987, 1996, 2006), founder of the Core Knowledge Foundation (1986). The Core Knowledge Foundation states as its mission,

> "By outlining the precise content that every child should learn
> in language arts and literature, history and geography,
> mathematics, science, music, and the visual arts, the Core
> Knowledge curriculum represents a first-of-its kind effort to
> identify the foundational knowledge every child needs to reach
> these goals – and to teach it, grade-by-grade, year-by-year, in a

coherent, age-appropriate sequence" (retrieved 2014, http://www.coreknowledge.org/learn-about-us).

Although the Core Knowledge Foundation makes the claim that its efforts are "a first-of-its kind" this is not quite true. In fact, an examination of the curriculum statement of virtually any publicly funded primary or high school in the United States, Canada, Great Britain, Australia or New Zealand, or any other country that you might wish to name will quickly reveal a list of subjects that are considered essential for all children to learn. They are often called the core curriculum or the compulsory subjects. The list of core subjects typically includes English (or the first language of the culture, including reading, writing and literature), history, mathematics, computer studies, natural sciences, social sciences, music, fine arts and perhaps a foreign language.

There are numerous contemporary curricula which exemplify an essentialist perspective. A particularly good example is that of the curriculum developed by the Australian Curriculum, Assessment and Reporting Authority (ACARA), an Australian federal government authority. ACARA states that

"The Australian Curriculum describes what young Australians should learn as they progress through schooling. It is the foundation for their future learning, growth and active participation in the Australian community. It sets out essential knowledge, understanding, skills and capabilities and provides a national standard for student achievement in core learning areas" (retrieved 2014, http://www.australiancurriculum.edu. au/). (Information for Figure 4.2 is from the ACARA website, F-10 Curriculum, retrieved 2014, http://www.australiancurricu-lum.edu.au/Curriculum/Overview).

Virtually all of the historical debates in educological literature about core curriculum that have taken place, and continue to take place in current times as ongoing arguments, are borne out of an essentialist perspective. The push for common standards, standardized testing and achievement of minimum competencies are expressions of an essentialist perspective.

(1) *Analysis of the Situation.* From the essentialist perspective, it is clearly a fact of human existence that we live within some society, and as individuals, we exemplify through our habits of

Figure 4.2: The Australian Curriculum: An Example of a Contemporary Curriculum Designed from an Essentialist Perspective

Australian Curriculum Overview: Foundation Year to Year 10 [Kindergarten through Grade 10]			
Learning areas	*General capabilities*	*Cross-curriculum priorities*	*Year level*
▪ English ▪ Mathematics ▪ Science ▪ Humanities and Social Sciences ▪ History ▪ Geography *Awaiting final endorsement* ▪ Humanities and Social Sciences ▪ Economics and Business ▪ Civics and Citizenship ▪ The Arts ▪ Technologies ▪ Health and Physical Education ▪ Languages Other Than English	▪ Literacy ▪ Numeracy ▪ Information and Communication Technology (ICT) capability ▪ Critical and creative thinking ▪ Personal and social capability ▪ Ethical understanding ▪ Intercultural understanding	▪ Aboriginal and Torres Strait Islander histories and cultures ▪ Asia and Australia's engagement with Asia ▪ Sustainability	Foundation Year Year 1 Year 2 Year 3 Year 4 Year 5 Year 6 Year 7 Year 8 Year 9 Year 10

thought and behavior (without self consciousness or self awareness) our individual version of the wider culture of our society.

Within all cultures, there are universal features. (Edward T. Hall, 1959). Each of us identifies as a member of a cultural group (e.g. as American, French, Chilean, etc.), and we have an ethnocentric attitude (e.g. on first contact with members of some other culture, we find them strange, intriguing, different, comical, perhaps even dangerous; we regard ourselves as normal). We share a common language and common ways of communication within our community (e.g. we speak as our first language Russian or Turkish or English). We organize ourselves and associate with each other in accordance with the customs and norms of our culture. We participate within an economic system and achieve our subsistence cooperatively within what we take to be normal arrangements for the production and distribution of goods and services (e.g. Kalahari bushmen hunt and gather and share their catch with their extended family; American computer programmers work in offices, exchange time for money and use the money to access goods and services). We express our sexuality and play our sex roles in accordance with the mores and norms of our culture. We manage our space and establish our territoriality in ways consistent with our culture. We have a sense of time and temporality that is common to our culture. We participate in recreation and play in ways that are acceptable within our culture. We organize for our personal and communal defense and protection. We worship and practice our religion (or religions) in ways that are considered normal for our culture. We use tools and techniques common to our culture. As we grow from children to adults, through the processes of socialization, enculturation and unofficial education, we come to be who we are without self consciousness and without self awareness of who we have become, of what we value and take to be normal and why we take it to be valuable and normal. We accept things as they are and can not even imagine doing things differently.

Socialization, enculturation and unofficial education are effective means of learning spoken language in early childhood, developing cultural identity and becoming habituated to sexual and social roles. The three processes are effective in developing acceptance of traditional customs, norms, values and habituated ways of doing things. But socialization, enculturation and unofficial education are ineffective means of freeing the mind from superstitution and prejudice and freeing it for rational thought, systematic inquiry, innovation and invention.

To be liberated, one needs to have *freedom from* and *freedom for* (Elizabeth Steiner [Maccia], 1981). Emancipated slaves of the American South after the Civil War (1860-65) were free from the restraints of slavery. But without literacy and numeracy, without knowing how to gain and exercise political power, without capital and access to the means of production, they could do little with their freedom. They had freedom from the restraints of slavery. But they did not have freedom for taking well informed, intelligent, rational action to access the legal system, to improve their economic, social and political situation, and to defend themselves against violence and oppression. Their situation in those post war years is a clear example of a people with freedom from but not freedom for.

Placement by birth, immigration or emancipation in a democratic society is an insufficient condition for an individual to be free. To be free, one needs to have freedom for as well as freedom from. Liberation from unjust and unreasonable restraints gives freedom from. A liberal education gives freedom for. It frees the mind for inquiry, rational action, innovation and invention. The process of official education (i.e. studying under guidance in schools, colleges and universities) provides the means for a liberal education. Through liberal education, individuals can transcend the limitations of their superstitions, prejudices and irrationalities learned from unofficial education, enculturation and socialization.

A liberal education allows access to the knowledge that cultures accumulate in books and literature over the generations and the centuries. Numeracy and literacy (and in contemporary times the use of computers) are basic to living the life of a free person within a democratic society. So too is an understanding of history, languages, literature (fiction and nonfiction), mathematics, natural sciences, social sciences, the fine arts and music. These funds of knowledge are complex. It takes time, patience and sustained study, moving from the simple to the complex, to learn, understand and master them. Once the children's liberal education has become well developed, then, as youth and young adults, their vocational education can be implemented.

Children are too immature and inexperienced to make well informed, intelligent and wise choices about what to study and learn. Well informed, well educated, mature adults have the responsibility and obligation to choose what children should learn and to guide them in their learning. As children mature and develop into youth and young adulthood, then it is appropriate to allow them more choice within a range of alternatives for study.

(2) *Specification of Intended Learning Outcomes.* From the essentialist perspective, desirable learning outcomes include sound levels of literacy and numeracy. They include the ability to think critically, analyze and conduct systematic inquiry. They include a sound understanding of history, languages, literature (fiction and nonfiction), mathematics, uses of computers, natural sciences, social sciences, the fine arts and music, health education and physical education. They include commitment to a sound set of values, including a sense of responsibility, honesty, integrity, justice and fairplay.

(3) *Justification of Intended Learning Outcomes.* From the essentialist perspective, the nomination of intended learning outcomes is made in relation to what is necessary to live the life of a responsible adult within a democratic society.

(4) *Allocation of Time.* From the essentialist perspective, the teachers, curriculum supervisors and curriculum developers have the responsibility to determine allocation of time. They should specify the total time, pace and sequence in relation to the ability of the pupils or students to achieve the intended learning outcomes.

(5) *Specification of Content.* From the essentialist perspective, the content should be organized in recognized and established subjects, viz. English, history, mathematics, computer sciences, natural sciences, social sciences, languages, fine arts and music, health education and physical education.

(6) *Nomination of Resources.* From the essentialist perspective, resources should be sourced and or created by the teacher and curriculum providers. Resources should be appropriate to the age level and learning ability of the students.

(7) *Specification of Learning Opportunities.* From the essentialist perspective, teachers have the obligation and responsibility to select the learning activities that evidence indicates are the most effective in assisting students achieve the intended learning outcomes.

(8) *Assessment and Evaluation.* The teachers or external assessment authorities have the responsibility to devise assessment activities that demonstrate student achievement of intended learning outcomes. System wide, state wide, nation wide and international comparisons of student achievement are desirable to gain a sense of whether students are achieving what they should and whether educational institutions are performing as well as they should.

Curriculum from the Perennialist Perspective. From the perennialist's perspective, the issues which each new generation confronts are much the same. Only the contemporary details differ. Is honesty always the best policy? Can conflict always be resolved peacefully? To what extent must individual freedoms be curtailed for the greater good of the community? To what extent can individuals be held accountable for their actions? What are my civic duties? Is patriotism ever a bad thing? What worthwhile purposes should I pursue in my life? What should be my core values? When is war justifiable? To what extent should I heed the advice of my parents and to what extent should I disregard it? What is love? How do we decide the right thing? What does it mean to be good? What is democracy? How does it differ from other forms of government? Is it the best form of government? The best way to answer these questions is for us to come to our own conclusions. The most appropriate means to reaching our own conclusions is to study the original works of those who have grappled with these very questions, and with the assistance of a skilled tutor who asks the appropriate questions, develop authentic, well informed and rationally defensible answers for which we have justified true belief.

Notable proponents of the perennialist perspective in the 20th century were Robert Maynard Hutchins, Mortimer Adler, Max Weismann, Strongfellow Barr, Scott Buchanan, Mark Van Doren and Sir Richard Livingstone.

Robert Maynard Hutchins (1936, 1943, 1952, 1953, 1961) initially studied at Yale and subsequently served as Dean of Yale Law School (1927-1929). At the age of 30, he was appointed President of the University of Chicago, and served in that position for 16 years (1929-1945). He then served as Chancellor of the university for another six years (1945-1951). Of his many reforms at the University of Chicago, the most significant was the restructuring of the undergraduate program into a liberal arts program based on the study of original classical authors. The program came to be referred to as the *Hutchins Plan of Great Books*. The content of the program consisted of what was deemed to be classical literature (the Great Books). The preferred teaching methods incorporated the Socratic method, i.e. tutors asking well formed questions to guide students in clarifying their thinking (their conversation with the Great Books) and arriving at their own well informed, rationally defensible conclusions. Other innovations included early aged admission (i.e. under 18 years of age) to the liberal arts program and comprehensive examinations on a periodic basis. In addition to his leadership role at the University of Chicago, Hutchins was Chairman of the Board of Editors of *Encyclopaedia Britannica* for 31 years (1943 to 1974). He served as Editor in Chief of *Great Books of the Western World* (a series which was first published by Encyclopaedia Britannica, Inc. in 1961) and *Gateway to the Great Books* (a series first published by Encyclopaedia Britannica, Inc. in 1963). Hutchins also served as coeditor (with Mortimer Adler) of *The Great Ideas Today*, a series first published by Encyclopaedia Britannica, Inc. in 1961 which noted connections between current issues and the *Great Books*. After he left the University of Chicago, Hutchins served as head of the Ford Foundation (1951-1959), then founded and worked with the Center for the Study of Democratic Institutions in Santa Barbara, California until his death (1959-1977). After Hutchins departed from the University of Chicago (1951), the university restructured the undergraduate program and abandoned much of the Hutchins Plan. But the plan is followed to a large extent to the present day at Shimer College in Chicago and St. John's College at its two campuses in Annapolis, Maryland and Santa Fe, New Mexico.

Mortimer J. Adler (1937, 1938, 1940, 1958, 1961, 1982, 2000, 2004) was one of Hutchins' most important colleagues. Hutchins recruited Adler to the University of Chicago in 1930. They collaborated in the development of the undergraduate liberal arts program at the university and developed the *Great Books of the Western World* (a series of books first published by Encyclopaedia Britannica, Inc. in 1952). Adler co-founded (with Robert Hutchins) the Great Books Foundation (1947), an organization devoted to the promotion of liberal education for children, youth and adults through the study of classical literature. Adler served on the Board of Editors for the *Encyclopaedia Britannica*, beginning in 1949, and he followed Hutchins as Chairman of the Board of Editors in 1974. In 1982, Adler published *The Paideia Proposal* in which he advocated and elaborated upon a liberal arts education program for primary and secondary school children. He was a co-founder of the Center for the Study of the Great Ideas (1990) in cooperation with his longtime colleague and fellow philosopher, Max Weismann.

Stringfellow Barr (1962) was an author and historian. Among his many achievements, he was President of St John's College (Annapolis, Maryland, 1936-1946), President of the Foundation for World Government (1948-1958) and in the 1950s, a professor of classics at Rutgers College (Newark, New Jersey). In 1937, Barr and his colleague from the University of Chicago, Scott Buchanan (1927, 1929, 1932), restructured the undergraduate program at St. John's College and transformed it into a liberal arts program based on Socratic teaching methods and the Great Books of philosophy, history, religion, mathematics, natural science, social science, music, poetry and literature. This curriculum continues today at St. John's campus at Annapolis, Maryland, and its more recent campus (founded in 1964) at Santa Fe, New Mexico.

Mark Van Doren (1943) was a Professor of English at Columbia University, New York for nearly 40 years (1920-1959). He distinguished himself for his inspirational teaching and his views on the value of a liberal education. Sir Richard Livingstone (1916) served as a fellow and tutor at Corpus Christi College at Oxford University in the 1920s. He was Vice-Chancellor of

Queen's University for nine years (1924-1933). In 1933, Livingstone returned to Oxford University, became President of Corpus Christi College, then Vice-Chancellor of Oxford University. He served as Vice-Chancellor for three years (1944-1947). Livingstone advised governments about education policy and, in his writings and lectures, argued vigorously in defense of the benefits of a classical liberal education.

(1) *Analysis of the Situation.* From the perennialist perspective, the most valuable attribute of humankind is its ability to reason. Rationality is the most important trait of any human being, and it should be developed to its fullest extent. Each generation encounters its own issues and challenges. The details of those issues differ from generation to generation, but the issues themselves, as categories, remain the same. Each and every generation is confronted, for example, with these questions: What is justice? What is fairness? What is good? What purposes are worth pursuing? What forms of government are best? How can conflict be resolved peacefully? Is war ever justified? What are one's civic responsibilities? What responsibilities does one have towards one's parents? What is love? Where does one's responsibilities end and another's begin? To what extent should society look after individuals and to what extent should individuals look after themselves? What is democracy? These questions and many others are perennial issues for humankind. Some of the best minds throughout the ages have addressed these questions and recorded their thoughts about them. The published record of these thoughts constitutes the Great Books. It is wise to consider those thoughts contained in the Great Books, study them closely, come to understand them thoroughly and take them into account as we develop our own reasoning and conclusions about the big questions which confront us as human beings.

(2) *Specification of Intended Learning Outcomes.* From the perennialist perspective, desirable learning outcomes are those which enable a free person to participate in the civic life of a democratic society. Traditionally those learning outcomes have been known as the liberal arts.

The liberal arts have a long history, beginning with ancient Athens. The liberal arts were the skills deemed essential for free men (as opposed to slaves) to fulfill their civic responsibilities in Athenian society. They were grammar, rhetoric and logic, i.e. the skills necessary to acquit one's self in public debate, legal disputes and jury duty. In Europe of the Middle Ages, the original three liberal arts came to be referred to as the *trivium*. European medieval universities added four additional arts (the *quadrivium*), viz. skills in arithmetic, geometry, music and astronomy. These were the seven liberal arts.

In contemporary times, the liberal arts remain the skills that are necessary for a free person to take part in civic life as a virtuous, articulate, well informed and rational person. The modern liberal arts are those which derive from an understanding of history, philosophy, languages, literature, mathematics, natural sciences, social sciences, the fine arts and music.

From the perennialist perspective, desirable learning outcomes include sound levels of literacy and numeracy. They include the ability to think critically, analyze and conduct systematic inquiry. They include commitment to a sound set of values, including a sense of responsibility, honesty, integrity, justice and fairplay. Above all, the most important learning outcome is the ability to use one's rationality in resolving the important issues in life in light of what other important thinkers have thought about the same issue.

(3) *Justification of Intended Learning Outcomes.* From the perennialist perspective, the nomination of intended learning outcomes is made in relation to what is necessary to live the life of a responsible, free and rational adult. Important issues are not resolved by quoting scriptures, following custom and tradition, exercising blind prejudice and suppressing dissent. They are resolved by open discussion, well informed debate and soundly reasoned argument.

(4) *Allocation of Time.* From the perennialist perspective, the teachers, curriculum supervisors and curriculum developers have the responsibility to determine allocation of time. They should specify the total time, pace and sequence in relation to the ability of the pupils or students to achieve the intended learning outcomes.

(5) *Specification of Content.* From the perennialist perspective, the content should be organized into recognized and established subjects (funds of knowledge), viz. English, history, mathematics, natural sciences, social sciences, languages, fine arts and music (and more recently, computer sciences).

(6) *Nomination of Resources.* From the perennialist perspective, learning resources should consist of the original works of great thinkers of Western Civilization (versus secondary sources or descriptions, summaries and analyses of what authors have written). The resources should be in the original language of the authors or in faithful and competent English translations of the authors. The authors should include ancient Greeks and Romans, e.g. Homer, Aeschylus, Sophocles, Euripides, Aristophanes, Herodotus, Thucydides, Plato, Aristotle, Hippocrates, Galen, Euclid, Archimedes, Marcus Aurelius, Epictetus, Lucretius, Virgil. They should include authors from the European Middle Ages, Renaissance and Early Modern period, e.g. Thomas Aquinas, Dante Alighieri, Geoffrey Chaucer, Niccolo Machiavelli, Thomas Hobbes, Francois Rabelais, William Shakespeare, Miguel de Cervantes, Sir Francis Bacon, René Descartes. They should include modern authors, e.g. Adam Smith, Edward Gibbon, Immanuel Kant, Antoine Lavoisier, Michael Faraday, Herman Melville, Charles Darwin, Karl Marx, William James, Sigmund Freud, Søren Kierkegaard, Friedrich Nietzsche, Alexis de Tocqueville, Mark Twain, Henrik Ibsen, William James.

(7) *Specification of Learning Opportunities.* From the perennialist perspective, teachers should use the Socratic method. They have the obligation and responsibility to select learning activities that will challenge students to address important questions, consider carefully what others (i.e. what Western civilization's most insightful contributors) have said about that question and come to their own well informed and rationally defensible conclusions about the questions.

(8) *Assessment and Evaluation.* The teachers have the responsibility to devise assessment activities that give students the opportunity to demonstrate their achievement of intended learning outcomes. The assessment may take the form of extended written essays, a treatise and/or an extended oral examination on one or a few important questions. The purpose of the assessment is to demonstrate the extent to which students can present a rationally defensible position in relation to important issues in life in light of what other important thinkers have thought about the same issue.

A Knowledge Base for Resolving Issues Arising from Constructing a Curriculum

In 1939, the distinguished American educologist, Harold Benjamin (1893-1969), published *The Saber-Tooth Curriculum*. It has since become a classic in educological literature about curriculum. Benjamin used the pseudonym of J. Abner Peddiwell to address the issue of how blind irrational acceptance of tradition in educational institutions impedes much needed innovations in curriculum.

Through his alter ego of Dr. J. Abner Peddiwell, Benjamin constructs an allegory about schools in the Stone Age that continue to teach skills of fish-grabbing, horse-clubbing and tiger-scaring long after the disappearance of clear streams for fishing, the migration of horses and the extinction of saber-tooth tigers. To adapt to new circumstances, tribesmen innovate net-making, snare-setting and pit-digging for catching fish, antelope and bears. They suggest that the schools discard teaching the old skills and start teaching the new skills, the ones that are directly relevant to contemporary circumstances. But the wise old men of the tribe object to introducing the teaching of the new skills on the basis that the new skills are merely training, not genuine education. The elders argue that the purposes of the traditional skills of fish-grabbing, horse-clubbing and tiger-scaring are not to develop these skills *per se*, but rather to develop the more generalized characteristics of agility, strength and courage. It is impossible, they maintain, to develop these generalized characteristics from teaching the newer skills of net-making, snare-making and pit-digging, which are merely vocational in nature.

What Benjamin manages to achieve with his allegory is to identify most of the issues that arise in constructing, implementing and evaluating a curriculum. A curriculum is never constructed in a social and cultural vacuum. It always has a history behind it. There are always questions as to what to retain from the past, what to address in the present and what to anticipate for the future. The larger community in which schools function always has expectations about what, how and whom the schools should teach and in what ways the schools should be held accountable. Within the community, there are always champions of innovation and advocates of tradition.

To deal with curriculum issues intelligently, one needs to be well informed about curriculum and education. One needs to able to mount a rationally defensible argument for a curriculum. And one needs to find some reference group within the community that will provide intellectual, social, political and financial support for the curriculum. Improvement of curriculum is not only an intellectual process. It also involves social, political and financial forces as well.

The educology of curriculum has a role to play in the intellectual process of curriculum design, development, implementation and evaluation. It is an important fund of knowledge which contributes to informing discussions, inquiry, design, development, implementation and evaluation of curriculum. The educology of curriculum is a subfund of educology, and educology is the fund of knowledge about the educational process. Educology is developed and organized from an educological perspective. The educological perspective treats the educational process as the dependent variable, and it examines how other factors or variables affect the educational process. In relation to curriculum, the fundamental question that can be posed from an educological perspective is,

"What are the effects of curriculum (or a particular curriculum) on the educational process?"

This fundamental question implies a number of derivative questions.

(1) What are the meanings of terms used in discourse about curriculum (or a particular curriculum) and the educational process and how does the use of those terms affect curriculum and education? This question is addressed by the analytic philosophical educology of curriculum.

(2) What are good and bad (or relatively good and bad) effects of curriculum (or a particular curriculum) on the educational process? This question is addressed by the normative philosophical educology of curriculum.

(3) How has curriculum (or a particular curriculum) affected the educational process in the past? This question is addressed by the historical educology of curriculum.

(4) How does curriculum (or a particular curriculum) currently affect the educational process in contemporary societies and cultures? This question is addressed by the scientific educology of curriculum.

(5) What practices for planning, developing, implementing and evaluating curriculum (or a particular curriculum) are effective in achieving desired results and/or states of affairs in the educational process? This question is address by the praxiological educology of curriculum.

Answers to these five questions constitutes the educology of curriculum, The educology of curriculum provides a fund of knowledge that serves as a basis for decision making about curriculum design, development, implementation and evaluation.

In matters of the educational process and curriculum, experience is highly prized. While it is true that experience with the educational process and curriculum is important for developing educological understanding, naïve experience alone is insufficient in and of itself. All of us experience disease, for example, but this does not qualify us as medical practitioners. We occupy space and exist in time, but this experience does not transform us into physicists. We are living organisms, and we experience life amongst other living organisms, but this does not make us biologists. So it is with educological knowing and understanding. Naïve experience with education is insufficient to make us educologists.

To develop educological understanding, one must engage in experiences with an educological perspective so that the educologically significant features of the experience may be discerned, reflected upon and analyzed. To develop a range of knowing about the educational process and curriculum, one must study educology (including the educology of curriculum) as well as have experience with the educational process and curriculum. Rational constructive action within and for curriculum and the educational process requires educological understanding. Without that understanding, action can be taken, of course, but not rational action. If such action is constructive, it will be by accident, for it will not be by one's qualitative, quantitative and procedural knowing about the educational process and curriculum.

The way to rational constructive action with and for curriculum and the educational process is through developing an extensive range of educological knowing (in its three kinds, six forms and three levels) about the educational process and curriculum. An extensive range of educological knowing requires appropriate experience with curriculum and the educational process. Appropriate experience is made appropriate when it is undertaken with an educological perspective. The development of the educological perspective requires the study of educology, i.e. the reading, the analysis and the comprehension, the reflection upon and the intelligent action in relation to warranted assertions about the educational process and about curriculum within the process. It is educology which provides clear characterizations, factual descriptions, valid explanations, sound justifications, reliable predictions and effective prescriptions about the educational process and curriculum. Educology provides the cognitive structure for sound reasoning about education and curriculum and for taking rational constructive action in and for education and curriculum.

Bibliography

Adler, Mortimer J. (1937: *What Man Has Made of Man: A Study of the Consequences of Platonism and Positivism in Psychology.* New York: Longmans.

Adler, Mortimer J. (1938): *St. Thomas and the Gentiles.* Milwaukee, Wisconsin: Marquette University Press.

Adler, Mortimer J. (1940): *How to Read a Book: The Art of Getting a Liberal Education.* New York: Simon and Schuster.

Adler, Mortimer J. (1958): *The Idea of Freedom: A Dialectical Examination of the Conceptions of Freedom.* Garden City, New York: Doubleday.

Adler, Mortimer J. (1961): *Great Ideas from the Great Books.* New York: Simon and Schuster.

Adler, Mortimer J. (1982): *The Paideia Proposal: An Educational Manifesto.* New York: MacMillan Publishing Company.

Adler, Mortimer J. (Edited by Max Weismann) (2000): *How to Think about the Great Ideas: From the Great Books of Western Civilization.* Chicago: Open Court.

Adler, Mortimer J. (Editor) (2004): *Great Books of the Western World.* 60 Volumes. London: Encyclopaedia Britannica, Inc., U.K.

Allen, Dwight W. and Seifman, Eli (Eds.) (1971): *The Teacher's Handbook.* Glenview, Illinois: Scott, Foresman and Company.

Ameh, Catherine Onyeka (1986): "Chapter 1: Science Teachers' Concepts in Science: An Educological Perspective," in James E. Christensen (Ed.), *Educology 86: Proceedings of a Conference on Educational Research, Inquiry and Development with an Educological Perspective, Canberra, July 10-12, 1986.* Sydney: Educology Research Associates, pp. 5–18.

Ameh, Catherine Onyeka (1988): "An Educological Approach to Identifying Teachers' Understanding of Science Concepts," *International Journal of Educology*, Vol. 2, No. 1, pp. 75-84. Sydney: Educology Research Associates.

Ameh, Catherine Onyeka (1991): "An Educology for Science: Teaching Sciences in the 90's," *International Journal of Educology*, Vol. 5, No. 1, pp. 53-60. Sydney: Educology Research Associates.

Ameh, Catherine Onyeka (1997): "The Challenges to Effective Teaching of Secondary School Science and Technology Subjects in Nigeria: An Educology of Teacher Preparation," *International Journal of Educology*, Vol. 11, No. 1, pp. 45-64. Sydney: Educology Research Associates.

Ameh, Catherine Onyeka (2002): "Harmful Traditional Practices in Nigeria and Measures for Eradication: An Educology of Home Education," *International Journal of Educology*, Vol. 16, No. 1, pp. 1-10. Sydney: Educology Research Associates.

Anegbe, Catherine Onyeka and Dabit, S. I. (1996): "The Need for an Education Program Which Contributes to the Implementation of National Population Control in Nigeria: An Educology of Social and Economic Policies," *International Journal of Educology*, Vol. 10, No. 2, pp. 144-158. Sydney: Educology Research Associates.

Apple, Michael and Beane, James A. (Eds.) (2007): *Democratic Schools: Lessons in Powerful Education.* Second Edition. Portsmouth, New Hampshire: Heinemann.

Axtelle, George (1975): *George E. Axtelle Papers, 1924-1974.* Carbondale, Illinois: University Archives, Southern Illinois University. http://archives.lib.siu.edu/?p=collections/findingaid &id=456&q=...&rootcontentid=5557

Bagley, William C. (1934): *Education and the Emergent Man: A Theory of Education with Particular Application to Public Education in the United States.* Nelson Education Series. New York: T. Nelson and Sons.

Barnhart, Clarence L. (Ed.) (1975): *World Book Dictionary.* Vol. I. Chicago: Field Enterprises Educational Corporation.

Barr, Stringfellow (1962): *The Pilgrimage of Western Man.* New York: J.B. Lippincott Company.

Bauer, Norman J. (1988): *Foundational Studies as a New Liberal Art Form: Educology.* Washington, D.C., ERIC Clearinghouse. Paper presented at the Annual Convention of the American Educational Studies Association (Toronto, Canada, November 2, 1988).

Bayles, Ernest (1960): *Democratic Educational Theory.* New York: Harper and Brothers, Publishers.

Bayles, Ernest (1966): *Pragmatism in Education.* New York: Harper and Row.

Becker, Wesley C. and Engelmann, Siegfried (Winter, 1995-6): "Sponsor Findings from Project Follow Through," *Effective School Practices*, Vol. 15, No. 1. Eugene, Oregon: Association for Direct Instruction (ADI).

Becker, Wesley C.; Engelmann, Siegfried; and Thomas, Don R. (1971): *Teaching: A Course in Applied Psychology.* Chicago, Illinois: Science Research Associates.

Becker, Wesley C.; Engelmann, Siegfried; and Thomas, Don R. (1975a): *Teaching Vol. 1: A Modular Revision of Teaching.* Chicago, Illinois: Science Research Associates.

Becker, Wesley C.; Engelmann, Siegfried; and Thomas, Don R. (1975b): *Teaching Vol. 2: Cognitive Learning and Instruction.* Chicago: Science Research Associates.

Benjamin, Harold (1939, 2004): *The Saber-Tooth Curriculum.* By J. Abner Peddiwell. Forward by Harold Benjamin. Introduction by John Goodlad. New York: McGraw-Hill.

Bereiter, Carl (Winter, 1995-6): "A Constructive Look at Follow Through Results," *Effective School Practices*, Vol. 15, No. 1. Eugene, Oregon: Association for Direct Instruction (ADI).

Berkson, Isaac B. (1958): *The Ideal and the Community.* Westport, Connecticut: Greenwood Press.

Bestor, Arthur E. (1953): *Educational Wastelands: The Retreat from Learning in Our Public Schools.* Champaign, Illinois: University of Illinois Press.

Bettelheim, Ruth (10 November, 2010): "Outdated Teaching is Failing Our Children," *USA Today*. http://usatoday30.usatoday.com/ news/opinion/forum/2010-11-10-column10_ST1_N.htm

Biggs, John B. (1975): "Professional Development or Practice," A paper presented to the Annual Conference of the South Pacific Association for Teacher Education, Macquarie University, Sydney, Australia. Cited in "Preface," p. vi, in James E. Christensen (Ed.), *Perspectives on Education as Educology.* Washington, D.C.: University Press of America.

Biggs, John B. (1976): "Educology: Theory of Educational Practice," *Contemporary Educational Psychology,* Vol. 1, pp. 274-284.

Biggs, John B. (1981): "Educology: The Science of Effective Education," in J.E. Christensen (Ed.), *Perspectives on Education as Educology.* Washington, D.C.: University Press of America.

Bloom, Benjamin S. (Ed.) (1956): *Taxonomy of Educational Objectives, The Classification of Educational Goals, Handbook I: Cognitive Domain.* New York: Longman.

Bloom, Benjamin S. (1968): "Learning for Mastery," *Evaluation Comment*, Vol. 1, No. 2, p. 112.

Bloom, B.S.; Hastings, J.T.; and Madaus, G. (1971): *Handbook on Formative and Summative Evaluation of Student Learning.* New York: McGraw-Hill.

Bloom, Benjamin S. (1974): "An Introduction to Mastery Learning Theory," in J.H. Block (Ed.), *Schools, Society, and Mastery Learning.* New York: Holt, Rinehart & Winston.

Bode, Boyd H. (1921): *Fundamentals of Education.* New York: The Macmillan Company.

Bode, Boyd H. (1927): *Modern Educational Theories.* New York: The Macmillan Company.

Bode, Boyd H. (1938): *Progressive Education at the Crossroads.* New York: Newson & Company.

Brady, Laurie (1987): "An Educological Examination of Curriculum Models and Related Variables,"*International Journal of Educology*, Vol. 1, No. 1, pp. 33-44. Sydney: Educology Research Associates.

Brady, Laurie (1988): "An Educology of Teaching Models Approach," *International Journal of Educology*, Vol. 2, No. 1, pp. 67-74. Sydney: Educology Research Associates.

Brady, Laurie (1989): "An Educological Analysis of Curriculum Design,"*International Journal of Educology*, Vol. 3, No. 1, pp. 81-92. Sydney: Educology Research Associates.

Brady, Laurie (1991): "An Educology of School Management: The Professional Development Objectives of School Principals," *International Journal of Educology*, Vol. 5, No.2, pp. 97-107. Sydney: Educology Research Associates.

Brady, Laurie (1995): "Outcome Based Education: Imposing a Model for Curriculum Development,"*International Journal of Educology*, Vol. 9, No. 2, pp. 189-192. Sydney: Educology Research Associates.

Bragg, Raymond B. et al. (May-June, 1933): "Humanist Manifesto." *New Humanist.* Chicago: The Humanist Fellowship. (http://americanhumanist.org/Humanism/Humanist_Manifesto_I)

Brameld, Theodore (1950): *Patterns of Educational Philosophy.* Yonkers on Hudson, NY: World Book.

Brameld, Theodore (1955): *Philosophies of Education in Cultural Perspective.* New York: Holt, Rinehart and Winston.

Brameld, Theodore (1956): *Toward a Reconstructed Philosophy of Education.* New York: Holt, Rinehart and Winston.

Brameld, Theodore (1957): *Cultural Foundations of Education – An Interdisciplinary Approach.* New York: Harper & Brothers.

Brameld, Theodore (1965): *Education as Power.* New York: Holt, Rinehart and Winston.

Breed, Frederick S. (1939): *Education and the New Realism.* New York: The Macmillan Company.

Brezinka, Wolfgang (1981): "Chapter 1: Meta-Theory of Education: European Contributions from an Empirical-Analytic Point of View," in J.E. Christensen (Ed.), *Perspectives on Education as Educology.* Washington, D.C.: University Press of America, pp. 7-26.

Brezinka, Wolfgang (Translated by James Stuart Brice) (1992): *Philosophy of Educational Knowledge: An Introduction to the Foundations of Science of Education, Philosophy of Education and Practical Pedagogics.* Dordrecht: Kluwer Academic Publishers.

Brezinka, Wolfgang (Translated by James Stuart Brice) (1994): *Basic Concepts of Educational Science: Analysis, Critique, Proposals.* New York: University Press of America.

Brezinka, Wolfgang (Translated by James Stuart Brice) (1997): *Educational Aims, Educational Means, Educational Success: Contributions to a System of Science of Education.* Aldershot: Avebury.

Buchanan, Scott (1927): *Possibility.* London: K. Paul, Trench, Trubner & Company Limited.

Buchanan, Scott (1929): *Poetry and Mathematics.* New York: The John Day Company.

Buchanan, Scott (1932: *Symbolic Distance in Relation to Analogy and Fiction.* London: K. Paul, Trench, Trubner & Company Limited.

Buchanan, Scott (1938: *The Doctrine of Signatures: A Defense of Theory in Medicine.* New York: Harcourt Brace and Company.

Buchanan, Scott (1972): *Truth in the Sciences.* Charlottesville, Virginia: University of Virginia Press.

Bruner, Jerome S. (1960): *The Process of Education.* Cambridge, Massachusetts: Harvard University Press.

Bruner, Jerome S. (1971): *The Relevance of Education.* New York, N.Y.: W.W.Norton & Company.

Bruniges, Michele (June, 2005): "What's driving curriculum reform in Australia?" a paper delivered to the Curriculum Corporation Conference, Brisbane. http://www.curriculum.edu.au/verve/_resources/Bruniges_edited.pdf

Burant, Terry; Christensen, Linda; Salas, Kelley Dawson; and Walters, Stephanie (Eds.) (2010): *The New Teacher Book: Finding Purpose, Balance, and Hope During Your First Years in the Classroom.* Second Edition. New York: Rethinking Schools.

Butler, John (1966): *Idealism in Education.* New York: Harper and Row.

Cantor, Jeffrey A. (1992): *Delivering Instruction to Adult Learners.* Toronto: Wall & Emerson.

Carnine, Douglas W.; Silbert, Jerry; Kame'enui, Edward J.; and Tarver, Sarah G. (2009): *Direct Instruction Reading* (5th Edition). Upper Saddle River, New Jersey: Pearson.

Cazden, C.B. (1986): "Classroom Discourse," in M.C. Wittrock (Ed.), *Handbook of Research on Teaching*, Third Edition. New York: Macmillan Publishing Company.

Childs, John L. (1931): *Education and the Philosophy of Experimentalism.* New York: The Century Company.

Childs, John L. (1958): *American Pragmatism and Education.* New York: Henry Holt and Company.

Childs, John L. (1958): *An Assessment of the Experimentalist Educational Theory.* Columbus, Ohio: The College of Education, the Ohio State University.

Christensen, James E. (1975): "Educational Research as Educology," *Australian Educational Researcher* (Australian Association for Research in Education), Vol. 2, No. 4, pp. 18-20.

Christensen, James E. (1977): "A Conversation about Education as Educology, Guest Editorial," *Educational Studies: A Journal of the American Educational Studies Association.* Vol 8, No. 1, pp. v-xii.

Christensen, James E. (1981): *Curriculum, Education, and Educology.* Sydney: Educology Research Associates.

Christensen, James E. (1981): *Education and Human Development: A Study in Educology.* Sydney: Educology Research Associates.

Christensen, James E. (1981): "Chapter 6: Educology and Some Related Concepts," in J.E. Christensen (Ed.), *Perspectives on Education as Educology.* Washington, D.C.: University Press of America, pp. 121-158.

Christensen, James E. (Ed.) (1981): *Perspectives on Education as Educology.* Washington, D.C.: University Press of America

Christensen, James E. (March, 1982): "The Educology of Curriculum". *Collected Original Resources in Education* (Taylor and Francis Group).

Christensen, James E. (23-27 November, 1983): "Cognition, Knowing, and Understanding: Levels, Forms, and Range." *Proceedings of the National Conference of the Australian Association for Research in Education.* Canberra, ACT: AARE.

Christensen, James E. (March, 1986): "Educational Research with an Educological Perspective," A paper presented to the Annual Conference of the American Educational Research Association, Chicago, Mar 31-Apr 4, 1985," *Resources in Education* (ERIC: Education Resources Information Center): Accession Numbers ED 263197, TM 850688.

Christensen, James E. (June, 1986): "Comparative Educology: A Bridging Concept for Comparative Educational Inquiry," A paper presented to the Fifth World Congress of Comparative Education, Paris, 2-6 Jul, 1984, *Resources in Education* (ERIC: Education Resources Information Center): Accession Numbers ED 266542, EA 018220.

Christensen, James E. (Ed.) (1986): *Educology 86: Proceedings of a Conference on Educational Research, Inquiry and Development with an Educological Perspective, Canberra, July 10-12, 1986.* Sydney: Educology Research Associates.

Christensen, James E. (1987): "Education, Educology and Educological Discourse: Theory and Structure for Education and Constructive Action in Education," *International Journal of Educology* , Vol. 1, No. 1, pp. 1-32, Sydney: Educology Research Associates.

Christensen, James E. (1992): "Education for Freedom: A Philosophical Educology,"*International Journal of Educology*, Vol. 6, No. 2, pp. 97-131. Sydney: Educology Research Associates.

Christensen, James E. (2013): *Education, Knowledge and Educology.* Los Gatos, California: Smashwords, an e-book available at http://www.smashwords.com/books/search?query= education+knowledge+educology

Christensen, James E. and Fisher, James E (1978): "An Organizational Theory for Schools of Teacher Education and Faculties of Education," *Australian Journal of Education*, Vol. 22, No. 1, pp. 52-71, Australian Council for Educational Research.

Christensen, James E. and Fisher, James E (1979): *Analytic Philosophy of Education as a Sub-Discipline of Educology: An Introduction to its Techniques and Application.* Washington, D.C.: University Press of America.

Christensen, James E. and Fisher, James E (1981): "Chapter 12: Educology as an Organizational Concept for Schools of Teacher Education, College of Education, and Faculties of Education," in J.E. Christensen (Ed.), *Perspectives on Education as Educology*. Washington, DC: University Press of America, pp. 263-300.

Christensen, James E. and Fisher, James E. (1983): *Organization and Colleges of Education: An Educological Perspective*. Sydney: Educology Research Associates.

Christensen, James E. and Fisher, James E. (1988): "The Need for Educological Research in the Areas of Secondary School Retention Rates, Educational Pathways and Recurrent

Education," *International Journal of Educology*, Vol. 2, No. 2, pp. ix-xii. Sydney: Educology Research Associates.

Christensen, James E. and Fisher, James E. (1989): "Educology and the Educological Perspective," *International Journal of Educology*, Vol. 3, No. 1, pp. ix-xv. Sydney: Educology Research Associates.

Christensen, James E. and Fisher, James E. (1990). "Three Critical Distinctions for Advancing Educology," *International Journal of Educology*, Vol. 4, No. 1, pp. vi-viii. Sydney: Educology Research Associates.

Christensen, James E. and Fisher, James E. (1990): "Educology for Initial Teacher Education and for Professional Development of Practising Teachers - Changing Needs, Changing Demands," *International Journal of Educology*, Vol. 4, No. 2, pp. vi-xvii. Sydney: Educology Research Associates.

Christensen, James E. and Fisher, James E. (1991): "A Challenge for Educologists of Curriculum," *International Journal of Educology*, Vol. 5, No. 1, pp. vi-ix. Sydney: Educology Research Associates.

Christensen, James E. and Fisher, James E. (1991): "An Educology of Values, Goals and Action Plans," *International Journal of Educology*, Vol. 5, No. 2, pp. vi-ix. Sydney: Educology Research Associates.

Christensen, James E. and Fisher, James E. (1992): "The Educology of the Work Place," *International Journal of Educology*, Vol. 6, No. 1, pp. vi-xi. Sydney: Educology Research Associates.

Copperman, Paul (1978): *The Literacy Hoax: The Decline of Reading, Writing and Learning in the Public Schools and What We Can Do about It.* New York: William Morrow & Co.

Counts, George (1930): *The American Road to Culture: Social Interpretation of Education in the United States.* New York: John Day Company.

Counts, George (1932): *Dare the Schools Build a New Social Order?* New York: John Day Company.

Craig, John (2007): "Curriculum Synchronicity: Alignment, Improvement and Accountability," Australian Council for Educational Leaders (ACEL), October 2007. http://www.acel.or.au/conf07/papers/CurriculumSynchronicity

Cross, K. Patricia (1992): *Adults as Learners: Increasing Participation and Facilitating Learning.* San Francisco: Jossey-Bass.

Demiashkevich, Michael J. (1935): *An Introduction the Philosophy of Education.* New York: American Book Company.

Denton, David E (1981): "Chapter 17: A Renewed Call for a Society of Educologists," in James E. Christensen (Ed.), *Perspectives on Education as Educology.* Washington, DC: University Press of America, pp. 375–380.

Dewey, John (1916): *Democracy and Education.* New York: The Macmillan Company.

Doyle, W. (1986): "Classroom Organization and Management," in M.C. Wittrock (Ed.), *Handbook of Research on Teaching,* Third Edition. New York: Macmillan Publishing Company.

Eco, Umberto (1976): *A Theory of Semiotics.* Bloomington, Indiana: Indiana University Press.

Educology Newsletter (April 1, 2009): Vol. 1, No. 1. College of Education, University of Illinois, Chicago Campus. (Retrieved 2009) http://education.uic.edu/newsletter/20090401/

Ehle, Maryann (1986): "Chapter 3: The Educology of Self Perception," in James E. Christensen (Ed.), *Educology 86: Proceedings of a Conference on Educational Research, Inquiry and Development with an Educological Perspective, Canberra, July 10-12, 1986.* Sydney: Educology Research Associates. pp. 34–50.

Elder, Rachel Ann (1971): "Three Educologies." (Mimeographed.) A paper written for Far West Laboratory for Educational Research and Development. San Francisco, California. Cited in "Preface," p. vi, in James E. Christensen (Ed.), *Perspectives on Education as Educology.* Washington, D.C.: University Press of America.

Engelmann, Siegfried (1969): *DISTAR Reading: Teacher's Guide with Directions for Student Materials.* Chicago: Science Research Associates.

Engelmann, Siegfried (1992): *War Against the Schools' Academic Child Abuse.* Portland, Oregon: Halcyon House.

Engelmann, Siegfried (2007): *Teaching Needy Kids in our Backward System.* Eugene, Oregon: ADI Press.

Ennis, Robert T. (1969): *Logic in Teaching.* Englewood Cliffs, New Jersey: Prentice-Hall, Inc.

Fenstermacher, Gary D. and Soltis, Jonas F., with contributions from Matthew N. Sanger (2009): *Approaches to Teaching.* Fifth Edition. Thinking about Education Series. New York: Teachers College Press.

Fisher, James E. (1981): "Chapter 13: The Concept of Educology and the Classification System used in *Educational Studies,*" in J.E. Christensen (Ed.), *Perspectives on Education as Educology.* Washington, DC: University Press of America, pp. 301–327.

Fisher, James E. (1986): "Chapter 4: Toward a Theory of Language for Educology and Education," in J.E. Christensen (Ed.), *Educology 86: Proceedings of a Conference on Educational Research, Inquiry and Development with an Educological Perspective, Canberra, July 10-12, 1986.* Sydney: Educology Research Associates, pp. 51–72.

Fisher, James E. (1991): "The Territory of Educology," *International Journal of Educology*, Vol. 5, No. 1, pp. 18-45. Sydney: Educology Research Associates.

Fisher, James E. (1992): "Mapping Observations about Education in the Home: An Educology of Home," *International Journal of Educology*, Vol. 6, No. 1, pp. 53-93. Sydney: Educology Research Associates.

Fisher, James E. (1992): "An Introduction to Home Educology and Home Education in the USA, Part I," *International Journal of Educology*, Vol. 6, No. 2, pp. 170-207. Sydney: Educology Research Associates.

Fisher, James E. (1993): "An Introduction to Home Educology and Home Education in the USA, Part II," *International Journal of Educology*, Vol. 7, No. 2, pp. 139-196. Sydney: Educology Research Associates.

Fisher, James E. (1996): "The Domain of Educology," *International Journal of Educology*, Vol. 10, No. 1, pp. 66-143. Sydney: Educology Research Associates.

Fisher, James E. (1998-2001): "An Outlined Introduction to the Universal and Unifying Experiential Research Methodology in the Domain of Educology: The Discipline of Educology Introduced to Graduate Students in Educology," *International*

Journal of Educology, Vol. 12-15, pp. 59-76. Sydney: Educology Research Associates.

Fisher, James E. (1998-2001): "Educology Contributing to the Development of the New Democracy in Lithuania," *International Journal of Educology*, Vol. 12-15, pp. 77-79. Sydney: Educology Research Associates.

Fisher, James E. (2001): "Contributing Paper 1.1 in History and Philosophy of Educology, Part I (A paper used as the basis for a series of seven lectures to faculty and doctoral students in educology at Vytautas Magnus University (VMU) in December, 2001)," *Pedagogika*. Kaunus, Lithuania: Vytauto Didziojo universiteto leidykla.

Fisher, James E. (2003): "A General Sketch of a Semiotically Understood and Oriented Organic Experiential Philosophy of Educology for Developing Democracies in the World," *International Journal of Educology*, Vol. 17, No. 1&2, pp. 1-40. Sydney: Educology Research Associates.

Fisher, James E. and Reinhart, Marian (1981): "Chapter 14: Educology and the Teaching of Mathematics," in James E. Christensen (Ed.), *Perspectives on Education as Educology*. Washington, DC: University Press of America. pp. 328–340.

Freire, Paulo (Translated by Myra Berman Ramos) (1970, 2007): *Pedagogy of the Oppressed.* 30th Anniversary Edition. New York: The Continuum International Publishing Group.

Gagné, R.M. (1977): *The Conditions of Learning.* Third Edition. New York: Holt, Rinehart and Winston.

Gagné, R.M.; Briggs, L.; & Wager, W. (1992). *Principles of Instructional Design.* Fourth Edition. Fort Worth, Texas: HBJ College Publishers.

Giroux, Henry A. and Purpel, David E. (Eds.) 1983: *The Hidden Curriculum and Moral Education: Deception or Discovery?* Berkeley, California: McCutchan Publishing Corporation.

Gorovitz, Samuel and Williams, Ron G. (1969): *Philosophical Analysis.* 2nd Edition. New York: Random House.

Green, Thomas F. (1971): *The Activities of Teaching.* New York: McGraw-Hill.

Gribble, James (1969): *Introduction to Philosophy of Education.* Boston: Allyn and Bacon.

Gronlund, N.E. (1991): *How to Write and Use Instructional Objectives*. Fourth Edition. New York, NY: Macmillan.

Grossen, Bonnie (Winter, 1995-6): "The Story Behind Project Follow Through," *Effective School Practices*, Vol. 15, No. 1. Eugene, Oregon: Association for Direct Instruction (ADI).

Hall, Edward T. (1959): *The Silent Language.* Garden City, N.J.: Doubleday and Co.

Harding, L.W. (Ed.) (1951): *Anthology in Educology*. Dubuque, Iowa: Wm. C. Brown, Co

Harding, L.W. (Ed.) (1956): *Essays in Educology*. Dubuque, Iowa: Wm. C. Brown, Co

Harding, L.W. (Ed.) (1964): *More Essays in Educology*. Columbus, Ohio: Association for the Study of Educology.

Harding, L.W. (Ed.) (1965): *Educology: The Fourth Collection*. Columbus, Ohio: Association for the Study of Educology.

Harel, Idit and Papert, Seymour (Ed.) (1991): *Constructionism*. Norwood, New Jersey: Ablex Publishing.

Hiatt, Diana Buell (1986): "Chapter 7: Curricular Decision Making with an Educological Perspective: Theory into Practice," in James E. Christensen (Ed.), *Educology 86: Proceedings of a Conference on Educational Research, Inquiry and Development with an Educological Perspective, Canberra, July 10-12, 1986*. Sydney: Educology Research Associates.

Hirsch, Eric D. (1987): *Cultural Literacy: What Every American Needs to Know.* Boston: Houghton Mifflin Company.

Hirsch, Eric D. (1996): *The Schools We Need and Why We Don't Have Them.* New York: Doubleday.

Hirsch, Eric D. (2006): *The Knowledge Deficit: Closing the Shocking Education Gap for American Children.* New York: Houghton Mifflin Company.

Hirst, Paul H. (1965): "Liberal Education and the Nature of Knowledge," in R.D Archambault (Ed.), *Philosophical Analysis and Education.* London: Routledge and Kegan Paul.

Hirst, Paul H. (1969): "The Logic of the Curriculum," *Journal of Curriculum Studies*, Vol. 1, No. 2, pp. 142-158.

Hirst, Paul H. (1974): *Knowledge and the Curriculum.* London: Routledge and Kegan Paul.

Hirst, Paul H. and Peters, R. S. (1970): *The Logic of Education.* London: Routledge and Kegan Paul.

Holt, John (1964): *How Children Fail.* New York: Dell
Publishing Company.

Holt, John (1967): *How Children Learn.* New York: Pitman
Publishing Company.

Hospers, John (1953): *An Introduction to Philosophical Analysis.*
Englewood Cliffs, New Jersey: Prentice-Hall, Inc.

Hullfish, H. Gordon (1960): *Toward a Democratic Education.*
Columbus, Ohio: The College of Education, the Ohio State
University.

Hullfish, H. Gordon (1961): *Problems of Educational Freedom.*
Bloomington, Indiana: Division of Research and Field
Services, Indiana University.

Hullfish, H. Gordon and Smith, Philip G. (1968): *Reflective
Thinking: The Method of Education.* New York: Dodd, Mead
and Company.

Hunter, Madeline (1994): *Mastery Teaching: Increasing
Instructional Effectiveness in Elementary and Second Schools,
Colleges, and Universities.* Thousand Oaks, California: Sage
Publications.

Hutchins, Robert Maynard (1936): *The Higher Learning in
America.* New Haven, Connecticut: Yale University Press.

Hutchins, Robert Maynard (1943): *Education for Freedom.*
Baton Rouge, Louisiana: Louisiana State University Press.

Hutchins, Robert Maynard (1952): *The Great Conversation: The
Substance of a Liberal Education, Vol. 1.* Chicago, Illinois:
Encyclopaedia Britannica, Inc.

Hutchins, Robert Maynard (1953): *The University of Utopia.*
Chicago: The University of Chicago Press.

**Hutchins, Robert Maynard and Adler, Mortimer J. (Eds.)
(1961):** *The Great Ideas Today.* Chicago: Encyclopaedia
Britannica.

***International Journal of Educology,* (1987)**: Vol. 1, No. 1.
Sydney: Educology Research Associates. ISSN 08180563.

Jackson, Philip W. (1968): *Life in Classrooms.* New York:
Teachers College Press.

Johnson, David W. and Johnson, Roger T. (1975): *Learning
Together and Alone: Cooperation, Competition, and
Individualization.* Englewood Cliffs, New Jersey: Prentice
Hall.

Johnson, David W.; Johnson, Roger T.; and Holubec, Edythe. (2008): *Cooperation in the Classroom*, Eighth Edition. Edina, Minnesota: Interaction Book Company.

Joyce, Bruce and Weil, Marsha (2011): *Models of Teaching.* Eighth Edition. Upper Saddle River, New Jersey: Pearson Publishing.

Kandel, Isaac L. (1930): *History of Secondary Education.* Boston: Houghton Mifflin.

Kandel, Isaac L. (1933): *Comparative Education.* Boston: Houghton Mifflin.

Kandel, Isaac L. (1943): *The Cult of Uncertainty.* New York: Macmillan.

Kandel, Isaac L. (1955): *The New Era in Education.* Boston: Houghton Mifflin.

Kilpatrick, William Heard (1918): *The Project Method: The Use of the Purposeful Act in the Educative Process.* New York: Teachers College, Columbia University.

Kilpatrick, William Heard (1949): *Modern Education: Its Proper Work.* New York: John Dewey Society.

Kilpatrick, William Heard (1951): *Philosophy of Education.* New York: Macmillan.

Kneller, George F. (1964): *Introduction to the Philosophy of Education.* New York: John Wiley & Sons.

Kneller, George F. (1966): *Logic and Language of Education.* New York: John Wiley & Sons.

Knowles, Malcolm S. (1970): *The Modern Practice of Adult Education: Andragogy Versus Pedagogy.* New York: Association Press.

Koerner, James D. (1963): *The Miseducation of American Teachers.* Boston: Houghton Mifflin.

Koerner, James E. (1968: *Reform in Education: England and the United States.* New York: Delacorte Press

Kohl, Herbert (1967): *36 Children.* New York: New American Library.

Kohl, Herbert (1969): *The Open Classroom.* New York: A New York Review Book.

Kohlberg, L. (1963): "The Development of Children's Orientations Toward a Moral Order: Sequence in the Development of Moral Thought," *Vita Humana*, 6:11-33.

Kohlberg, L. (1964): "Development of Moral Character and Ideology," in M.L. Hoffman and L.W. Hoffman (Eds.), *Review of Child Development Research*, Vol. 1. New York: Russell Sage Press.

Kotarbiński, Tadeusz (Translated from the Polish by Olgierd Wojtasiewicz) (1965): *Praxiology; An Introduction to the Sciences of Efficient Action.* London: Pergamon Press.

Krathwohl, D.R., et al. (1956): *Taxonomy o f Educational Objectives: The Classification of Educational Goals: Handbook II: Affective Domain.* New York: David McKay Company, Inc.

Kridel, Craig (Ed.) (2010): *Encyclopedia of Curriculum Studies. Volume 1.* New York: Sage Publications.

Kurtz, Paul and Wilson, Edwin H. (September-October, 1973): "Humanist Manifesto II." *The Humanist.* Washington, D.C.: American Humanist Association. (http://americanhumanist.org/ Humanism/Humanist_Manifesto_II)

Lehrer, K. and Paxon, Jr., T. (April, 1968): "Knowledge: Undefeated Justified True Belief," *Journal of Philosophy*, Vol LXVI, No. 8.

Livingstone, Richard (1916): *A Defence of Classical Education.* London: Macmillan and Company.

Livingstone, Richard (1941): *The Future in Education.* Cambridge: Cambridge University Press.

Levine, David; Lowe, Robert; Peterson, Robert W.; and Tenorio, Rita (Eds.) (1995): *Rethinking Schools: An Agenda for Change.* New York: The New Press.

Lucas, George (1999?): *A Word from George Lucas: Edutopia's Role in Education.* Edutopia.org. http://www.edutopia.org/ word- from-george-lucas-edutopias-role-in-education

Luke, Allan (1999): "Education 2010 and new times: Why equity and social justice still matter, but differently," a paper presented to the Education Queensland Online Conference, October 20, 1999.

Maccia, George (1967): "Science and Science of Education," in George F. Kneller (Ed.), *Foundations of Education, Second Edition.* New York: John Wiley & Sons.

Maccia, George (September, 1973a): "Contributions of Epistemology Toward a Science of Education." A paper presented to the International Congress of the International Association for the Advancement of Educational Research. Paris: The University of Paris.

Maccia, George (September, 1973b): "Epistemological Considerations of Educational Objectives." A paper presented to the Philosophy of Education Section of the XVth World Congress of Philosophy. Varna, Bulgaria.

Maccia, George (November, 1973c): "Educological Epistemology." A paper presented to the 1973 annual meeting of the Ohio Valley Philosophy of Education Society. Cincinnati, Ohio.

Maccia, George (21-22 October, 1977): "Education for Humanity." A paper presented to a Symposium on Philosophy of Education, the Philosophical Society. Fredonia, New York: State University of New York.

Maccia, George (1981): "Chapter 2: The Genesis of Educology," in James E. Christensen (Ed.), *Perspectives on Education as Educology*. Washington, DC: University Press of America, pp. 27–50.

Maccia, George (1991): "A Philosophical Educology: Education and Dialectics of Person,"*International Journal of Educology*, Vol. 5, No. 1, pp. 71-84. Sydney: Educology Research Associates.

Maccia, George (1992): "Education for Humanity: A Philosophical Educology," *International Journal of Educology*, Vol. 6, No. 1, pp. 1-10. Sydney: Educology Research Associates.

Magee, John B. (1971): *Philosophical Analysis in Education.* New York: Harper & Row, Publishers.

Margaret, K.T. (1999): *The Open Classroom: A Journey through Education.* Hyderabad, India: Orient Longman Private Limited.

Mager, Robert (1990): *Preparing Instructional Objectives.* London: Kogan Page Ltd.

Marzano, Robert J. and Pickering, Debra J. with Daisy E. Aredondo, Guy J. Blackburn, Ronald S. Brandt, Cerylle A. Moffett, Diane E. Paynter, Jane E. Pollock and Jo Sue Whisler (1997): *Dimensions of Learning: Teacher's Manual.* Second Edition. Alexandria, Virginia: Association for Supervision and Curriculum Development (ASCD) and

Aurora, Colorado: Mid-continent Regional Educational
Laboratory (McREL).

**Marzano, Robert J. and Pickering, Debra J. with Daisy E.
Aredondo, Guy J. Blackburn, Ronald S. Brandt, Cerylle A.
Moffett, Diane E. Paynter, Jane E. Pollock and Jo Sue
Whisler (1997):** *Dimensions of Learning: Trainer's Manual.*
Second Edition. Alexandria, Virginia: Association for
Supervision and Curriculum Development (ASCD) and
Aurora, Colorado: Mid-continent Regional Educational
Laboratory (McREL).

McKeon, R. (Ed.) (1941): *The Basic Works of Aristotle.* New
York: Random House.

McManaman, Angela (October 4, 2012): "New Principal
Discusses Future, Focus, Traditions of La Escuela Fratney,"
schoolmattersMKE.com Milwaukee, Wisconsin.
http://schoolmattersmke.com/new-principal-discusses-future-
focus-traditions-of-la-escuela-fratney/

Mill, John Stuart (1846): *A System of Logic*, Book VI, Chapter
III, Paragraph 4.

Monshouwer, Anton (1981a): "Chapter 3: The Formal Structure
of an Emerging Science of Education, Part I: Some Opinions
about the Scientific Status of a Science of Education," in James
E. Christensen (Ed.), *Perspectives on Education as Educology.*
Washington, DC: University Press of America, pp. 51–86.

Monshouwer, Anton (1981b): "Chapter 7: The Formal Structure
of an Emerging Science of Education, Part II: The Concept of
Science," in James E. Christensen (Ed.), *Perspectives on
Education as Educology.* Washington, DC: University Press of
America, pp. 159–196.

Montessori, Maria (1947a, 1989) *Education for a New World.*
The Clio Montessori Series. Santa Barbara, California: ABC
CLIO.

Montessori, Maria (1947b, 1989) *To Educate the Human
Potential.* The Clio Montessori Series. Santa Barbara,
California: ABC CLIO.

Montessori, Maria (1949): *The Absorbent Mind.* Adyar, India:
The Theosophical Publishing House.

Morrison, Henry C. (1924): *The Teaching Technique of the
Secondary School.* Ann Arbor, Michigan: Edwrds Brothers.

Morrison, Henry C. (1926): *The Practice of Teaching in the Secondary School.* Chicago: The University of Chicago Press.

Morrison, Henry C. (1943): *American Schools: A Critical Study of Our School System.* Chicago: The University of Chicago Press.

Neff, Frederick (1966): *Philosophy and American Education.* New York: The Center for Applied Research in Education, Inc.

Nel, Berdine F (1980): *From Fundamental Pedagogics to Educology: A Solution or a Substitution.* Durban, Natal: South African Association for Advancement of Education.

Null, J. Wesley (2003): *A Disciplined Progressive Educator: The Life and Career of William Chandler Bagley.* New York: Peter Lang.

Page, Bill (October, 2008): "Curriculum Happens," *teachers.net*, Vol 5, No 10. http://www.teachers.net/gazette/OCT08/page/

Papert, Seymour (2001): *Project-Based Learning.* Edutopia Staff. http://www.edutopia.org/seymour-papert-project-based-learning

Pastuovic, Nikola (1995): "The Science(s) of Adult Education,". *International Journal of Lifelong Education,* Vol. 14, No. 1, pp. 273.291. Routledge Taylor & Francis Group.

Perry, James F (1981): "Chapter 9: Praxiology of Education as a Branch of Educology," in James E. Christensen (Ed.), *Perspectives on Education as Educology.* Washington, DC: University Press of America. pp. 213–222.

Perry, James F (1986): "Chapter 11: What Works for What, and Why: Praxiology of Education," in James E. Christensen (Ed.), *Educology 86: Proceedings of a Conference on Educational Research, Inquiry and Development with an Educological Perspective, Canberra, July 10-12, 1986.* Sydney: Educology Research Associates. pp. 163–182.

Peterson, Bob (2007): "La Escuela Fratney: A Journey Toward Democracy," in Michael Apple and James A. Beane (Eds.), *Democratic Schools: Lessons in Powerful Education.* Second Edition. Portsmouth, New Hampshire: Heinemann.

Piaget, Jean (1926): *The Language and Thought of the Child.* London: Routledge & Kegan.

Piaget, Jean (1948): *The Moral Judgment of the Child.* New York: Free Press.

Piaget, Jean (1953): *The Origin of Intelligence in the Child.* New Fetter Lane, New York: Routledge & Kegan Paul.

Piaget, Jean (1971): "The Theory of Stages in Cognitive Development," in D. Green, M. Ford and G. Flamer (Eds.), *Measurement and Piaget.* New York: McGraw-Hill, pp. 1-11.

Pietig, Jeane (1975): "Is Foundations of Education a Discipline?" *Educational Studies*, Vol. 6, No. 1/2, pp. 1-2.

Pool, Theo Oudkerk (1986): "Chapter 12: Teacher Education in an Educological Perspective," in James E. Christensen (Ed.), *Educology 86: Proceedings of a Conference on Educational Research, Inquiry and Development with an Educological Perspective, Canberra, July 10-12, 1986.* Sydney: Educology Research Associates, pp. 182–220.

Pukelis, Kestutis and Savickiene, Izabela (2005): "The Challenge of Establishing a Common Set of Terms for Discourse, Inquiry, and Research in Educational Science: An Analytically Oriented Philosophy of Educology," *International Journal of Educology.* Educology Research Associates. Lithuanian Special Issue: pp.14–27.

Qvarsell, Birgitta (2003): "Cultures as a Construction for Educational Research," in Birgitta Qvarsell and Christoph Wulf (Ed.), *Culture and Education. European Studies in Education,* Volume 16. Munster, Germany: Waxman, pp. 13–24.

Raup, R. Bruce; Axtelle, George; Benne, Kenneth D.; and Smith, B. Othanel (1950): *The Improvement of Practical Intelligence: The Central Task of Education.* New York: Harper.and Brothers. Originally published as the 28th yearbook of the National Society of College Teachers of Education under the title, *The Discipline of Practical Judgment in a Democratic Society*, 1943.

Reigeluth, Charles M. and Merrill, M. David (1981): "Chapter 10: Instructional Science and Technology: Their Context within Educology and Some Ideas for Their Future Development," in James E. Christensen (Ed.), *Perspectives on Education as Educology.* Washington, DC: University Press of America. pp. 223–250.

"Report of the Task Force on Academic Standards Guidelines for Professional Academic Instruction in Foundations of

Education, Educational Studies and Education Policy Studies," (1977): *American Educational Studies Association Newsletter*, Vol. 3, No. 3, pp. 2-6.

Rickover, Hyman G. (1959): *Education and Freedom.* Boston: E.P. Dutton.

Rickover, Hyman G. (1962): *Swiss Schools and Ours: Why Theirs are Better.* New York: Little, Brown and Company.

Rickover, Hyman G. (1963): *American Education, a National Failure; The Problem of Our Schools and What We Can Learn from England.* Boston: E.P. Dutton.

Robertson, Richard (1954): *Definition.* Oxford: Oxford University Press.

Rogers, Carl (1969): *Freedom to Learn: A View of What Education Might Become.* First Edition. Columbus, Ohio: Charles Merrill.

Rosenshine, Barak and Stevens, Robert (1986): "Chapter 13: Teaching Functions," in Merlin C. Wittrock (Ed.), *Handbook of Research on Teaching* (Third Edition): A Project of the American Educational Research Association. New York, N.Y.: Macmillan Publishing Company, pp. 376-391.

Rugg, Harold (1931): *Culture and Education in America.* New York: Harcourt, Brace.

Ryle, Gilbert (1949): *The Concept of Mind.* New York: Barnes and Noble.

Scheffler, Israel (1960): *The Language of Education.* Springfield, Illinois: Charles C. Thomas, Co.

Scriven, Michael (1967): "The Methodology of Evaluation," in R.W. Tyler, R.M. Gagné & M. Scriven (Eds.), *Perspectives of Curriculum Evaluation*, pp. 39-83. American Educational Research Association (AERA) Monograph Series on Curriculum Evaluation, No. 1. Chicago: Rand-McNally.

Scriven, Michael (1991): *Evaluation Thesaurus.* Fourth Edition. Thousand Oaks, California: Sage Publications, Inc.

Short, Edmund C. (1981): "Chapter 16: Analysis of Educology and Educological Inquiry," in James E. Christensen (Ed.), *Perspectives on Education as Educology.* Washington, DC: University Press of America, pp. 351–374.

Sizer, Theodore R. (1984): *Horace's Compromise: The Dilemma of the American High School.* Boston: Houghton Mifflin Company.

Sizer, Theodore R. (1992): *Horace's School: Redesigning the American High School.* Boston: Houghton Mifflin Company.

Sizer, Theodore R. (1997): *Horace's Hope: What Works for the American High School.* Boston: Houghton Mifflin Company.

Slavin, R.E.; Madden, N.A.; Dolan, L.J.; Wasik, B.A.; Ross, S.; Smith, L.; and Dianda, M. (1996): "Success for All: A Summary of Research," *Journal of Education for Students Placed at Risk,* Vol. 1, No. 1, pp. 41-76.

Smith, B. Othanel and Robert H. Ennis (1961): *Language and Concepts in Education.* Chicago: Rand McNally and Co.

Smith, B. Othanel and Meux, Milton O. (1960): *A Study of the Logic of Teaching.* Urbana, Illinois: Bureau of Educational Research, College of Education, University of Illinois.

Smith, B. Othanel; Shores, J. Harlan; and Stanley, William O. (1951): *Fundamentals of Curriculum Development.* New York: World Book Company.

Smith, B. Othanel; Stanley, William O.; and Shores, J. Harlan (1950): *Social Diagnosis for Education.* New York: World Book Company.

Smith, Mortimer B. (1954): *The Diminished Mind.* Chicago, Illinois: The Henry Regnery Company.

Snyder, Benson R. (1971): *The Hidden Curriculum.* New York: Alfred A. Knopf.

Steiner Maccia, Elizabeth (1964): "Logic of Education and Educatology: Dimensions of Philosophy of Education," *Proceedings of the Philosophy of Education Society.* Lawrence, Kansas: Philosophy of Education Society.

Steiner Maccia, Elizabeth (Sep 1970): "Towards Educational Theorizing without Mistake," *Studies in Philosophy and Education,* Vol. 7, No. 2, pp. 154-157.

Steiner [Maccia], Elizabeth (1972): "The Non-Identity of Philosophy and Theory of Education," in John Martin Rich (Ed.), *Readings in the Philosophy of Education, Second Edition.* Belmont, California: Wadsworth Publishing Company.

Steiner [Maccia], Elizabeth (1977): "Educology: Its Origins and Future," A paper presented to the Annual Meeting of the

American Educational Research Association, New York, N.Y., Apr 3-8, 1977. *Resources in Education* (ERIC: Education Resources Information Center): Accession Numbers ED 141201.

Steiner [Maccia], Elizabeth (1978): *Logical and Conceptual Analytic Techniques for Educational Researchers.* Washington, DC: University Press of America.

Steiner [Maccia], Elizabeth (1981a): *Educology of the Free.* New York: Philosophical Library.

Steiner [Maccia], Elizabeth (1981b): "Chapter 4: Logic of Education and of Educatology: Dimensions of Philosophy of Education," in James. E. Christensen (Ed.), *Perspectives on Education as Educology.* Washington, DC: University Press of America. pp. 87–100.

Steiner [Maccia], Elizabeth (1981c): "Chapter 5: Educology: Thirteen Years Later," in James E. Christensen (Ed.), *Perspectives on Education as Educology.* Washington, DC: University Press of America. pp. 101–120.

Steiner [Maccia], Elizabeth (1986): "Chapter 13: Crisis in Educology," in James E. Christensen (Ed.), *Educology 86: Proceedings of a Conference on Educational Research, Inquiry and Development with an Educological Perspective, Canberra, July 10-12, 1986.* Sydney: Educology Research Associates, pp. 221–228.

Stones, Edgar. (1979): *Psychopedagogy: Psychological Theory and the Practice of Teaching.* London: Methuen.

Sundahl, Deborah (2004): *Better Sex Video.* Knowle, West Midlands, UK: Isis Media.

Taba, Hilda (1962): *Curriculum Development; Theory and Practice.* New York: Harcourt, Brace & World.

Taba, Hilda (1966): *Teaching Strategies and Cognitive Functioning in Elementary School Children.* Cooperative Research Project 2404. San Fancisco, California: San Francisco State College.

Taylor, Paul W. (1961): *Normative Discourse.* Englewood Cliffs, N.J.: Prentice-Hall.

Tenorio, Rita (2004): "Curriculum Is Everything That Happens," in Kelley Dawson Salas and Rita Tenorio (Eds.), *The New Teacher Book: Finding Purpose, Balance, and Hope During*

Your First Years in the Classroom. First Edition. Milwaukee, Wisconsin: Rethinking Schools.

Tenorio, Rita (2010): "What can I do when a student makes a racist or sexist remark?" in Terry Burant, Linda Christensen, Kelley Dawson Salas and Stephanie Walters (Eds.), *The New Teacher Book: Finding Purpose, Balance, and Hope During Your First Years in the Classroom.* Second Edition. New York: Rethinking Schools.

Thayer, V.T. (1928): *The Passing of the Recitation.* Boston, Massachusetts: D.C. Heath.

Thayer, V.T. (1944): *American Education under Fire.* New York: Harper and Brothers.

Thayer, V.T. (1954): *Public Education and its Critics.* New York: The Macmillan Company.

Thayer, V.T. (1965): *Formative Ideas in American Education: From the Colonial Period to the Present.* New York: Dodd, Mead & Company.

Thomas, Lawrence G. (Ed.) (1972): *Philosophical Redirection of Educational Research.* Chicago, Illinois: National Society of the Study of Education. University of Chicago Press.

Trumbo, Dalton (1939): *Johnny Got His Gun.* Philadelphia: J.B. Lippincott & Co.

Tyler, Ralph (1949): *Basic Principles of Curriulum and Instruction.* Chicago, Illinois: University of Chicago Press.

Van Doren, Mark (1943): *Liberal Education.* New York: Henry Holt and Company.

Vygotsky, Lev S. (Edited by Alex Kozulin) (1934, 1986): *Thought and Language.* Revised Edition. Cambridge, Massachusetts: Massachusetts Institute of Technology.

Walton, John (1981): "Chapter 15: Educology: An Academic Discipline," in James E. Christensen (Ed.), *Perspectives on Education as Educology.* Washington, DC: University Press of America. pp. 341–350.

Wilson, John (1969): *Language and the Pursuit of Truth.* Cambridge: Cambridge University Press.

Wilson, John (1971): *Thinking with Concepts.* Cambridge: Cambridge University Press.

End

About the Author

James E. Christensen completed his BA in history at the University of California, Berkeley, 1963. He subsequently completed his California Secondary Teaching Credential and taught high school in Kenya from 1964 to 1966 as part of the United States Agency for International Development (USAID) Teachers for East Africa Project (TEA). He returned to the USA and taught at Fountain Valley High School in the Huntington Beach High School District in California from 1966 to 1969. During that time he also completed his MA in history at California State College (now California State University), Long Beach. In 1972, he completed his PhD in education (i.e. educology) at the University of California, Los Angeles, and took up his first university teaching appointment as an Assistant Professor at Southern Illinois University, Carbondale, where he taught philosophy of education (i.e. philosophical educology) and comparative education (i.e. comparative educology, or the educology of societies and cultures). In 1974, he emigrated to Australia. From 1974 to 1989, he taught the educology of curriculum, instructional methods and assessment & evaluation at Charles Sturt University, Wagga Wagga, NSW, in the School of Education. While on study leave from CSU in 1979, he taught at Colgate University, Hamilton, New York (in comparative educology), and in 1991, he taught at Newcastle University, Australia (in the educology of society). In 1987, he founded the *International Journal of Educology*, and from 1987 to 2003, he served as co-editor (with James E. Fisher) of the *IJE*. In 1992, he left university teaching to work in private enterprise. His lifelong research interests have focused on the questions of whether knowledge about education is possible, if so, what kinds of knowledge are possible, how can that knowledge be formed and how can it be organized in ways which are useful and fruitful for those who want to understand the educational process and take constructive action in improving education.

Connect with James E. Christensen online at:

educologist@gmail.com
http://www.jamesechristensen.com
http://www.facebook.com/JamesEChristensen

Other Publications by the Author

Other e-Books by the Author

***Education, Knowledge and Educology* (2013):** Kindle Direct Publishing. This e-book addresses the questions of:
(1) What is education?
(2) What is knowledge about education?
(3) How can knowledge about education be organized in ways so that it can be used fruitfully to take rational action in the educational process to pursue and achieve worthwhile intentions and purposes?

This book is available as an e-book and paperback at Amazon.com and other retail outlets.

Books

Christensen, James E. (1981): *Curriculum, Education, and Educology.* Sydney: Educology Research Associates. ISBN 094978401X

Christensen, James E. (1981): *Education and Human Development: A Study in Educology.* Sydney: Educology Research Associates. ISBN 0949784001

Christensen, James E. (Ed.) (1981): *Perspectives on Education as Educology.* Washington, D.C.: University Press of America ISBN 0819113934

Christensen, James E. (Ed.) (1986): *Educology 86: Proceedings of a Conference on Educational Research, Inquiry and Development with an Educological Perspective, Canberra, July 10-12, 1986.* Sydney: Educology Research Associates. ISBN 0949784052

Christensen, James E. and Fisher, James E. (1979): *Analytic Philosophy of Education as a Sub-Discipline of Educology: An Introduction to its Techniques and Application.* Washington, D.C.: University Press of America. ISBN 0819108022

Christensen, James E. and Fisher, James E. (1983): *Organization and Colleges of Education: An Educological Perspective.* Sydney: Educology Research Associates. ISBN 0949784028

Articles

Christensen, James E. (1975): "Educational Research as Educology," *Australian Educational Researcher* (Australian Association for Research in Education), Vol. 2, No. 4, pp. 18-20. ISSN 03116999

Christensen, James E. (1977): "A Conversation about Education as Educology, Guest Editorial," *Educational Studies: A Journal of the American Educational Studies Association.* Vol 8, No. 1, pp. v-xii. ISSN 0031946

Christensen, James E. (1981): "Chapter 6: Educology and Some Related Concepts," in J.E. Christensen (Ed.), *Perspectives on Education as Educology.* Washington, D.C.: University Press of America, pp. 121-158. ISBN 0819113934

Christensen, James E. (March, 1982): "The Educology of Curriculum". *Collected Original Resources in Education* (Taylor and Francis Group). ISSN 03086909

Christensen, James E. (23-27 November, 1983): "Cognition, Knowing, and Understanding: Levels, Forms, and Range." *Proceedings of the National Conference of the Australian Association for Research in Education.* Canberra, ACT: AARE.

Christensen, James E. (June, 1986): "Comparative Educology: A Bridging Concept for Comparative Educational Inquiry," A paper presented to the Fifth World Congress of Comparative Education, Paris, 2-6 Jul, 1984, *Resources in Education* (ERIC: Education Resources Information Center): Accession Numbers ED 266542, EA 018220.

Christensen, James E. (March, 1986): "Educational Research with an Educological Perspective," A paper presented to the Annual Conference of the American Educational Research Association, Chicago, 31 Mar-4 Apr, 1985,"*Resources in Education* (ERIC: Education Resources Information Center): Accession Numbers ED 263197, TM 850688.

Christensen, James E. (1987): "Education, Educology and Educological Discourse: Theory and Structure for Education and Constructive Action in Education," *International Journal of Educology*, Vol. 1, No. 1, pp. 1-32, Sydney: Educology Research Associates. ISSN 08180563

Christensen, James E. (1992): "Education for Freedom: A Philosophical Educology,"*International Journal of Educology*, Vol. 6, No. 2, pp. 97-131. Sydney: Educology Research Associates. ISSN 08180563

Christensen, James E. and Fisher, James E (1978): "An Organizational Theory for Schools of Teacher Education and Faculties of Education," *Australian Journal of Education*, Vol. 22, No. 1, pp. 52-71, Australian Council for Educational Research. ISSN 00049441

Christensen, James E. and Fisher, James E (1981): "Chapter 12: Educology as an Organizational Concept for Schools of Teacher Education, College of Education, and Faculties of Education," in J.E. Christensen (Ed.), *Perspectives on Education as Educology*. Washington, DC: University Press of America, pp. 263-300. ISBN 0819113934

Christensen, James E. and Fisher, James E. (1988): "The Need for Educological Research in the Areas of Secondary School Retention Rates, Educational Pathways and Recurrent Education," *International Journal of Educology*, Vol. 2, No. 2, pp. ix-xii. Sydney: Educology Research Associates. ISSN 0818 0563

Christensen, James E. and Fisher, James E. (1989): "Educology and the Educological Perspective," *International Journal of Educology*, Vol. 3, No. 1, pp. ix-xv. Sydney: Educology Research Associates. ISSN 0818 0563

Christensen, James E. and Fisher, James E. (1990): "Three Critical Distinctions for Advancing Educology," *International Journal of Educology*, Vol. 4, No. 1, pp. vi-viii. Sydney: Educology Research Associates. ISSN 0818 0563

Christensen, James E. and Fisher, James E. (1990): "Educology for Initial Teacher Education and for Professional Development of Practising Teachers - Changing Needs, Changing Demands," *International Journal of Educology*, Vol. 4, No. 2, pp. vi-xvii. Sydney: Educology Research Associates. ISSN 0818 0563

Christensen, James E. and Fisher, James E. (1991): "A Challenge for Educologists of Curriculum," *International Journal of Educology*, Vol. 5, No. 1, pp. vi-ix. Sydney: Educology Research Associates. ISSN 0818 0563

Christensen, James E. and Fisher, James E. (1991): "An Educology of Values, Goals and Action Plans," *International Journal of Educology*, Vol. 5, No. 2, pp. vi-ix. Sydney: Educology Research Associates. ISSN 0818 0563

Christensen, James E. and Fisher, James E. (1992): "The Educology of the Work Place," *International Journal of Educology*, Vol. 6, No. 1, pp. vi-xi. Sydney: Educology Research Associates. ISSN 0818 0563

Printed in Great Britain
by Amazon

18894446R00161